Moscow's Muslim Challenge

MICHAEL RYWKIN

Moscow's Muslim Challenge

SOVIET CENTRAL ASIA

M.E. Sharpe Inc.
ARMONK, NEW YORK
LONDON

Copyright © 1982 by M. E. Sharpe, Inc.
80 Business Park Drive, Armonk, New York 10504

Library of Congress Cataloging in Publication Data

Rywkin, Michael.
    Moscow's Muslim challenge.

    Bibliography: p.
    Includes index.
    1. Soviet Central Asia—Politics and government. I. Title.
DK859.R98   957′.08   81-14414
ISBN 0-87332-196-0

Printed in the United States of America.

Contents

List of Maps, Figures, and Tables *vi*

Preface *vii*

Acknowledgments *x*

CHAPTER ONE
Tsarist Times *3*

CHAPTER TWO
The Revolution *20*

CHAPTER THREE
The Basmachi Revolt *34*

CHAPTER FOUR
The Economic Scene *45*

CHAPTER FIVE
Population and Manpower *58*

CHAPTER SIX
The National-Religious Symbiosis *84*

CHAPTER SEVEN
Culture *93*

CHAPTER EIGHT
The Sociopolitical Setting *108*

CHAPTER NINE
Government *122*

CHAPTER TEN
The Terminology of Nationality Politics *138*

Conclusion *149*

Notes *155*

Selected Bibliography *173*

Index *177*

About the Author *186*

List of Maps, Figures, and Tables

Maps:
1. Central Asia in the Early Nineteenth Century   6
2. The Turkestan ASSR and People's
     Republic of Khorezm   41
3. Political-Ethnic Map   62-63

Figures:
1. Growth of Population by Main National Groups   61
2. Births by Ethnic Groups   65
3. Expected Number of Children   70

Tables:
1. Cattle   46
2. Cotton and Grain in Uzbekistan   47
3. Cotton and Grain Production   48
4. Industrial Output   49
5. Selected Economic Indicators   50
6. Welfare Colonialism   51
7. Native Working Class   53
8. The Private Sector in Housing   55
9. Private Plot Agriculture in Uzbekistan   56
10. Population before the Revolution   59
11. Percentage of Non-Muslims   64
12. Divorce   66
13. Soviet Population Dynamics   67
14. Muslims in the USSR by Language Groups   68-69
15. Soviet Manpower Prospects for the 1980s   71
16. Muslim and Non-Muslim Populations   77
17. Migration Balances for Selected Republics   78
18. Out-migration from Central Asia   81
19. Central Asian Nationalities in the RSFSR   82
20. Fluency in the Russian Language   98
21. European Settlers Speaking Local Languages   99
22. The Colonial *Nomenklatura*   126
23. Exclusive Competence of Republic Ministries   130
24. Content Analysis of National Anthems   144
25. Stages of Historical and National Development   146

Preface

Soviet Central Asia has come out of the backyards of history and now clamors for our attention. Bordering on both China and the Muslim Middle East, it appears on every map of the oil-producing countries of the Persian gulf as a huge northern mass suspended over its southern neighbors, a palpable geopolitical weight. Even more noteworthy is the fact that the area is inhabited by Muslim peoples, linked by race, religion, and tradition less to the Soviet northwest than to an Islamic south. And the numbers of Soviet Muslims are swelling, altering the internal ethnic balance in the USSR: by the year 2000 every second child born in the country is expected to be of Muslim origin. Practically unassimilable and indifferent to most Soviet values, the growing masses of Soviet Muslims (especially those of Central Asia) present a potential challenge to the Russian-dominated social order established in the USSR.

Obviously Muslims are not alone in their opposition to that order. Ukrainians, Georgians, Lithuanians, Latvians, Estonians, Jews, and Volga Germans are, in fact, more vocal than the Muslims. But Ukrainians, even when nationalistic, are still culturally, linguistically, and ethnically close to the Russians and, whenever out of their own republic, regarded as akin to the latter. The small Baltic nations, deprived of independence by the 1939 Soviet-Nazi agreement, are simply not numerous enough to challenge Russian domination. Jews and Germans, though they have lived in Russia for several centuries, are torn between assimilation and emigration; they are increasingly attracted by the latter. Proud Georgians, difficult to deal with, still regard historically Christian Russia as a "lesser evil" in comparison to their Muslim neighbors to the south.

In order to subdue nationalist ferment within its borders,

Moscow has attempted to mold the peoples of the USSR into a "new Soviet people" grouped around a Russian ethnic core, adopting the Soviet variant of Russian culture as its common base and the Russian language as its *lingua franca*. The general reaction to this program among the non-Russian nationalities has been quite unreceptive, with the Soviet Muslims among the most negative. Moscow's efforts have succeeded in creating some distance between Soviet Muslims and their foreign coreligionists, but an even greater gap remains between the Russians and their Muslim compatriots.

Well aware of the need for special political and administrative tools to control its dependencies, Moscow has devised methods that were neither colonial in the traditional sense nor free of colonial features: non-Russian lands inherited from the tsars were given an equal patina of autonomy but different degrees of actual say in their own affairs, depending on their reliability at the moment and the stability of their historic association with Russia. Their progress and modernization were promoted, but central economic control over the area was preserved; opportunities for personal advancement were enhanced, but key positions, whenever politically sensitive, were kept in Russian hands; national cultures were encouraged, but their content was purged to suit the larger Soviet purpose. This became known as the Soviet nationality policy.

Applied more thoroughly to Soviet Central Asia than elsewhere, under Stalin it fostered the creation of Muslim national republics dotted with developing economies and trained elites but deprived of final decision-making power in their own affairs. Education, industrialization, and modernization, consistently promoted and aided by Moscow almost since the beginning of Soviet rule, beneficial as they were, did not sway Muslim allegiances in Russia's favor. It is doubtful that the cooptation of Muslim elites into the ruling party apparatus, a process accelerated since Stalin's death, has produced better results.

The absence of political allegiance is not automatically translatable into political unreliability without the objective circumstances that promote dissent. The current level of disaffection would not turn the Soviet Central Asia of the 1980s into an insurgent Afghanistan or Islamic revivalist Iran. But in the two decades remaining in this century, propelled by an unprecedented demographic boom, the political, economic, and cultural weight of Soviet Islam will inexorably grow. By the year 2000 the sheer numerical strength and the continuing unassimilability of the Soviet Muslim masses will present the Soviet state with its greatest internal challenge: the survival of the empire inherited from the tsars.

This book presents the cumulative results of continuous study of Russian policies in Soviet Central Asia and of the principal developments either affected by or affecting such policies. My first book on the subject, *Russia in Central Asia*, was based on an analysis of Stalin's methods of control as applied to this area. Here I have adapted those parts of *Russia in Central Asia* which are still relevant, especially in the first three historical chapters and in the introductory passages of some other chapters. The present book is divided into four parts: historical (the first three chapters), economic and demographic (Chapters 4 and 5), cultural (Chapters 6 and 7), political and ideological (the last three chapters).

The reader will find a selected bibliography on pages 173-76.

Acknowledgments

I owe my thanks to my own university, the City College of New York, for granting me a sabbatical leave to complete this work; to Columbia University in New York City, Bibliothèque de Documentation Internationale Contemporaine in Nanterre, and Radio Liberty in Munich for access to their respective research facilities (and to John Hazard, Seweryn Bialer, and Jaan Penaar who facilitated this task); to a dozen or so of my colleagues in the profession (and in particular Hélène Carrère d'Encausse and James Critchlow) for providing me with valid interpretations; to the organizers of valuable professional conferences both here and abroad (Edward Allworth, Steven Grant, Stephan Horak, Edward Mortimer, Yaacov Ro'i), for giving me the opportunity to air my views in public and expose them to the criticism of my peers.

I also owe my thanks to recent émigrés from the Soviet Union (such as Boris Kamenetsky and others too numerous to mention) who graciously gave me their time and provided me with personal insights otherwise unobtainable.

My thanks also go to my rather numerous Soviet critics who, by taking issue with specific points in my previous writings, attracted my attention to the importance of particular problems.

Finally, I wish to thank Tanya Mairs for editorial work in preparing the last draft, Joseph Hollander, the editor in charge of this volume, for final editing, and Shirley Burton, our departmental secretary at CCNY, who patiently retyped the text at preliminary stages.

Moscow's
Muslim
★Challenge

CHAPTER ONE

Tsarist Times

1. Before the Conquest
(From the 1550s to the 1850s)

Russian attempts to establish relations with Central Asia can be traced back as far as the sixteenth century; they follow the conquest of the Astrakhan khanate by the troops of Tsar Ivan the Terrible (1556).[1] The first traveler from Moscow to penetrate the area (1558—59) was an English merchant, Jenkinson. After 1565 several Russian missions went to Bukhara, Khiva, and Samarkand, and emissaries from the Central Asian states appeared in Moscow seeking privileges for their merchants.

The interregnum of the Time of Troubles (1605—13) did not slow Russian movements eastward to Siberia, but neither was it conducive to new diplomatic openings in Central Asia. When order had been reestablished in Moscow, an envoy of the Emir of Bukhara arrived in 1619 to seek contacts with the first tsar of the new dynasty, Michael Fedorovich Romanov. To reciprocate, a Russian envoy, Ivan Khokhlov, was sent to Bukhara in 1621.

Mutual interest was, however, too limited and travel too difficult to warrant any steady relations, and contacts between Moscow and Central Asia remained sporadic. After the Russians had reached the Pacific Ocean in their eastward penetration of Siberia, a boyar from the Russian Caspian Sea harbor of Astrakhan, Ivan Fedotov, was sent to Khiva (1669), and the brothers Pazukhin to Bukhara and Balk (Balsh). In 1675 another Russian emissary, Vasilii Daudov, and his party reached Bukhara.

With Peter the Great on the throne and the subsequent Westernization of Russia, Russian interest in Central Asia, although superficial, increased. The new tsar was influenced by his natural curiosity, his passion to establish commercial relations with every possible country, and by his knowledge of the colonial exploits of Western European nations. He therefore wanted a more active policy with regard to Central Asia. During his reign, in 1695 a Russian merchant by the name of Semen Malenkii reached India by way of Central Asia but died on his return trip, unable to match the feat of his seafaring predecessor, Afanasii Nikitin (1469).

The year 1700 brought two new developments which further increased Peter's interest in Central Asia. The first was a rumor about gold deposits in Central Asia, in the Amu Darya area, and the second, an odd request for Russian protection by Shah Niaz of Khiva, who was then involved in one of the endless feudal wars that usually plagued the area. At war with Sweden and Turkey, Peter had to postpone any positive action. But in 1715 he sent an expedition to the Kazakh Steppe, along the Irtysh and Erket rivers, and in 1716 a few forts were built on the Irtysh. Finally, in 1717 an expedition under the command of Prince A. Bekovich-Cherkasskii went to Khiva. This expedition, 6,655 men strong, was equipped at a cost of a quarter of a million rubles. They were instructed to study the flow of the Amu Darya, to reroute the river, if possible, to flow back to the Caspian Sea, and to build a fort on the Amu Darya shores. In addition, Bekovich-Cherkasskii was to induce the rulers of Khiva and Bukhara to accept nomad Kazakhs, friendly to Russia, into their personal guards. The Khivans, who never considered their old offer too seriously, since it was made amid internal struggles, showed little enthusiasm for the Russians. Under the pretext of providing adequate living quarters, the Russians were split into small units and massacred. Most of those who escaped perished in the desert, and only a few found their way back home. All that was left was a small fort on the eastern shore of the Caspian Sea, which was abandoned two years later. The tragic end of the Khivan venture did not discourage the tsar; in 1718 his envoy, Florio Beneveni, arrived in Bukhara and stayed there until the emperor's death in 1725.

With the death of Peter the Great and the consequent evacuation of the Persian Caspian Sea shore by Russian troops (1732), Russia temporarily discontinued all attempts to penetrate Central Asia, concentrating her efforts on extending her influence in the Kazakh Steppe, an enormous, sparsely inhabited area located between Siberia and Central Asia proper. The 1731 acceptance of nominal Russian sovereignty by the Kazakhs of the Lesser Horde, wandering in the steppes southeast of the Ural River, was the first step in that direction. A series of forts was built on the Ural River in 1735, facing the newly acquired but unruly "vassals." Russian Cossacks settled around these forts and around the previously built Irtysh forts. The first have since been known as Ural and Orenburg Cossacks, the latter as Siberian Cossacks. The Kazakhs of the Lesser Horde, separated by fortifications from Russian territory, maintained their old way of life. The Middle Horde accepted Russian sovereignty in 1740 and then changed in favor of Chinese sovereignty in 1742, but soon thereafter renounced both. From then on, for three quarters of a century, the political picture of the area remained static. Russia was unwilling at that time to undertake any new ventures in the steppes and deserts of Kazakhstan. The Kazakhs in the steppe and the Cossacks around the forts maintained an uneasy truce with the Russian garrisons in the forts, detailed to preserve peace and order. The Kazakhs were more disturbed by the unfriendly Cossack attitude than by nominal Russian sovereignty, which even the Middle Horde came gradually to accept.

The first important Russian intervention in Kazakh affairs occurred at the turn of the century, when Emperor Paul I approved the break off of the western part of the Lesser Horde from the main body. The new group became known as the Bukeev Horde. At the same time, in accordance with his new alliance with Napoleon, Paul I organized an expedition of 22,500 Don Cossacks, under General Vasilii Orlov, to Orenburg with the mission to proceed through Bukhara and Khiva to India. Although the main goal of the expedition was to attack the British in India, instructions were given to Orlov to take possession of Bukhara and to liberate Russian slaves in Khiva. This plan was not new; in 1791 Catherine the Great had considered a similar scheme. The assassination of Paul and the reversal of Russian foreign policy stopped the expedition, but diplomatic contacts with Central Asia were now in progress. A Cossack officer, Teliatnikov, on a mission from St. Petersburg, managed to reach Tashkent in 1797, and the next year a Tashkent mission journeyed to Russia to discuss not only commercial but political relations as well.[2]

Following the victory over Napoleon and Russia's emergence as a great power in Europe, a radical change in Russian policy occurred toward the Kazakh Steppe. The Emperor Alexander I decided to transform Russia's relationships with the

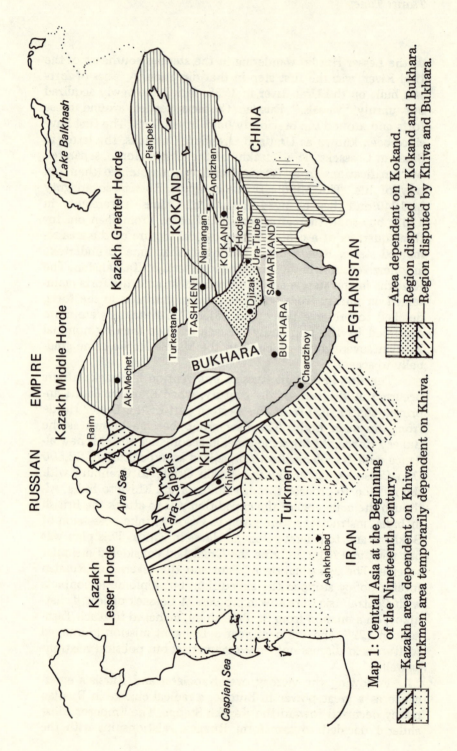

Map 1: Central Asia at the Beginning
of the Nineteenth Century.

— Area dependent on Kokand.
— Region disputed by Kokand and Bukhara.
— Region disputed by Khiva and Bukhara.

— Kazakh area dependent on Khiva.
— Turkmen area temporarily dependent on Khiva.

Lesser and Middle Hordes. A special Kazakh code was drafted in 1822 by his otherwise liberal advisor, Speranskii. The khanate of the Middle Horde was abolished, and its territory, inhabited by about a half million people, was divided into Russian administrative units with a mixed Russian-native administration. Russian military jurisdiction was established over all criminal offenses as well as over all civil litigations involving over twenty rubles. Acquisition of new slaves among Kazakhs was prohibited. Russian sovereignty over the area ceased to be nominal and became a reality. Two years later (1824) the half million nomads of the Lesser Horde were affected by similar reforms, but local administration was left in the hands of three native "sultans," each to be responsible for a part of the territory. Simultaneously, Cossacks were permitted to use "hot pursuit" in following unruly Kazakh bands into their own territory. Kazakh pasture lands near Russian fortifications were expropriated and given to the Cossacks.

Such an abrupt end of Kazakh independence led to numerous revolts. Kaip Gallia Ishimov, son of a former khan of the Lesser Horde, rose against the Russians in 1818—20 and again in 1827—29, trying to reestablish the khanate by accepting the sovereignty of the Central Asian Khan of Kokand. Isatai and Makambat led revolts in the Bukeev Horde in 1836—38, and Sardzhan in the Middle Horde in 1832—36. At the same time (1834), Russian Orenburg authorities built the Novo-Aleksandrovsk fort on the eastern shore of the Caspian on the spot which had been abandoned since the days of Bekovich-Cherkasskii.

In order to "encourage trade" between the Cossacks, engaged in agriculture, and the Kazakhs, traditionally nomad cattle breeders, the latter were forbidden to cultivate their land. This discriminatory policy, which was enforced during the 1830s, forced the Kazakhs to buy Russian bread at high prices and to sell their cattle at low prices.

In 1837 the Russian government, in order to improve the collection of taxes from the Kazakhs of the Lesser Horde, established a hut tax of 1.50 rubles, and the old method of collecting taxes through the intermediary of Kazakh authorities was discarded.

Dissatisfaction with Russian policies brought about a large-scale revolt in 1838 in western and northern Kazakhstan, which was especially fierce in the Akmolinsk area. The Kazakhs, led by the energetic Kenesary, kept the area in turmoil until 1845.

Kenesary wanted to return to the pre-1822 relations, that is, to a purely nominal Russian sovereignty. Unable to force Russian consent, Kenesary sought cooperation from the three khans of Turkestan and tried to destroy Russian forts and Cossack settlements. Finally defeated, he moved south into the territory of the Greater Horde, which was still outside Russian control, where he perished in a local skirmish.

In the meantime Russia continued to attempt to establish diplomatic and commercial relations with the states of Kokand, Bukhara, and Khiva, south of the Kazakh Steppe. The Russian minister of commerce, Count Rumiantsev, dreamed of large-scale economic penetration into the area. Central Asian khanates were visualized as potential counterparts of what India was for England.

Thus in 1803 an armed caravan under Lieutenant Gaverdovskii tried to reach Bukhara or even Kabul from Siberia, but, on encountering Kazakh resistance, turned back. In 1819 Captain Muraviev reached Khiva on a mission from the Russian proconsul of the Caucasus, General Ermolov.[3] And in 1820 a Greek in the Russian service, Negri, reached Bukhara and managed to obtain useful information as well as official reassurances of smoother commercial relations. But a new caravan, sent in 1824 in an attempt to foster such relations, lost all its merchandise. Finally, in 1819, when an Asian Department had been established in the Ministry of Foreign Affairs, its Second Section was charged with handling relations with all areas east of Persia, which included Central Asia.

In 1833 a very energetic general, V. A. Perovskii, became governor of Orenburg, and a more active policy was started toward Central Asia. In 1835 Jan Witkewicz, an officer of Polish origin, exiled to Siberia, was sent by the Russian government to Central Asia. Witkewicz, hoping to gain amnesty, was very enterprising. He reached Bukhara and from there went to Afghanistan, staying from 1837 to 1839 and successfully counteracting the intrigues of a British agent named Burns, who was the first Westerner since Marco Polo to reach the mountains of Pamir. In 1839 an armed conflict broke out between Britain and Afghanistan. British troops took Kandahor and Kabul. Russia was far from pleased and felt justified compensating herself. General Perovskii was given orders to move on Khiva, to replace the khan with a more compliant one, to obtain trade privileges, and to free Russian prisoners. The 6,000-man expeditionary force included 150 Bashkir and 1,000 Kazakh auxiliary troops, with

12,000 camels. Perovskii failed, however, to reach Khiva and, after losing over a thousand men and almost all the camels in the desert, turned back, lucky to avoid the fate of his predecessor of 120 years before, Bekovich-Cherkasskii. Shortly afterward, he was dismissed.

The British were no more successful in Afghanistan. Initial victories were followed by defeat in 1841. Although both Russia and Britain had a difficult start, neither gave up. Britain continued its penetration of Afghanistan, and new Russian missions went to Bukhara (Major Butenev) and Khiva (Captain Nikiforov). Meanwhile, despite numerous attempts by Russian merchants, commerce between Russia and the khanates remained in the hands of Central Asian merchants, the Russians encountering too many obstacles in dealing directly with the Muslims.[4]

By 1847, two years after the Kenesary revolt, the Russians felt secure enough to make a major move toward Central Asia. General Obruchev, military governor of Orenburg since 1842, constructed Fort Raim (Aralskoe) on the northern shore of the Syr Darya River. Two vessels were brought by land to the Aral Sea and reassembled there. The fort became the main base for further Russian penetration into Central Asia. In the years following, several new forts were built on the banks of the Syr Darya, bringing Russia 500 miles closer to the khanates of Turkestan by eliminating the protective no man's land of the "hungry steppes" between the Ural and Syr Darya rivers. Reappointed governor of Orenburg, Perovskii, not only followed in Obruchev's footsteps but even accelerated Russian penetration. The line of forts was completed in 1853 with the seizure of Ak Mechet (Perovsk) from Kokand in reprisal for a raid by nomad Kokand Kazakhs on the Russian Fort Raim.

The other arm of the huge Russian pincer movement was moving south from Siberia along the Chinese borders, through the lands of the Middle Horde and across Lake Balkhash. In this way the Russians succeeded in forcing the Kazakhs of the Greater Horde to shift their allegiance from Kokand to Russia (1847). Pushing further south, they erected Fort Vernoe (now Alma-Ata, the capital of Kazakhstan). It was the first of a new line of forts that the Russians constructed to seal the northern borders of Kokand. Kazakh revolts which spread in the Russian rear among the nomads, like the Iset and Beket revolts of 1850—54 in the Middle Horde area, were suppressed with much difficulty.[5]

Thus in the middle of the nineteenth century, the backward, medieval khanates of Khiva, Bukhara, and Kokand, quarreling among themselves and deprived of the protective buffer of the Kazakh Steppes, found themselves face to face with a great European power—Russia—ready and eager for an easy colonial acquisition.

2. *The Conquest*

The three khanates, disunited since mid-seventeenth century, had no well-defined borders. The Emir of Bukhara ruled a large territory between the Syr Darya and Amu Darya rivers, with the exception of a vast desert area south of the Aral Sea. The heart of his country was the rich valley of Zeravshan, in which lay the historic cities of Bukhara and Samarkand. The country had a population of about two and a half million, half of them Uzbeks, one third Tadzhiks, and about one tenth Turkmen. As elsewhere in Turkestan, the population was Sunni Muslim, except for a Shiite minority among the Tadzhiks and for the Tadzhik-speaking Bukhara Jews.

The lands of the Khan of Khiva were located south of the Aral Sea, on both shores of the Amu Darya, with the oasis of Khiva in the center. Its population was about three quarters of a million and consisted of Kara-Kalpaks, Turkmen, Kazakhs, and Uzbeks.

Kokand occupied vast territories between the Syr Darya and the Chinese Sinkiang Province, with the center in the rich Fergana Valley and in the Tashkent Oasis. With a population of about three million, mostly Uzbeks, Kazakhs, and Kirghiz, it included the largest city in Central Asia, Tashkent (one hundred thousand inhabitants).

Nomad Turkmen, between the Caspian Sea and the Amu Darya River, and those Kazakhs in the northern steppes who were not yet under Russian protection, recognized the authority of the khans only intermittently.

The political and social structure of the three khanates was medieval. The land, divided into three main categories—state (*amliak*), which predominated, private (*miulk*), and clerical (*vakf*)—was most often cultivated by impoverished tenants who were allowed to retain only between one half and one fifth of the crop. Irrigation, essential in the area, was under the control of state functionaries. Many peasants were landless.[6] Economic activity was mostly of a local character. Slavery existed throughout the territory. The military and administrative organization of the khanates was backward, and only Khiva, because of its smaller territory, had achieved a certain degree of centralization. The outlying provinces (*vilayets*) of Bukhara and Kokand were constantly challenging the central authority. Uzbek political supremacy in a multinational situation led to national conflicts. In addition, the three khans were usually quarreling with one another.

The 1855 Russian defeat in the Crimean War spurred the Russian drive into Turkestan in an attempt to redeem Russian national and military honor and gain commercial advantages. Throughout the entire operation the Ministry of Foreign Affairs, fearful of potential trouble with England, called for caution, while the Russian military, eager for recognition, glory, and promotions, advocated further advances. Both sides were most often at odds, competing for the emperor's ear. Thus a mission to Khiva and Bukhara under Colonel Ignatiev recommended to St. Petersburg a policy of "surer and more powerful protection of our interests."[7]

The Russians, avoiding direct hostilities with Bukhara and Khiva, started a series of local operations at the Kokand borders. Moving south along the Syr Darya River toward the Kirghiz Mountains, they took Tokmak and Pishpek in 1860, Djulek and Yany-Kurgan in 1861, Turkestan City, Aulie-Ata, and finally Chimkent in 1864. The local Russian field commander, General Cherniaev, established at Chimkent, tried on his own initiative to take Tashkent by surprise, but failed. The exasperated Kokand government was unwilling to relinquish its major centers, Tashkent and the Fergana Valley, without a full-scale war. St. Petersburg was hesitant, but in 1865 a separate Turkestan Province under the jurisdiction of the remote Orenburg governor-general was created. In June, taking advantage of conflicting instructions, General Cherniaev, with 1,950 men and twelve cannons, marched on Tashkent and took the city by assault. The 30,000 Muslim defenders, with sixty-three cannons, were unable to inflict serious losses on the Russians. This victory had a demoralizing effect on the natives and enhanced Russian prestige.

"A civilized mission," insisted Gorchakov. "Asiatic peoples respect nothing but visible and palpable force."[8] But the Emir of Bukhara, frightened by Russian victories and openly provoked by Cherniaev's advance into his territory, finally decided to act. He asked the Russians to evacuate Tashkent and detained the Russian mission in Bukhara. At the same time, the weak Khan of Kokand was replaced, with Bukhara's backing, by their choice, Khudoyar Khan. Armed Bukharan bands harassed Russian communications as far as Tashkent. Cherniaev was dismissed in 1866 for overstepping his authority, but the war with Bukhara could no longer be avoided.

Russian forces defeated the Bukharan troops at Irdjar. They took Khodjent and Ura Tiube and defeated the Bukharans again at Yany-Kurgan. This was followed by a reorganization of the conquered territory. Turkestan Province was made into a separate governorship-general, with the capital at Tashkent, and then divided into two provinces, Syr Darya and Semireche (1867). (In 1868 the Kazakh Steppe were also divided into Russian-style administrative units under military governors.) General Kaufman, an aggressive army commander and an excellent administrator, was made the first governor-general of Turkestan. He was given the administrative, military, financial, and diplomatic powers of a genuine viceroy. In January 1868 Kaufman concluded a peace treaty with Kokand but pursued the fight against Bukhara. In May, with 3,500 men, he took the historic city of Samarkand almost without a fight and, following the course of the Zeravshan River, reached Katta-Kurgan. The Bukharan army, almost 50,000 strong, outflanked the Russians and attacked Samarkand but failed to break the resistance of its 658-man garrison. In June Bukhara was forced to sign a peace treaty which made this khanate a vassal of Russia. Bukhara was also required to cede both Samarkand and Katta-Kurgan.

Following a decision made prior to Cherniaev's move against Tashkent, Russian Caucasian troops crossed the Caspian Sea and established the fort and the harbor of Krasnovodsk (1869). It served as a base for future advances across the Turkmen desert. Only Khiva was left untouched; protected by arid deserts, it was still inaccessible. At the same time, an agreement concluded between Russia and Persia gave St. Petersburg full freedom of action against the Turkmen tribes. As expressed by Teheran,

Sa Majesté préfère avoir de ce coté la pour limitrophe un pouvoir civillisé comme la Russie.[9]

In 1873, however, despite the Russian Foreign Ministry's peaceful declarations,

> The Emperor not only does not wish to take possession of Khiva, but has given definite orders that such an eventuality be prevented.[10]

General Kaufman moved against Khiva, entered the city, and forced the khan to accept a Russian protectorate (August 1873). Included in the terms were the cession of the western part of his territory and the payment of a contribution. Simultaneously, acting from Krasnovodsk, Russian troops pacified the Caspian coast (1870—73).

Thus, eight years after the fall of Tashkent, all three khans of Turkestan had become vassals of Russia, and a large part of their territories had been made into a Russian province.

Widespread dissatisfaction with the new state of affairs led to a revolt against the unpopular Khudoyar Khan in Kokand. His son, Nasreddin, was proclaimed khan, and a holy war began against the Russians. Russian troops, under Colonel Skobelev, were quick to act. Skobelev defeated the natives at Makhram, entered the Fergana Valley, and took all the main cities of the valley one after another—Namangan, Andizhan, Kokand, Margelan. In reprisal for the revolt, Russia incorporated the Khanate of Kokand into Russian Turkestan and exiled the unfortunate Khudoyar Khan (1876). As a reward for his victories, Colonel Skobelev was promoted to general and made governor of the new Fergana Province of Turkestan.

During the same year Russian troops pacified the Kirghiz tribes in the east and in 1877 took Kzyl-Arvat in the Teke Oasis of Turkmenia. Skobelev, proud of his success, submitted a plan for the invasion of India to General Kaufman. However, having established itself in Central Asia, Russia was unwilling to risk a war with Britain by following Skobelev's aggressive plans. Britain acted swiftly: Queen Victoria was proclaimed "Empress of India" (1877) in a manifest indication of British intentions to stand firm in the area. This did not prevent the Russians from testing British patience at the Afghan borders. In 1878 General Stoletov of the Russian Transcaspian Force was sent with a diplomatic mission to Kabul to prepare the ground for possible Russian military penetration. Russian units were on the move in the entire area. Only the Congress of Berlin was able to call a halt to further Russian intervention in Afghanistan.

In 1879 Russian troops moved against the Teke Turkmen tribes but then suffered a defeat at Geok-Tepe. However, the pacification of Turkmenia continued. In 1880 the Russians began to build a strategic railroad from the Caspian Sea to the hinterland, and a new expedition under General Skobelev was sent against the recalcitrant Teke Turkmen. Eleven thousand men attacked the fort of Geok-Tepe and, after a fierce battle, took it in January 1881, slaughtering scores of defenders along with their families. This was the last large-scale battle of the campaign.

In 1881 the Russians created the Transcaspian Province from the Turkmen territory and pushed the Transcaspian Railroad from the Caspian coast to Kzyl-Arvat.

General Kaufman died a year later, having witnessed the success of his policy. In 1884 the last strongholds of native resistance, the Turkmen oases of Mary and Tedjen, recognized Russian authority. A year later the Transcaspian Railroad had reached Mary. The conquest of Central Asia was achieved. Russia offered to negotiate a frontier with British-dominated Afghanistan. For that purpose a mixed English-Russian commission was set up. While the commission was still being formed, a clash occurred in March 1855 at the Kushka River between Russians and Afghans led by British advisors. The conflict, however, was not allowed to get out of hand. In 1887 the border between Afghanistan and Russian Central Asia was finally determined.

By 1886 the Turkestan governorship-general was divided into three parts: Syr Darya Province, Fergana Province, and Zeravshan District (since 1887 Samarkand Province). The railroad reached Samarkand in 1888.[11] All of Central Asia was pacified and subjected to the "White Tsar."

3. *Tsarist Policy*

Tsarist internal policy in Central Asia was calculated to ensure continued domination by keeping peace and order in the area and interfering as little as possible with the native customs and way of life. Even Russian urban settlements were kept separate, albeit adjacent to local cities.

Soon, however, three problems emerged which were to dominate the development of the area. The first was the cotton boom in Turkestan. The needs of the Russian and Polish textile industry for cheap domestic cotton, the fertility of the rich soil of the Fergana Valley, and the successful introduction of American cotton (around 1884) in the area made cotton a key product. Second was the problem of so-called "surplus lands" in the Kazakh Steppe and in Kirghizia. There the lands of the nomads, wherever suitable for agriculture, were bought, seized, or expropriated by the Russians. The number of Russian settlers in the steppe grew rapidly, while the natives, classified as primitive *inorodtsy* (*peuples allogènes*) like the American Indians, were forced to move out into less desirable areas. The third problem was common to both Turkestan and the Steppe Region—the fact that Central Asia had become a choice market for Russian-manufactured goods. Commerce between Russia and Central Asia shifted from the hands of the previously favored Muslim merchants into the hands of the now privileged Russians, who were finally free to dominate the market.

These three factors—cotton, surplus land, and markets— were focal points for the years ahead. The total land under American cotton cultivation increased sixfold from 1886 to 1890. Imported cotton, free of duty until 1878, then taxed only 2.4 rubles per quintal, was hit with a 6-ruble import duty in 1887 and a 24-ruble levy in 1903. The Russian textile industry, which imported 96 percent of all of Russia's cotton needs in 1886, was importing only 48.7 percent by 1914. The rest was supplied by Central Asia, where the area under cotton cultivation grew from 13,200 hectares in 1886 to 597,200 hectares in 1914.[12]

The cotton boom had a decisive influence on other fields of activity. First, the increase in cotton production was paralleled by growth in the grain deficit. Central Asia, previously self-supporting in grain, had to rely increasingly on grains imported from Russia. Industrial development was also centered around cotton. In fact, cotton mills employed two thirds of all industrial workers and accounted for over three fourths of the total industrial production of Central Asia in terms of value. While exporting cotton, Central Asia was increasing its imports of Russian cotton textiles.

The cotton boom created a real basis for a money economy. Central Asian markets were opened to Russian industrial goods. Unable to compete with Western manufacturers on equal terms, Russian manufacturers were in need of a protected market with tariff barriers to check foreign competition. Central Asia was perfect in this respect. By 1907 it had become an important buyer of grains, sugar, lumber, iron, and steel products as well as of manufactured goods from metropolitan Russia.[13]

The problem of land surplus was the most complicated one. Prior to the 1861 abolition of serfdom in Russia, the only Russians who settled in Kazakh territory were the free Cossacks, and they settled only along the lines of fortifications on the edge of the Kazakh Steppe. After the emancipation, peasants from Tomsk and Tobolsk provinces started to settle in northern Kazakhstan. Peasants from Samara, Saratov, Voronezh, Kursk, Kiev, Orel, Tambov, Chernigov, and the Don provinces followed, especially after the 1891 famine. By 1893 the total number of newcomers had reached 200,000.[14]

At this point Russian authorities decided to give the colonization movement a more orderly character. A new ordinance in 1891 strengthened the Russian administrative hold in the steppe, and a special regulation was issued governing further colonization. The next Russian move was sending an expedition to the Kazakh steppe (1895) in order to establish a "land fund" for new settlers out of land "not needed" by the mostly nomad natives. This was the first organized step toward dispossessing the natives. The commission was not too careful in making a distinction between "needed" and "not needed" land. Pressure was applied to make the natives relinquish "superfluous" land. Russian immigration increased. Every spring wagon loads of weary peasants crossed the Ural Mountains and went down to the virgin lands of Kazakhstan in search of a new life. But in 1898 an outbreak of religious fanaticism in the Andizhan area temporarily shattered Russian confidence.[15]

In 1902 a new commission was sent to Turkestan. The commission found that large areas of land in the steppe of Semireche were "not needed" by the natives and could qualify as surplus land. It was also understood that Russian farms required much more land than native farms because Russian peasants used extensive methods of agriculture and planted mainly grains.[16]

Until then the number of Russian Cossacks and peasants in Semireche was small (only 2,500 by 1883). There were also some workers who had remained in that area after the building of a canal, as well as refugees from the 1891–92 famine in Russia. The findings of the commission and the mass arrival of Russian peasants after the collapse of the 1905 Russian Revolution led to an accelerated expropriation of native land. In 1908 a second commission was sent to the steppe, headed by Count K. K. Palen, which led to a new increase in Russian colonization. Thus between 1903 and 1911 the Russian rural population of Semireche increased from 95,000 to 175,000, and the number of Russian rural settlers in Syr Darya Region reached 45,000. The expropriation of Kazakh and Kirghiz lands was made easier by a legal device based on the highly questionable assumption that all the lands in the steppe formerly belonged to the khans and not to private owners, and therefore, after the Russian conquest the tsar became the rightful heir to all the legal titles to the land.[17]

The taking over of "surplus lands" was most often done under harsh administrative pressure and resulted in forcing the natives out of their own land. Not only nomads but even settled Kazakhs and Kirghiz were faced with these measures. The takeover of "surplus lands" was again accelerated after a visit to the area by Prime Minister P. A. Stolypin in 1910. It is estimated that between forty and forty-five million hectares of Kazakh land were taken over prior to the Revolution. The main areas of seized land were western, northern, and eastern Kazakhstan and, after 1905, Semireche and Syr Darya as well. The land expropriation resulted in yearly famines among the Muslims between 1910 and 1913.[18] The annual income of the average Russian farm was twice as large as that of an average Kazakh farm in the same area. The real difference was greater, however, since most of the Kazakh wealth was concentrated in the hands of the tribal aristocracy, which accounted for less than 4 percent of the total native population.

The expropriation of "surplus lands" continued after the beginning of World War I. Then in 1916 the tsarist government, in need of manpower, decided to draft Central Asian Muslims, traditionally free from draft obligation, into labor units. This was the last straw. A revolt flared in Kazakhstan under the leadership of Amangeldy Imanov, Abdu Gafar Dzhambosyn, and Kasym Ospan. The revolt spread to the Dzhizak District of Samarkand and to the Fergana Valley. The total number of rebels may have reached 50,000 by October. In November they almost took the town of Turgai, but failed and returned to the steppes.[19]

Meanwhile a conference on the revolt was held by General Kuropatkin, governor-general of Turkestan. At this conference it was decided to expel all the natives who took part in the revolt from their land into eastern Kirghizia. Their lands were to be opened to immediate Russian settlement. The resettlement decision was carried out while the revolt was still in progress. In fact, a few days before the February (1917) Revolution, Russian punitive troops were still pursuing the remnants of rebel units. A quarter of a million Kazakhs and Kirghiz fled to Chinese Turkestan or died of famine.[20] The termination of land expropriations and of Russian settlement of the area became the main aspiration of Kazakh and Kirghiz nationalists in the years to come.

But it was only after the 1905 Revolution that Muslim nationalist movements that stemmed from the Tatars and the Azeri Turks began to surface in Turkestan and in the Kazakh steppe. The leaders of the movement, known as *jadids* (among them Abdurauf Fitrat, Münnever Quari, and Faizullah Khodzhaev), set up their first political organization in Bukhara in 1909 ("Young Bukharans"). Anti-Russian in their attitudes and looking to the "Young Turks" of the Ottoman Empire for inspiration, they resembled the "Muslim socialists" of our time.

In the steppe the attitude was less anti-Russian, more pro-Western and liberal than socialist politically, with two dominant personalities——Ali Khan Bukeykhanov and Akhmed Baytursun. In 1912 they formed the Alash Orda Party, which was to cooperate with the Russian liberal bourgeoisie.[21]

The tsarist conquest of Central Asia did not result from consistent policies established in St. Petersburg and pursued by one administration after another. Nor was the reverse true: no *"concours de circonstances"* was solely responsible.

What most influenced Russian moves was a whole range of attitudes that went unchanged for centuries, persisting regardless of policy shifts by changing administrations. Among these attitudes we can discern the following:

1. An instinctive drive aimed at filling the geopolitical gap created by the collapse of the Great Tatar Horde. Only the Pacific Ocean, Japan, China, and, later, British India were perceived as substantial obstacles to further penetration. Everything in between was viewed as kind of no man's land open to Russian advance (*"Nos frontières marchent avec nous."*[22]).

2. A historical spirit of *"reconquista"* as far as the territories once conquered by the Horde were concerned. Tatars, Mongols, Bashkirs, Kazakhs, or Uzbeks were indiscriminately viewed as heirs to that Horde.

3. A growing feeling of the superiority of St. Petersburg Russia over all the non-Christian *"inorodtsy,"* with their "barbaric Asian" morals and habits.

4. A traditional anti-Turkish stand, easily translatable into anti-Islamic attitudes.

5. The perception that the relatively few people inhabiting Asiatic areas to the east and southeast of Russia (the present-

day demographic explosion is a recent development) were an easy target for control and exploitation once the area was conquered.

These attitudes not only influenced the Russian colonial conquest and further governance of the area but, albeit in a residual form, managed to survive the Revolution itself.

CHAPTER TWO

The Revolution

1. *The Two Revolutions*

"The February Revolution reached Turkestan by cable," states
G. Safarov, the best authority for the revolutionary period.[1]
General Kuropatkin, the tsarist governor-general of Turkestan,
tried to cling to power but was replaced by a committee of the
provisional government composed of five Russians and four
local Muslims. Almost simultaneously a "council (soviet) of
workers and soldiers" was set up in Tashkent similar in structure to the metropolitan soviets. It was made up of various
left-wing elements, but mainly Mensheviks and Social Revolutionaries (SRs). Right-wing groupings countered this move by
organizing "committees of public safety" in several towns.

The Muslims had little to do with all this. Nationalist
Muslims gathered around religious *ulema* groups, the only ones
expressing an open desire for independence. Liberal Muslim
groups, unwilling to jeopardize the support of the new liberal
Russian regime, avoided this issue. Extreme radicals among the
Muslims were few, and they were represented by two small
groups: the "Union of Toiling Muslims" in Fergana and Ittihad
in Samarkand.

Muslim congresses were called by Muslim nationalists in
May and September. The May congress pronounced itself in
favor of the creation of an autonomous federated republic of
Turkestan (within the new Russia) based on national autonomy
and the shariat (Muslim religious law). It was decided to stop
the planting of American cotton, the growing of which was as-
sociated with colonialism. The replacement of cotton by grains
was equated with the liberation of Turkestan from economic
dependence on Russia.[2] The congress elected a Central Muslim

Council, dominated by *jadids*, with Mustafa Chokay as chairman. Chokay immediately began forwarding a series of demands to Tashkent. Included were the transfer of judicial authority into Muslim hands and the abolition of separate European courts, electoral equality for Muslims and Russians, removal of Russian troops, and establishment of an independent legislative assembly in Turkestan.

The Tashkent Committee of the provisional government, on which these demands were made, was already on its way out. During September the soldiers of the two Siberian regiments stationed in Tashkent held a meeting with the leftist workers of the Tashkent Railroad Repair Shops. They demanded that essential goods be requisitioned from local capitalists, that workers be in control in factories, that banks be nationalized, and that power be transferred to the Tashkent Soviet.

The provisional government decided to react. General Korovnichenko, the commander of the Turkestan military district, was ordered to move his troops on Tashkent. Under his command armored trains and Cossack cavalry entered the city. An uneasy truce was established between Korovnichenko on one side and the soviet, shielded by the two regiments of Siberian infantry, on the other. Korovnichenko was slowly gaining control when the Bolsheviks took power in Petrograd. This prompted Korovnichenko to force the issue. Two days later he had the Tashkent Soviet arrested and ordered the disarming of the prosoviet Siberian infantry. The first regiment, taken by surprise, was disarmed successfully, but the second, reinforced by railroad workers, met force with force. In the resulting fierce battle the Siberian units gained the upper hand, thereby restoring the soviet to power.

The Menshevik-SR soviet, once again in command, refused to recognize the new Bolshevik regime in Petrograd. To strengthen its prestige among the Muslims, the soviet established two organizations with resounding names and a minimum of authority: the Executive Committee and the Krai-Soviet (Territorial Council), in both of which the nationalist *ulema* Muslims were given half the seats.

Within the soviet, Bolsheviks, Mensheviks, and SRs quarreled. The Bolsheviks wanted to set up a purely proletarian regime as in metropolitan Russia. In an area where the only organized proletariat was Russian and where the mass of local population consisted of small proprietors—peasants, artisans, and small merchants—such a dogma had a strong flavor of colonialism.[3] The moderate socialist Mensheviks advocated local autonomy based on a large degree of self-government for local authorities and on universal suffrage. The left-wing SRs were interested in a peasant government which, under local conditions, would have amounted to government by the rural Russian settlers of Semireche. The settlers of Semireche, in turn, wanted either autonomy or union with Siberian anticommunists. The Bolshevik minority in the soviet was unwilling to accept the policies of the Menshevik-SR majority or to tolerate the sharing of power with the Muslim nationalists, even on paper. On November 19, 1917, the Bolsheviks created their own government and a rival of the Tashkent Soviet, the Council of People's Commissars, composed of seven Bolsheviks and one left-wing SR. All were Russians.

Muslim nationalists were quick to follow. Their Fourth All-Muslim Congress met in Kokand on November 26 and 27 and created the Muslim Provisional Government of Autonomous Turkestan, with Tanyshbaev as premier and Chokaev as minister of foreign affairs. The Kokand cabinet included one non-Muslim, the finance minister Herzfeld. However, the new Muslim government, the third contender for power in Turkestan, lacked both troops and money and consequently was unable to back its bid for power with the necessary force.

The course of events in the Kazakh Steppe also did not favor the Muslims. The February Revolution found them divided between the liberal-nationalist Alash Orda Party (Mirzhakup Dulatov, Alikhan Bukheikhanov, and Baitursunov), which received the support of the provisional government, and the radical elements that had survived the Russian suppression of the 1916 revolt (Amangeldy Imanov and others). The few local leftists, such as Dzhangeldyn, joined the radicals.

A number of Kazakhs and Kirghiz, who had fled the country after the 1916 revolt, started to return to their homes. Their former properties were, however, already occupied by Russian settlers. Serious strife developed between the returning natives and the new settlers, who preferred the use of force to surrendering their recently acquired property. Local Russian garrisons, poorly disciplined, ineffectually tried to keep some semblance of peace.

During this period two Kazakh congresses had been held in Orenburg. Through this medium the Kazakh nationalist party, Alash-Orda, formulated new demands: expulsion of Russian settlers, termination of the draft, and return to native administration of education. The emerging idea of national autonomy had little time to develop. The success of the October Revolution threw the whole area into a new turmoil.

2. *The Struggle for Survival*

The young Soviet regime in Turkestan was almost immediately cut off from Soviet Russia by the anticommunist Cossack troops of Ataman Dutov and remained so, with a few short interruptions, until the fall of 1919. The only solid support for the new regime came from the Russian workers of the Tashkent Railroad Repair Shops and the troops of the local garrison.

On December 13, Mohammed's birthday, the Muslim nationalists organized a demonstration in Tashkent in which some Russian anticommunists also participated. Soldiers dispersed the demonstrators, killing eighteen people in the process, but renewed recognition had been won, since the Tashkent Council of People's Commissars decided to appease the Muslims by offering to call a Turkestan constituent assembly.

Meanwhile, the Kokand Muslim government, plagued by the lack of military force and in need of military alliances, decided to join the "Southeastern Union of Cossacks, Mountain Caucasians, and Peoples of the Steppe." This organization had been created on paper by the anticommunist General Kaledin. As the latter, busy with his own problems, supplied no troops, the Kokand government made an "opening to the left" by giving a third of the seats in its Muslim Congress to the freshly organized Kokand Muslim Soviet, a left-wing organization modeled on the Russian soviets of workers' and soldiers' deputies.

While the Kokand government was maneuvering for support, anticommunist Cossack troops finally began moving eastward from the Caspian Sea toward Taskhent. The Tashkent Soviet threw its military forces against the Cossacks and routed them near Samarkand. Freed from that menace, the Tashkent Soviet finally decided to liquidate its embarrassing Muslim competitor. Soviet troops returning from Samarkand were ordered to Kokand. The Kokand government reacted by attacking the small Russian garrison within the city in the hope of destroying it before the arrival of the main Soviet force. This action was unsuccessful. In the meantime the Soviet troops under Commissar Perfilev—consisting mostly of ragged units fresh from their Samarkand victory—reached the city. The hastily assembled defenders were made up of local Uzbek inhabitants, as well as some Teke-Turkmen, Caucasian Lezgin mountaineers, and a few Persians, reinforced by local Muslim guerrillas under Irgash-bey. To further confuse the whole affair, the weak Kokand Muslim Soviet made an eleventh-hour attempt to take power in Kokand, hoping thereby to deprive the Russian troops of their reason for attack. The attempt failed, and the Soviet troops assaulted the city on February 5, supported by a local Russian and Armenian mob. The Muslim defenders were routed. A real "pogrom" ensued, accompanied by looting and rape. The local Muslim population became deeply alienated from the Soviets.

The Tashkent Soviet made no attempt to win back the Muslims. During the winter famine of 1917—18 little effort was made to relieve the urban Muslim population with the requisite foodstuffs. In the villages Russian troops requisitioned food in what was, at that time, the accepted "war communism" pattern. All cotton was surrendered under penalty of death. Muslim peasants suspected of sympathy with the nationalist guerrillas were shot. The Russian revolutionary slogan *svoboda* (freedom) became known among the Muslims as *svobodka* (little freedom) and was given the meaning of lawlessness and looting.[4] The result was pitiful: all the countryside, cities, and railroads were soon in Irgash-bey's hands.[5] The basis for the future nationalist Basmachi Revolt was laid.

The next step of the Tashkent Soviet was an attempt to penetrate Bukhara, where the emir maintained his authority undisturbed by the two revolutions in Russia. On February 28, 1918, the chairman of the Turkestan Council of People's Commissars, F. I. Kolesov, arrived in Bukhara from Tashkent to visit the emir. As he expected, his demands for cooperation were rejected. However, Kolesov had carefully stationed his troops in advance, should military action against Bukhara be necessary. His attack on March 2 routed the Bukharan defenders, and the Soviet troops penetrated the city. Again, as they had in Kokand, the troops looted the city. At this point the outraged population decided to back up the otherwise unpopular emir, and the invaders were, in their turn, routed. Several hundred innocent Russian inhabitants of Bukhara were then slaughtered by the Muslim mob before the emir's troops could intervene and stop the massacre.

The Soviet setback was followed by the signing of an agreement between the emir of Bukhara and the Soviet regime of

Tashkent for the recognition of Bukharan independence by the latter. In return the emir agreed to turn over anticommunist Russian agents to the Soviets and to exchange prisoners without compensation. The truce was clearly a temporary solution, as the emir continued to help the nationalist bands operating in Russian Turkestan, and the Tashkent Soviet continued to plot the emir's overthrow with the Bukharan radical groups.[6]

During this period the old Russian puppet, Khan Isfendiar, was deposed in Khiva by a very energetic opponent, Djunaid-Khan (January 1918). Djunaid put his own man on the Khivan throne and established contact with both the emir in Bukhara and the Basmachis in Russian Turkestan. In May he executed several left-wing Young Khivan leaders who were plotting against his regime.[7]

To a large extent these setbacks were due to the internal difficulties of the Tashkent Soviet government. Not only was the entire area in a state of economic collapse——a condition not helped by wholesale nationalization——but the popularity of the Tashkent Soviet authority among the Muslims and among many Russian settlers was at a very low ebb.

To remedy the situation Moscow sent an "extraordinary commissar" to Turkestan, P. A. Kobozev, to look into the situation. Under his guidance the Fifth Congress of Soviets in Tashkent proclaimed Turkestan a republic, part of the Russian Federation. A new thirty-six-man Central Executive Committee was elected, equally divided between Bolsheviks and left SRs, with Kobozev himself as chairman. Seven Muslims were included, a token representation for their over 85 percent of the new republic's population. A Council of People's Commissars was also confirmed, with Kolesov still in charge. Of its sixteen seats only three were conceded to the Muslims.

In May events were more favorable for the Soviets. The Russian settlers of Semireche finally decided to move against the anticommunist Cossacks and create a Soviet regime in that area. This strengthened the position of the Tashkent Soviet, but the new Soviet regime of Semireche proved to be a rather embarrassing ally, as Semireche authorities were ridden with anti-Muslim and anti-Semitic prejudices, issued their own currency guaranteed by stocks of opium, and favored the distilling of bootleg vodka.

In Tashkent, Russian and Armenian nationalists, regardless of political allegiance, began to gather around the local Soviet regime as the only remaining "European" force in a sea of discontented natives. The struggle in Turkestan was followed along ever increasing nationalist lines, with the Muslims pitted against the Russians. Concepts such as revolution and communism were no longer of prime importance.

The number of communists in Tashkent was nominal; the First Party Conference, which took place in June 1918, counted only 250 party members in the entire city. Some insignificant gestures were made toward the Muslim masses. The Uzbek language was "recognized" as equal to Russian, and "confidence" was expressed in the Uzbek proletariat.[8] A seven-man Central Party Committee of the Turkestan Republic was elected, with only one Muslim member.

The same month an anti-Soviet revolt started in the main city of Turkmenia, Ashkhabad. Tashkent sent its own man, Commissar Frolov, who succeeded only in making the situation worse. Local Turkmen tribesmen and anticommunist Russian officers took over. The Transcaspian Soviet government was arrested and shot. Supported by British funds, an anti-Bolshevik Transcaspian government was set up to include anticommunist Russians, Armenians, and Turkmen. Soviet troops were soon ejected from Mary Oasis.

Soviet Turkestan was in a difficult position, caught between the Russian anticommunist forces in Orenburg and those in the Turkmen steppes, the Cossacks pressing on Semireche, and the Muslim nationalist Basmachi Revolt brewing in the valley of Fergana. In addition, the Soviet regime was affected by constant internal struggle. First, the left-wing SRs split with the Bolsheviks at the Sixth Congress of Soviets (Tashkent, October 1918); then old and young communists divided at the Second Party Congress (December 1918). In December the Basmachi showed a considerable growth in strength. Then an anticommunist revolt by Russian settlers had to be quelled in the Belovodsk District of Semireche. On the night of January 18, 1919, events again turned for the worse, as the military commissar of the Tashkent Soviet government, Osipov, attempted to take over the city. Even though the revolt failed and the defeated Osipov fled to Bukhara, morale fell very low, especially since the workers of the Tashkent Railroad Repair Shops had taken part in the attempted coup.

In February Moscow appointed a special temporary commission for Turkestan affairs. In addition to P. A. Kobozev, who was already heading the Tashkent Soviet government, two more communist officials were sent from Moscow, S. Z. Eliava and A. S. Kiselev. Meanwhile, the situation in Khiva was becoming tense. Since the middle of 1919 the Young Khivan and other anti-Djunaid elements had been allowed to gather on the Soviet side of the border. Tashkent, nevertheless, aware of its own weakness, felt it necessary at this time to sign a treaty with Djunaid-Khan recognizing Khivan independence (April 9, 1919). The Soviet delegation sent to Khiva was officially headed by a former Turkish officer, Mohammed Kazembek. The real head of the Soviet delegation was, however, a Russian communist, Khristoforov, who divided his attention between his official work in the delegation and behind-the-scenes propaganda activities against Djunaid-Khan.[9] He remained in Khiva as Tashkent's envoy but persisted in his intrigues and finally perished at the hands of Djunaid-Khan's men.

In the meantime a struggle between the pro-Muslim and colonialist factions was brewing in Tashkent. During the Seventh Congress of Soviets, after the left-wing SRs united with the communists, a national section was created within the party where Muslim communists were at last given a chance to express their views. However, natives pursuing the goal of self-determination, such as the Kirghiz, Turar Ryskulov and the Uzbek Tursunkhodzhaev, were not always sure enough of their safety to attend party meetings without safe-conduct passes, which were necessary in order to avoid arbitrary arrests by Russian chauvinists active within the Tashkent Soviet regime.

A fight between the pro-Muslims and the colonialists finally took place at the Third Congress of the Communist Party of Turkestan. While Moscow's Commissar Kobozev sided with the pro-Muslims, Kazakov, the new head of the Tashkent government, sided with the colonialists. One of the leaders of the colonialists was Uspenskii, a former member of the Black Hundreds (a violently reactionary organization) turned communist. The Tashkent Soviet also took the side of the colonialists. In order to overcome their opposition, Kobozev had a new Turkestan Party Committee elected which included seven Russians and three Muslims. The new Party Committee immediately clashed with the Tashkent government, while local Soviet authorities as well as the security forces continued to display their usual anti-Muslim bias. On July 12, 1919, Moscow cabled Tashkent demanding that Muslims be admitted into government bodies. On receiving the cable, Kazakov called a joint meeting of the heads of all the leading soviet, party, and governmental institutions in Tashkent. The result of the meeting was a victory for the colonialists. A reply was sent to Moscow stating that owing to local conditions, the admission of Muslims into local government bodies was impossible. It was also decided not to publish the contents of the Moscow cable.[10]

In September 1919 two congresses met in Tashkent: the Eighth Congress of Soviets and the Fourth Congress of the Communist Party of Turkestan. From these congresses came the organization of the *Kombedy* (committees of poor peasants) in the usual communist manner and the introduction of a state grain monopoly. Once again the new developments became a tool in the hands of Russian settlers and an excuse to confiscate food from the Muslim peasants. The Congress of Soviets was finally induced, however, to give the natives a majority in the Tashkent government.

In contrast with the political and economic dilemmas, the military situation had improved considerably. The Russian anti-communist forces had been thrown out of Turkmenia (July 1919). Admiral Kolchak was finally defeated in Siberia, and Turkestan was no longer isolated from the rest of the country.

3. *The Revolution Secured*

The arrival of Soviet troops from the north, which followed the reestablishment of communications between Turkestan and Russia proper, shifted the center of political power in Tashkent from the local authorities into the hands of Moscow's delegates and the military command of the freshly arrived Fourth Red Army. The Fourth Army Party Conference decided to overrule previous decisions by the Tashkent authorities concerning the nonparticipation of Muslims in local soviet organizations. In October 1919 a commission for Turkestan affairs was established by a Moscow decree signed by Lenin. No Muslims were included. S. Z. Eliava, a Georgian, was named chairman and placed in charge of external relations. V. V. Kuibyshev and M. V. Frunze were mainly concerned with military matters, Ia. E. Rudzutak with economic problems, and F. I. Goloshchekin with party affairs. Also included was G. I. Bokii. They began to arrive in Tashkent in November 1919. The Army Special Section took over the local Cheka (political police). The Ministry of Foreign Affairs of Turkestan, a symbol of far-reaching regional autonomy, was abolished and its functions transferred to the Department of External Relations within the commission itself. All supplies were channeled through the supply commission of the army, cutting the ground from under the feet of the Tashkent authorities.

In an attempt to stop the growth of Moscow's control in local Turkestan affairs, Russian settlers in and around Tashkent, including communists, began to advocate local autonomy and to court local Muslims. Tursunkhodzhaev, a native Muslim, was elected as first party secretary. The Fourth Army headquarters, the Tashkent government, and the Commission for Turkestan were now also courting the Muslim majority. The commission sent a project to Moscow harshly criticizing the previous activities of the Soviet regime in Turkestan. The latter was said to have been infected with "colonialist psychology," and the local Muslim population was said to condemn their policies as "a continuation of the actions of the agents of the old tsarist regime."[11]

Following the commission's recommendations, Moscow pressed for action on two main goals: elimination of colonialist attitudes among Russian settlers and of "feudal-patriarchal attitudes" among the Muslims. Land taken from the Kirghiz after the suppression of the 1916 revolt was to be given back. Landless peasants, regardless of nationality, were to be given land. To implement this policy, Russian settlers were to be disarmed. Speculators, former bourgeois, former tsarist policemen, and those among the old tsarist bureaucrats "who did not fit in the new Turkestan" were to be expelled and sent to concentration camps in Russia. Local Russian communists with "colonialist mentality" were to be transferred to Russia and replaced by communists from metropolitan Russia. Russians and Muslims were to be treated equally in the distribution of supplies by the state. This fresh approach was easy to proclaim but difficult, if not impossible, to implement.

The Commission for Turkestan Affairs, which had been so critical of colonialists and their methods, soon reverted to the very position it had previously condemned. A conflict developed between the commission and the Muslim communists of the Ryskulov group. The latter were this time backed by both the party and the government in Tashkent, where Muslims were now in the majority. Ryskulov, a friend of the Tatar nationalist-communist foe of Stalin, Mir-Said Sultan Galiev,[12] wanted it clearly understood that the arrival of the Fourth Red Army was not to be interpreted as a conquest of the area by Russian troops from metropolitan Russia. Ryskulov was also opposed to the idea of carrying the class struggle into the native community, especially during the period of decolonization.

In January 1920, at two parallel party conferences (one of them Muslim), Ryskulov pressed for renaming the Turkestan Republic the "Turkic Republic" and the party the "Turkic Party." Met with Frunze's rebuff, Ryskulov attempted to carry his arguments to Lenin himself. In June his delegates in Moscow argued for the suppression of the commission, the withdrawal of Russian army units, and the formation of a local Muslim Red Army, all without success. Unable to reach a working agreement with the commission, Ryskulov's group resigned from the government. A new Tashkent government was organized, with the more docile Rakhimbaev as chairman. He and a score of co-operative native communists were elected to the new Temporary Central Party Committee of Turkestan.

Moscow, aware of the difficulties in Tashkent, decided to send a new commission, which again contained no Muslims and consisted of Sokolnikov, Safarov, Kaganovich, and Peters. Under their auspices the Fifth Congress of the Communist Party of Turkestan and the Ninth Congress of Soviets (September 1920) reaffirmed the principle of class struggle within the Muslim community, thus rejecting Ryskulov's contention of similarity of interest between the bourgeoisie and the proletariat of a colonized nation. Shortly thereafter Ryskulov, at the First Congress of the Peoples of the East in Baku, continued to advocate his and Sultan Galiev's ideas of the necessity of a bourgeois nationalist revolution in the colonial east by arguing that the native proletariat in colonial areas was still much too weak to become a leading revolutionary force.[13]

As has since been demonstrated, both Sultan Galiev and Ryskulov were much in advance of their time and geographically misplaced. Only after Stalin's death, and then only with respect to Western colonial and underdeveloped areas, did Moscow accept their proposals as exemplifying the correct approach for the decolonization stage.

During 1920 things in Central Asia went quite differently. Safarov, the most pro-Muslim member of the new commission, but an opponent of Ryskulov, soon found himself in conflict with his Russian colleagues. Letters were exchanged with Moscow leaders, involving Lenin, who grew suspicious of chauvinistic tendencies displayed by Russian officials in Tashkent, including the new chairman of the commission, M. P. Tomskii, and a member of the same group, the Latvian communist Peters.[14]

In the meantime, with the civil war ending, the Soviets decided to reorganize Khiva along more convenient lines. Even before the arrival of the Fourth Red Army, local Soviet authorities had reached a behind-the-scenes agreement with Djunaid-
Khan's feudal rivals. In November 1919 a revolt began against
Djunaid, led by another Turkmen chieftain, Koshmamed-Khan,
which continued until the middle of December. By that time
the Soviets realized the inability of the rebels to win without direct Russian support, so on December 25 Soviet troops, led by
G. B. Skalov, crossed the Khivan borders. Three days later
Koshmamed-Khan became their official ally. After a month of
resistance Djunaid-Khan, with 400 men, fled to the Kara Kum
desert. The legal ruler of Khiva, Djunaid's puppet Seid-Adulla,
acquiesced to the new state of affairs. Despite his submission,
he was deposed on February 2, 1920, and replaced by a pro-
Soviet revolutionary committee (with the RSFSR emissary G. I.
Broido playing the leading role).[15] Shortly thereafter Djunaid-
Khan made a comeback, trying to take Khiva, but was repulsed.

On April 4 Khiva, already under Soviet control, was transformed into the People's Republic of Khorezm. In May this first
Soviet satellite received its first Soviet envoy, Iosif Moiseevich
Byk.[16] Byk arrived to find that the newly created Khorezm government consisted not of genuine communists but of patriotic
Young Khivan radicals. Two Young Khivans, Palvanniaz Yusupov and Sultanmuradov, had become, respectively, head of the
government and head of the revolutionary committee. The only
reliable man in the Khivan (Khorezm) government was old Djunaid's rival, Koshmamed-Khan, who became the deputy chairman of the revolutionary committee. The People's Republic of
Khorezm duly signed a treaty of alliance with Soviet Russia
(September 1920). Nevertheless a serious conflict was developing between the nationalist-minded Young Khivans and their
Russian "protectors."[17]

Having established a people's republic in Khiva, the Soviet
government decided to follow a similar approach in Bukhara.
On March 14, 1920, M. V. Frunze, the commander of the Turkestan Red Army, visited the emir, repeating the 1918 attempt
by Kolesov to persuade him to "coöperate" with the Soviets.[18]
This démarche, made only five weeks after the Soviets' takeover
of Khiva, yielded no positive results whatsoever. On the contrary, the emir sent an emissary to London in an attempt to
obtain British support. He also contacted anti-Soviet Muslim
guerrilla leaders from neighboring Soviet areas. Frunze and

Kuibyshev, for their part, aware of the need to preserve a Muslim facade for their projected intervention, forced reconciliation on the Young Bukharans and their communist counterparts (August).[19] The next month Frunze decided to act. Russian workers staged a revolt in a Bukharan town on the Turkestan-Bukharan border. Simultaneously the small revolutionary Young Bukharan group started a revolt in Bukhara itself, and, as in 1918, Russian troops were ready in advance. But this time they were not poorly disciplined Red Guards from Tashkent but regular units of Commander Frunze's army. They crossed the Bukharan border on the same day and, after a four-day battle, took the capital (September 1920). The emir fled south to the Tadzhik Mountains, and the People's Republic of Bukhara was established. Frunze, his task accomplished, was transferred to the Ukraine to command Soviet operations against the anticommunist forces in the Crimea.

Ten days later Kuibyshev arrived in Bukhara as the first official envoy of Moscow. The assignment of such a prominent Soviet leader to this position speaks for itself. Kuibyshev was not sent to Bukhara merely to be an envoy——he intended to rule.

On November 3, 1920, a treaty of military, political, and economic cooperation was signed between Moscow and the newly established Bukharan government, and in December Soviet troops started to move toward eastern Bukhara to throw out the emir.[20] Emir Said Alim Khan, who fled to Dushanbe (today the Tadzhik capital), was unable to resist. On the tenth of March he crossed the border to Afghanistan.[21]

Soviet domination over the area seemed to be secure at this point, but new obstacles——national communism in both Khiva and Bukhara and the Muslim nationalist revolt all over the area——were already looming in the path of the Soviet regime.

The October Revolution in Central Asia was initially a settlers' affair; this situation continued for two years, while Turkestan was cut off from the rest of the country by events of the Civil War. Menaced by the Whites, threatened by Muslim nationalism, and too weak to control the former Russian protectorates of Khiva and Bukhara, the authorities in Tashkent had only stranded Russian Army units, railroad workers, and a few leftist settlers to rely on. And the settlers' support had to be bought by protecting their privileges. The breaking of geographical isolation and the arrival of metropolitan troops brought basic changes. Under Lenin's prodding, Muslim participation rose from token to real, and hopes for true self-determination arose among the few Muslim intellectuals who joined the Revolution. Among them were Young Bukharans and Young Khivans fighting the reactionary regimes of their respective emirs.

But hopes for genuine self-determination were soon dashed. It is true that unlike the Tashkent settlers, Lenin stood for real autonomy with strong Muslim participation, but not beyond the limits needed to preserve the basic unity of the country and the centralized, Moscow-controlled authority of the party. Yet Lenin's concept of national autonomy, while limiting Muslim aspirations, left enough room to make further cooperation attractive. Quite a few Muslim leaders availed themselves of this opportunity, which prevented the Basmachis from monopolizing the allegiance of the Muslim masses and helped speed up the reconstruction process.

Later, Stalin's economic drives (forced collectivization, forced industrialization, mass implantation of new settlers into the area), combined with endless purges, created a new reality that had little in common with the Leninist beginnings.

CHAPTER THREE

The Basmachi
Revolt

The word *basmach*, which originally meant "bandit," was not new in Central Asia. Bandits had always roamed the countryside, attacking and plundering caravans, and had been especially brazen during troubled times. The Muslim nationalist Kokand government, before collapsing, had received the support of the local Basmachi leader, Irgash-bey. Later, some members of the Kokand government fled to the Basmachi, giving an ideological and patriotic coloring to their activity. Organized around local leaders, the Basmachi movement was similar to that in Algeria of the 1950s, where the term *fellagha* (peasant), originally used by the French to describe Algerian bandits, changed into a word for a nationalist patriot waging a war of liberation against colonial oppression. The impetus for the growth of the Basmachi movement was twofold: a struggle for national independence resulting from the destruction by the Soviets of the Kokand Muslim government and subsequent coloniallike outrages, and the economic crisis stemming from the ruin of cotton crops in the Fergana Valley, with its attendant famine.[1]

The initial phase of the Basmachi Revolt took place from February 1918, when the Muslim Kokand government was overthrown, to September 1920, when Soviet troops seized Bukhara. The Basmachi, active mostly in the Fergana Valley, initially included a large proportion of common criminals and were in no way models of good behavior.[2] But during this period the blunders made by the Tashkent Soviet government tended to work in the Basmachi's favor. Requisitions, the shooting of Muslim peasants suspected of being sympathetic to the Basmachi, and the looting by poorly disciplined Red troops were undermining Soviet prestige. Such slogans as "Turkestan for the Turks" and "Turkestan without violence" were popular among the native Muslim population. Many native Soviet officials defected. One of them, Madamin-bek, the head of the Soviet militia in the Fergana Valley town of Margelan, became a prominent Basmachi leader and a rival to Irgash-bey. In November 1918 he and an allied Basmachi group led by Khal-Hodja attacked the villages of Russian settlers in the valley. The local Russian settlers, in an attempt to fend off further raids, created an army of their own, and this force received official recognition and support from the Fergana Red Army headquarters. However, under the impact of the unpopular Soviet decree establishing the state grain monopoly, the Fergana peasant army began to grow restless. The Soviets, aware of this, tried to disarm them in June 1919 but failed. This in turn alienated the settlers.

In August the settlers' army demanded civil rights and the abolition of state grain monopolies and revolutionary tribunals. The Basmachi chieftain, Madamin-bek, supported these demands and joined his 7,000-man force to the peasant army. Their combined forces took the town of Osh in September. A temporary government for Fergana was created, with Madamin-bek as chairman and military commander, and as deputy chairman, Konstantin Monstrov, a former Soviet staff officer and the commander of the settlers' army. A joint Muslim and Russian anticommunist force seemed to be in the making in Fergana.

Soon, however, the entire military picture changed. Soviet metropolitan troops, led by Army Commander Mikhail Frunze, arrived in Turkestan. The Soviet regime in Tashkent was no longer isolated from the rest of Soviet Russia. Fresh Soviet troops were sent to Fergana Valley, and by the end of September they had retaken the few towns which had previously fallen into rebel hands. During this time the relations between the Russian settlers and the Basmachi had been deteriorating. In January Monstrov and his men surrendered to the Red Army. In a brilliant political move the Muslim Volga Tatar Red Brigade was sent to subdue the Basmachi. The latter began to surrender in large numbers: 2,600 in January, 3,000 in February. Those remaining were crushed on February 4. By the middle of March 1920 Madamin himself was forced to surrender. Only one important Basmachi chieftain, Kur-Shirmat, remained in the field. The revolt in the Fergana Valley appeared to be at an end. Former Basmachi units were transformed into "Soviet Basmachi" units of the First Uzbek Cavalry Brigade.[3]

The second period of the Basmachi Revolt started as a

consequence of Soviet military actions against Khiva and Bukhara. In April 1920 the People's Republic of Khorezm (Khiva) was proclaimed. In September the Emir of Bukhara fled to Dushanbe, and in turn, the People's Republic of Bukhara was established. Although the emir was unable to remain in Dushanbe and was forced to take refuge in Afghanistan (March 1921), his departure only increased nationalist resistance. Mullah Abdul-Kahar was appointed by the emir to head the resistance in Bukhara. Soviet attempts to induce, by negotiation, the remnants of Basmachi forces in the Fergana Valley to surrender also failed.

The Soviet takeover in Bukhara irritated the natives all over Central Asia. The action of Russian food-requisition squads and the untimely mobilization (summer 1920) of Muslim conscripts into the Soviet army resulted in mass defections of Muslims to the Basmachi. Basmachi forces began to grow from day to day, while Muslim Red Army units became increasingly unreliable. An order was given to disarm the First Uzbek Cavalry Brigade. The result was grave. The brigade (with few exceptions) joined the Basmachi. Under the leadership of a local chieftain, Kur-Shirmat, Basmachi strength increased. They were a force of 6,000 who knew the area, had an effective intelligence service, and what is most important, had the support of the local population. In the event of defeat they could disappear into the villages. As a result, the entire Fergana Valley was under their control. The Soviets dominated only the main cities and railroads.[4]

On February 22, 1921, army commander G. V. Zinoviev, head of the anti-Basmachi operations in Fergana, met with the Basmachi representatives but failed to obtain their surrender.[5] In April the Soviet situation temporarily improved. A Basmachi chieftain, Djany-bek, went over to their side. From his followers and from the remnants of the First Uzbek Cavalry Brigade a native regiment was formed. The winter of 1920—21 was severe. People became weary. In August and September peace parleys were held between the Soviets and the Basmachi, and the prospects for peace appeared encouraging. Meanwhile hungry Russian refugees poured into the area.[6] Elsewhere in Central Asia the situation was also very difficult. In Kazakhstan, despite aid from the American Relief Administration and the relaxation of economic pressures due to the introduction of the New Economic Policy (NEP), both the famine and the Basmachi were spreading.[7]

In Khiva, the local Communist Party was becoming more

and more nationalistic. In an upsurge of Uzbek-Turkmen ethnic feuds, Koshmamed-Khan, the leading local Soviet supporter, was shot. As a result, serious difficulties developed between his Turkmen followers and the Uzbek nationalist-communists, who were in power. Khivan authorities gave refuge to the Bashkir Muslim nationalist Zeki Validov (November 1920), who had fled there after the liquidation by the Russians of Volga Bashkir autonomy.

The Commission for Turkestan Affairs in Tashkent and Kuibyshev in Bukhara could no longer tolerate this state of affairs. In January a large group of party men, headed by a Russian communist, Safonov, arrived in Khiva on Kuibyshev's orders. Khivan communists tried to discredit the de facto "High Commissioner" Safonov in Moscow by alleging that he used violence in dealing with Muslim communists; but their efforts failed, and the integration of Khiva proceeded as planned by Tashkent. The political department of the Soviet Khivan Red Army assumed responsibility for party work in Khiva, supplanting the nationalist central committee. Finally, on the night of March 14, 1921, the Young Khivan government was deposed. Its members fled into the desert and joined their former enemy, Djunaid-Khan. The Soviets set up a new, more obedient Khivan government. A party purge followed. Of 2,000 party members, only sixty were judged reliable enough to retain their party cards. The republic's name was transformed from "people's republic" to "soviet republic," an important step forward on the road to complete integration.[8]

The result of the Khivan putsch intensified Muslim nationalist resistance to the Soviets in Bukhara. The Lokai Valley of Hissar became a hotbed of new Basmachi revolt. Ibragim-bek, a member of a local Uzbek tribe, organized the main Basmachi forces. New Basmachi chieftains arose both in the Tadzhik Mountains and in the Fergana Valley (Rakhman-Datkho, Khal-Hodja, Nurmat-Ali, and others). Muslim nationalist revolt spread across Central Asia.[9]

Some Russian officials, impatient with the slow process of Sovietization and the spread of the Basmachi revolt in Bukhara, began to toy with the idea of replacing the leadership of the people's republic with more pliable men. Fajzullah Khodzhaev, the head of the government of Bukhara and one of the few former *jadids* still on the Soviet side, warned the Turkcommission:

> We know that all obstinacy on our side and forcible measures on

yours will be fatal and lead to undesirable consequences for us and for you.

We wish no forceful upheavals, since we realize that Bukhara, after such an experiment, will relapse into a desert of destruction, without mentioning the [former] emir's statements and the whole range of revolts on tribal and national grounds.[10]

Moscow heeded this warning and concentrated on military means of quelling the Basmachi rebellion while throwing its political support to present Bukharan leaders.

The Soviets took drastic steps to stop the spread of the rebellion. S. S. Kamenev, the commander-in-chief of the Red Army, arrived in Central Asia to set up campaign plans against the Basmachi. In January 1922 an extraordinary dictatorial commission for east Bukharan affairs, with full powers in that area, was established by the "People's Government" of Bukhara, and it remained in force until May 28, 1924. At the same time, the Central Committee of the Communist Party in Moscow organized a special commission, consisting of I. V. Stalin (then People's Commissar for Nationalities), G. V. Chicherin (People's Commissar for Foreign Affairs), and V. V. Kuibyshev (who arrived from Central Asia), to study the materials presented by the Commission for Turkestan Affairs concerning the situation in Bukhara. The commission acted rapidly.

In February the Bukharan Communist Party was brought under the control of the Russian Communist Party. All the anti-Basmachi operations in Bukhara, Fergana, and elsewhere in Turkestan were unified. Validov, already expelled from Khiva, and other Bashkir and Tatar Muslim nationalists were expelled from Bukhara.

National Communism was, however, as strong among Young Bukharans as it had been among the Young Khivans. The newly organized satellite government of the People's Republic of Bukhara was torn between satisfaction at having eliminated the feudal regime of the emir and nationalist aspirations for more independence from the Russians. At the same time, on Moscow's instigation, Enver Pasha, one of the leaders of the defunct Young Turkish Government of Turkey, was sent to Bukhara. Son-in-law of the last sultan, army general, revolutionary, adventurer, and opportunist, he arrived on November 8, 1921, looked into the local situation, and soon decided to change sides. Enver, having left his former Soviet friends, reached the emir and was appointed commander-in-chief of his (or rather, Basmachi) forces in the field. The latter were, at that time, accumulating successes. In February a former Young Bukharan, Usman Hodja, head of the government of the Bukharan People's Republic, arrived in Dushanbe with 600 men. Dissatisfied with Soviet policy, he reached an agreement with the Basmachi and took over the town, overwhelming the malaria-ridden Soviet garrison. The Bukharan people's commissars of war and of the interior also went over to the Basmachi side. The Basmachi force, already 20,000 men strong in December 1921, was growing, and the local population was giving its support to them.[11] Muslim nationalist agitation was spreading even in Tashkent. In December the Soviets arrested the illegal Muslim Committee of National Union, operating in Tashkent since February and headed by the Tashkent mufti.[12]

The struggle between the Basmachi and the Soviet Russian troops was not between communists and anticommunists, as in Russia, but between Russians and Muslims. The Basmachi, despite some initial short-term opportunistic alliances with anticommunist Russian groups, were a native Muslim Turkestani movement. The Soviet troops fighting the Basmachi were, on the contrary, metropolitan troops of Russian nationality (with some Ukrainians and Tatars added). Native Turkestani soldiers were very few, their proportion less than that of Muslims in the French troops in Algeria. Uzbeks accounted for fewer than 5 percent in 1927, while Kirghiz, Turkmen, and other natives together numbered even fewer than that.[13] Even this small percentage was reached only after a big effort was made, in 1926, to create some native Turkestani Soviet units. From 1920 to 1926, during the crucial years of the revolt, the percentage of native soldiers in the Red Army in Turkestan was even lower.

During the spring of 1922 the revolt was approaching a climax. The government of the People's Republic of Bukhara, after the defection of Usman Hodja, was headed by Faizullah Khodzhaev, a former *jadid* who had taken part in the 1918 Kolesov expedition against Bukhara, and by Abdulhamid Arifov, a nationalist-communist who was not too willing to pursue the fight against the Basmachi with the requisite determination. The situation was getting dangerous for the Soviets, since they were faced with growing Basmachi strength and with nationalistic tendencies among the Muslim communists. The satellite government of Bukhara was forced to call for immediate Russian military assistance.[14]

In February a strong Basmachi force, under Mullah Abdul-

Kahar, started a revolt near Bukhara that endangered the security of the city.[15] Faced with an increasingly dangerous situation, the Soviets decided to take drastic steps. In March their war effort was subjected to a complete reorganization. A special anti-Basmachi force was created in eastern Bukhara. One infantry and two cavalry brigades, three infantry and one cavalry regiment, as well as auxiliary forces and the forces of the Bukharan People's Republic were included. In May a Central Asian bureau of the Central Committee of the Russian Communist Party was organized to coordinate the efforts of the communist parties of Turkestan, Bukhara, and Khiva. A prominent communist leader of Georgian origin, "Sergo" Ordzhonikidze, arrived in Bukhara from Moscow in May and sharply rebuked the hesitant policy of the Bukharan satellite government.[16] S. S. Kamenev, the commander-in-chief of the Red Army, coordinated military preparations in the area. Soviet troops soon moved against the main Basmachi forces of Ibragim-bek and Enver Pasha.

On the Basmachi side there was little agreement among the leaders. Enver Pasha, who dreamed of a Muslim empire, called himself "commander-in-chief of all the forces of Islam, son-in-law of the Khalif, and representative of the Prophet." Ibragim-bek, jealous of favors shown by the ex-emir to Enver, split with the latter. Faizullah Maksum, another important Basmachi leader, followed the same course. As a result Soviet troops recaptured Dushanbe and further pressed the rebels. On August 4, 1922, Enver was killed in an insignificant engagement. The new commander, Selim Pasha, selected by a Basmachi conference in Kabul,[17] and approved by the emir, was a Turk and a friend of Enver. Unrecognized by many Basmachi leaders (thereby failing to unite the movement), he committed suicide in the Piandj River. In the meantime a Basmachi terrorist attempt on the life of Faizullah Khodzhaev, new chairman of the Bukharan Council of People's Commissars, failed on July 7, 1922.[18]

The Soviet offensive was not limited to Tadzhikistan. An internal struggle between Uzbek and Kirghiz units in the Fergana Valley had weakened the Basmachi movement. On several occasions the Kirghiz chieftain, Muetdin, remained "neutral" during Soviet actions against Uzbek Basmachi. In November the foremost Uzbek Basmachi leader in the area, Kur-Shirmat, left Fergana and went to Afghanistan, leaving formal command to his Kirghiz rival, Muetdin. This attempt to unify the competing Basmachi groups failed. New fights began between Muetdin and the Uzbek chieftain, Israil, who was discon-

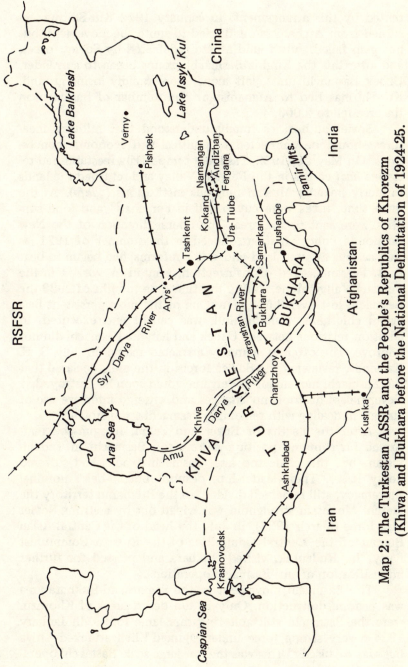

Map 2: The Turkestan ASSR and the People's Republics of Khorezm (Khiva) and Bukhara before the National Delimitation of 1924-25.

tented by this arrangement. In January 1922 Kur-Shirmat returned from Afghanistan and tried to unite the movement, but he again failed. July found Muetdin defeated by Soviet forces, and after this the Kirghiz Basmachi groups began to surrender. Uzbek Basmachi units, left alone, were rapidly losing ground. Kur-Shirmat fled to Afghanistan. The number of Basmachi in the area fell to 2,000.[19]

Soviet authorities finally understood that military measures should be connected to political and economic concessions. On May 26, 1922, Tashkent temporarily reestablished religious *kazi* courts in the Fergana Valley and returned the lands formerly held by Muslim religious institutions (*vakfs*). At the same time, taxes were cut in half in Fergana,[20] and food supplies were sent to the area. The liberal direction of the New Economic Policy, first introduced in the summer of 1921, as well as long-awaited land and water reforms, had begun to bear fruit. Peasants, tired of insurrection, wanted to work.[21] In the Fergana Valley alone, during the first nine months of 1923 the Basmachi lost over 3,500 men. One of the most persistent Basmachi chieftains, Rakhmankul, was caught and executed. In addition relations between Uzbek and Kirghiz Basmachi did not improve. The offer of amnesty attracted many. In July S. S. Kamenev, reviewing the Soviet forces in the area, declared that the Basmachi movement in Fergana would soon be destroyed.[22] Nevertheless he took no chances and ordered intensive use of aircraft in dealing with remaining Basmachi strongholds.[23]

After the deaths of Enver and Selim, Ibragim-bek reaffirmed his supreme position among the Basmachi in Tadzhikistan, but this came too late. Basmachi troops had suffered heavy losses. Their leadership, despite Ibragim-bek's nominal supremacy, still remained divided. In the Bukharan territory the Metchi Mountain stronghold was wiped out by a strong Soviet task force (March 1923). In July the head of the Central Asian Bureau of the Central Committee of the Russian Communist Party, Ia. Rudzutak, visited Bukhara and pressed for further intensification of anti-Basmachi operations.

The Basmachi movement in the Samarkand-Bukhara area was nearing destruction. Only in the desert areas of Khorezm were the Basmachi still able to gather large forces. In January 1924 a very strong force under Djunaid-Khan attacked Khiva but was repulsed.[24] This was the last large-scale Basmachi operation in Central Asia.

By 1925 Tadzhikistan, the center of the Basmachi revolt,

lay in ruin. Over 200,000 inhabitants had already fled to Afghanistan, leaving two thirds of the arable land abandoned. In relatively less affected Uzbekistan, one fourth of the land was abandoned.[25]

Ibragim-bek tried a comeback in 1925, but the country had been bled white, and the people were too tired to continue what was obviously a hopeless resistance. The peasants wanted peace at any price. From fifty-seven groups with 1,370 men, the Basmachi troops in Tadzhikistan dwindled to twenty-nine groups with 959 men (spring 1926).[26] The long-overdue land reform, finally carried out in Tadzhikistan in 1924, began to produce results favorable to the Soviet regime. A Communist Party organization was created that strengthened Soviet control in the area. After the 1926 campaign Soviet authorities were at last able to cut the number of troops engaged in mopping-up operations.[27] Reduced to small bands, many Basmachi took the still available opportunity of Soviet amnesty.[28] Their leaders, Ibragim-bek, Kuram-bek, and others, fled to Afghanistan. By 1927 the Basmachi forces in Tadzhikistan were reduced even further, but some small bands were still active, and a Basmachi chieftain, Rakhman, was still operating from across the border.[29]

In 1928 even Djunaid-Khan was forced to flee to Afghanistan. In Tadzhikistan Maksum, the new head of the Tadzhik Soviet government, was able to induce the peasants, already tired of the hopeless struggle, to return to their lands. About 33,000 peasants (out of 200,000 refugees) returned to Tadzhikistan from Afghanistan.[30] Fresh Russian cavalry units crushed the remnants of Basmachi troops in the countryside.[31]

The Basmachi movement, almost dead, was revived in 1929 by the Soviet action of forcing collectivization on reluctant peasants. Ibragim-bek himself was caught by Soviet troops in June 1931, but remnants of Basmachi groups, often reduced to banditry, survived until 1933.[32] After years of uneven struggle, all trace of military resistance was crushed. The local native population was finally subdued, and Soviet peace was established in Central Asia.

The Basmachi movement started as banditry, developed into a genuine national-liberation movement, then, when defeated, reverted to its origins. Present-day Soviet literature on the subject dismisses the central phase and obscures the Russian versus Muslim aspect of the anti-Basmachi struggle. Mikhail Frunze, the Russian *komandarm* who at one time led the fight against the revolt, was more objective. He saw it as "an armed protest against the new beginnings,"[33] which looked suspicious to the Muslim masses, frustrated in their hope for self-determination by the settler-dominated authorities of the Turkestan Republic.

The Basmachi were finally defeated by the military might of the Russian Red Army combined with more liberal policies initiated toward the Muslim majority, policies that lasted from the spring of 1922 until stifled by forced collectivization. But despite its murky origin and unglamorous end, the Basmachi movement was a national-liberation movement on a par with the many similar ones that have emerged in Asia and Africa since the end of World War II. It is worth noting that the descendants of the Basmachi took refuge in Afghanistan in the 1920s are now in the forefront of the guerilla battle against the Russian troops "pacifying" Afghanistan—sixty years later.

CHAPTER FOUR

The Economic Scene

A comprehensive study of the overall economic development of Soviet Central Asia lies beyond the scope of this book and beyond the competence of its author. Instead this chapter concentrates on those economic issues that have a direct bearing on nationality problems or, conversely, result from nationality policies, attitudes, or conflicts. Obviously such an approach overemphasizes controversial issues at the expense of objective achievements. Within such limits the latter cannot possibly be given the attention they otherwise deserve.

1. Collectivization and Its Consequences

The Central Asian economy emerged from the Revolution in a state of total chaos. In many areas production fell to 20 percent of the prerevolutionary level.[1] However, the liberal direction of the New Economic Policy (NEP) stimulated a recovery, despite the continuing Basmachi revolt. Two agricultural reforms were carried out after the establishment of the Soviet regime. The first one consisted of confiscating lands and water rights belonging to local *bais* (landlords) and distributing them to the *dekhane* (Muslim peasants). Started in 1921, then expanded in 1925—27, this reform fell short of expectations. It was, nevertheless, willingly accepted by the native peasant masses. Farmers' cooperatives, or *Koshchi* unions, organized on a voluntary basis by 1927, included 60 percent of peasant households. They helped the rural population buy necessary farm tools and market their products.[2] This period of economic stabilization was interrupted in 1929 by the social and economic revolution caused by the collectivization drive. Settled peasants were pressured to collectivize. Nomads were forced to settle *and* to join the collective farms. The previously successful farmers' cooperatives were abandoned. An American technician working in Kazakhstan at the time reported:

> When the Communist shock troops began to break up those herds and to put pressure on the nomad owners to pool their animals in so-called collective farms, the latter simply killed their animals. . . . The ex-nomads who survived this period were rounded up as the *kulaks* have been. . . . Many of them resisted dispossession; these were adjudged criminals, and sent to jail or shot.[3]

During this struggle the animal stock of the area was decimated. Millions of head of cattle were slaughtered by the peasants and the nomads; millions more perished in the resulting chaos. Precollectivization-sized herds were restored only in Khrushchev's day (see Table 1). At the same time, the yield of wheat in the cultivated areas of Kazakhstan dropped from the usual 5.7—6.3 centners per hectare to 4.0 in 1931 and 4.4 in 1932.[4] "Counterrevolutionary elements," *bais*, Basmachi, and other traditional villains were charged by the authorities with causing the hardships. Scores of native communists were removed for leniency and negligence. Others were executed for "bourgeois nationalism" because of their opposition to forced collectivization. Despite all the troubles, the bulk of private farming was collectivized between 1929 and 1932, with the percentage of collectivized land increasing in Uzbekistan from 1.2 in 1928—29 to 68.1 in 1932 and 95 in 1937; in Kazakhstan it rose from 2.7 in 1928 to 98.3 in 1935.[5] The rest of Central Asia followed.[6]

Table 1 **Cattle in Central Asia**
(in 1,000 head, pigs excluded)

	1929	Collectivization 1932–33	1941	1960	1979
Kazakhstan	36,000	5,029	11,488	33,633	42,183
Central Asia proper	23,151	9,120	16,167	24,623	31,379

Sources: Michael Rywkin, *Russia in Central Asia* (New York-London: Collier Macmillan, 1963), p. 64; *SSSR i soiuznye respubliki v 1976 godu* (Moscow: Statistika, 1977), pp. 106, 222, 237, 269; *Narodnoe khoziaistvo SSSR v 1978 g.* (Moscow: Statistika, 1979).

In 1942 Soviet authorities allowed former nomad cattle breeders to resume their traditional way of life, more appropriate to soil conditions in the area, but no retreat from the collective farm system was ever contemplated. The impact of collectivization on the traditional cattle-breeding economy of non-irrigated lands of Central Asia and the inability of post-World War II cattle breeding to keep pace with the threefold population increase between the 1926 and the 1979 censuses are obvious.

2. *Cotton and Grain Policies*

Since prerevolutionary days Central Asia has been the main cotton area of the USSR, accounting for about 90 percent of total production. Cotton is grown on irrigated lands, in valleys and oases. The heart of the cotton land is in the Fergana Valley.

One of the chief accusations leveled against the tsarist economic policy in Central Asia was that the latter had transformed the area into "a cotton appendix of Russia" (Lenin), just as British policy in Egypt was also directed at pushing cotton production at the expense of grain. But the Soviet government has always followed the same policy. This can be seen from Tables 2 and 3, showing the shifts in cotton and grain cultivation in Uzbekistan, the republic which accounts for about two thirds of the total cotton and for half of the silk in the country (no cotton is produced outside Central Asia).

The increase in cotton lands was closely connected with the decrease in the area occupied by grains, especially by rice, despite the fact that rice is the major component in the local diet. This shortage of rice was felt especially during the war years.

Table 2   **Cotton and Grain in Uzbekistan,**
Area under Cultivation (in 1,000 hectares)

Crop	1913	1938	1950	1965	1978
Cotton	423.5	917.2	955	1,549.9	1,824.0
All cereals	1,521	1,452.7	1,371	1,252.6	1,194.5
Rice only	161	80.4	52.8	55.3	94.2

Sources: Rywkin, p. 65; *Narodnoe khoziaistvo Uzbekskoi SSR v 1978 g. Statisticheskii ezhegodnik* (Tashkent: Uzbekistan, 1979), p. 92.

Table 3   **Cotton and Grain Production in Central Asia and Kazakhstan**
           (in 1,000 tons)

Grain	1913	1940	1961	Average 1971-75	1976-78
Kazakhstan	2,162	2,516	14,672	21,662	25,142
Central Asia proper	1,822	1,637	1,242	2,494	3,953
Cotton					
Kazakhstan	15	93	216	305	298
Central Asia proper	646	1,864	4,029	6,921	7,667

Sources: SSSR v tsifrakh v 1961 (Moscow: Statistika, 1962); *SSSR i soiuznye respubliki v 1978 g.* (Moscow: Statistika, 1979).

Faizullah Khodhzaev, the former head of the Uzbek government executed during the Great Purge (and duly rehabilitated
later), was made to confess his opposition to the policy of
cotton monoculture.[7] Khodzhaev and a number of local leaders
supposedly holding similar opinions were liquidated. The cotton
policy won out once and for all, and the economy of Central
Asia became integrated with that of the rest of the country.
Moreover, even in the 1970s only an insignificant part of Uzbek
cotton was processed locally (4-5 percent by the end of the
1970s). The rest was shipped to Russian textile mills.[8]

While increasing cotton production in Central Asia at the
expense of grains, Soviet planners have been strongly promoting
the development of grain-producing Siberian-type black soil
areas of northern Kazakhstan (see Table 3). This policy received
further impetus under Khrushchev. Hundreds of thousands of
party and Young Communist League (Komsomol) members
were sent to farm the area, despite adverse climatic conditions
resulting in a short growing season.[9] Elsewhere farming is limited to valleys and oases, while about 60 percent of the total
territory is made up of deserts.

3. *The Industrial Leap Forward*

The industrial development of Central Asia is recent. Prior to the October 1917 Revolution, Central Asia was a purely agrarian and cattle-breeding area, with only a few cotton-ginning and silk-spinning mills. The Soviet five-year plans, wartime transplantation of several large industrial enterprises, and especially post-World War II industrialization transformed the character of the region, projecting it into the industrial age (Table 4).

Table 4   **Industrial Output in Central Asia and Kazakhstan**

	1913		1940		1976		1978	
	In 1,000 tons	In % of total USSR output	In 1,000 tons	In % of total USSR output	In 1,000 tons	In % of total USSR output	In 1,000 tons	In % of total USSR output
Steel	—	0	11	0.06	6,010	4.15		
Coal	131	0.45	1,689	1.02	104,182	14.64		
Oil	260	2.52	1,433	4.61	39,894	7.68		
Cement	—	0	267	4.6	13,662	11		
Fertilizers (mineral)	—	0	2	0.06			13,396	13.67
Electroenergy (in million kwh)	7	0.35	1,310	2.7			114,402	9.52

Sources: Rywkin, p. 68; *SSSR i soiuznye respubliki v 1976 godu; SSSR i soiuznye respubliki v 1978 g.; Narodnoe khoziaistvo SSSR v 1978 g.*

But this leap forward brought the prospects for future industrial development of the area face to face with a number of limitations. As analyzed by a Russian economist who is a member of the Uzbek Academy of Sciences, despite its rich mineral resources and surplus manpower, the area suffers from:

1. limited water resources, the bulk of which are indispensable for agriculture;

2. distance from the main industrial regions of the country;

3. specific gaps in socioeconomic indicators as compared with the rest of the country.[10] (See Table 5.)

The gaps stem from a whole array of factors, such as the traditional local Muslim preference for nonindustrial occupations, lower labor productivity, the inclination toward nontechnical education, resistance to outmigration, limited female nonagricultural employment, and so on.

As a result of this situation and in order to maintain a de-

Table 5

Selected Economic Indicators

Republic	Industrial growth by 1979 (1970=100)		Capital investment per capita, in rubles (1979)	Retail trade turnover per capita, in rubles (1979)	Savings bank deposits, in rubles (1979)		Nonagricultural wages per capita, in rubles (1975)	Kolkhoz man-day wages, in rubles (1974 average)
	capital goods	consumer goods			per capita	average deposit		
	1		2	3	4		5	6
USSR as a whole	177	160	494	960	553	1,080	1,775	4.50[1]
RSFSR	174	153	585	1,055	608	1,054	1,860	4.60
Kazakhstan	165	159	530	822	378	1,017	1,792	6.71
Uzbekistan	174	201	330	596	198	1,015	1,677	4.72[2]
Kirghizia	194	164	267	682	260	971	1,651	5.51
Tadzhikistan	169	174	248	553	185	938	1,684	4.69
Turkmenistan	165	167	433	665	237	1,346	1,926	6.95

Sources: 1-4: Narodnoe khoziaistvo SSSR v 1979 g. (Moscow: Statistika, 1980); 5-6 Regional Development in the USSR, NATO Colloquium, 1979; 6: Narodnoe khoziaistvo Uzbekistan SSR v 1978 g.

[1] In 1978, 5.22.
[2] In 1978, 5.21.

sirable level of economic development in the area, Moscow has been increasingly forced to subsidize the Central Asian economy in a wide variety of ways, the most important of which is returning turnover taxes collected in the republics to republic budgets (see Table 6). Union republics, unlike the states of the

Table 6			**Soviet Central Asia: Welfare Colonialism**			Turnover tax collected and retained in budgets
	Net material product per capita (USSR = 100)		Total income per adult equivalent[1]		Growth of labor productivity (1970=100)	of republics, 1967-79 (average, in %)
Republic	1960	1978	1960	1978	1977	
Kazakhstan	88	82	98	85	134	100
Uzbekistan	75	56	82	77	133	92
Kirghizia	73	57	78	77	132	96
Tadzhikistan	66	50	72	72	120	90
Turkmenistan	107	60	85	92	135	99
RSFSR	107	114	107	109	144	45

Source: Soviet Economy in a Time of Change. A Compendium of Papers submitted to the Joint Economic Committee, Congress of United States, vol. 1, Washington, D.C., 1979.

[1] Children under 15 and retired persons counted at 50 percent.

United States, have no tax levy power but are given back a part of turnover tax moneys collected in their territory according to a centrally established, but variable, formula. The formula often tends to favor the non-Russian union republics, which get back a larger portion (or sometimes the totality) of their money.[11] Central Asia and Kazakhstan were generally allowed to keep almost 100 percent of the turnover tax that originated in their republics, as against a maximum of 45 percent for the RSFSR. This is something Russians view as another proof of their benevolence. Other union republics, however, tend to produce less tax money per capita than the RSFSR, resulting in smaller per capita sums available for their budgets, a fact that some Western analysts view as discriminatory.

Finally, permanent missions from individual republics to the USSR Council of Ministers in Moscow have been established in order to improve economic, scientific, and cultural contacts, a renewal of an earlier practice started in the 1920s. The last move was of limited practical importance but gives the appearance of increased concern for the individual republics.

4. The Native Working Class

The tremendous industrial development of Central Asia during the years of the Soviet regime has transformed the entire economy and created a large urban working class. The majority of nonagricultural employees in Central Asia remain nonnative, however, since the growth of the native working class has not yet matched the growth of industry. Of the nonagricultural cadres in Central Asia, nonnatives are in the majority among managers and technicians in industry and mining, white-collar workers, and skilled laborers. Natives, on the other hand, predominate as managers of consumer-good enterprises and cooperatives, as craftsmen in local industries, and as manual laborers. They are still just a small minority among those handling agricultural machinery. Thus in Uzbekistan, where so few Europeans work in agriculture, the number of Uzbeks classified as *mekhanizatory* ("machine operators") is still pitifully small: it did increase fivefold between 1939 and 1970, but only from 1.3 percent to 4.3 percent in 1959 and 6.7 percent in 1970.[12]

The process of increasing the native working class has been a slow one. Almost nonexistent at the time of the Revolution, still insignificant by the outbreak of World War II, it began to develop under the pressure of wartime manpower needs. Spurred by the rapid industrialization in the post-Stalin years, and despite many exaggerated claims, the Muslim working class is probably still in the minority in Soviet Central Asia (see Table 7). And considering that in 1972, 55.7 percent of all Soviet workers were doing manual labor (75 percent in agriculture), we can assume that among Muslim workers in Soviet Central Asia, the proportion was even higher.[13]

5. Russian Economic Strongholds

The largest factories in the republics, and obviously all those working for defense, are classified as "factories of all-Union importance" and are in most matters totally independent of local party authorities. The latter are prevented from interfering with their operation, and special party organizers of the USSR's Cen-

Table 7		Native Working Class				
		As % of total working class in the republic			As % of employees of titular nationality	
Republic		1939	1959	1973	1959	1970
Kazakhstan		27	19	n.a.	44	63
Uzbekistan		37	43	n.a.	27	39
Turkmenistan		25	34	37	22	32
Kirghizia		18	21	n.a.	22	41
Tadzhikistan		29	33	n.a.	18	37

Sources: Natsional'nye otnosheniia v SSSR na sovremennom etape. Na materialakh respublik Srednei Azii i Kazakhstana (Moscow: Nauka, 1979), p. 135; Iu. V. Bromlei, ed., *Sovremennye etnicheskie protsessy v SSSR* (Moscow: Mysl', 1972), p. 127; V. G. Kostakov and E. L. Manevich, eds., *Regional'nye problemy naseleniia i trudovye resursy SSSR* (Moscow: Statistika, 1978), p. 270.

tral Party Committee are in charge of their party organizations. The managers of such factories are selected for their ability to perform and for their standing in the party. Local ethnic pressures are for the most part disregarded. Thus in Central Asia these managers are predominantly Russians; a few Muslim directors appeared only after 1957, and their numbers, according to the émigrés from the area, are still very low.

Soviet style "affirmative action" measures are not enforced in such enterprises, thus protecting skilled Russian and other non-Muslim engineers, technicians, and workers from the demands of the still less prepared Muslim cadres and, by the same token, assuring a smoother production process.

The widespread presence of such enterprises in both Central Asia and Kazakhstan creates Russian oases directly connected to Mother Russia and shielded from undue local interference. But this state of affairs fuels tension between two competing ethnic groups: the better-qualified Russians, determined to preserve their entrenched positions, and the upwardly mobile natives, eager to assert their growing influence and use their newly acquired skills.

Yet there have been some concessions. Since 1965 the councils of ministers of individual republics have been allowed to "look into" Moscow's economic plans for enterprises of all-Union importance located on their territory and to make "suggestions" (only) in these matters.[14]

The exact proportion of enterprises of all-Union importance in the Central Asian economy as a whole is unknown. But, for example, in 1978 they accounted for 36.8 percent of all profit generated by industry located in the Uzbek Republic (as against 32.7 percent in 1965, 35.3 percent in 1970, and 35.2 percent in 1975, a rather stable one-third share).[15]

6. *Private Initiative: The Uzbek Example*

Income from private plots and per family earnings in Central Asia are higher than in the RSFSR, as is the average pay of collective farmers.[16] The role of private plots in Uzbek agricultural production is actually increasing. Conservative official figures speak of 15.2 percent of the gross output in 1965, 18.8 percent in 1970, and 20.9 percent in 1978.[17] More realistic Soviet Uzbek estimates are around 26 to 28.8 percent and account for a quarter of a collective farmer's income.[18] These figures may still be too low, given the USSR average of 25.2 percent of a collective farmer's income (1978) and the fact, stressed in other Soviet sources, that in the southern regions of the USSR, private plot production satisfies "to a large degree" both the food needs of the collective farmers *and* the collective farm market trade in the cities.[19]

Another center of private initiative is the collective farm market trade. In large Uzbek cities it has shown a constant increase, the amount of meat, vegetables, and fruits sold doubling between 1965 and 1974.[20] The volume of market trade in "second-hand goods," another source of private funds, is proverbial, especially in Tashkent. It too escapes the statistician's eye.

In addition, in 1974 average collective farm pay was higher in Uzbekistan than in the RSFSR (by 3 percent), and the cost of living was lower by 16.8 percent.[21] Uzbekistan is rich in fruits and vegetables (scarce in most of the RSFSR) and has climatic conditions that require much less clothing, covered housing space, and heating.

Starting in 1976 a more benevolent attitude toward private plots became a part of a growing positive attitude toward "legitimate" private initiative in general.[22] Beginning with January 1977, collective farmers were entitled to 1,500-ruble low interest ten-year loans (or approximately one fourth of the supposed cost of a basic 78-square-meter dwelling) for constructing private homes.[23] The June 1978 Resolution of the Central Committee of the CPSU and the USSR Council of Ministers concerning "the development of individual housing and the retention of cadres in the village" is in line with this new attitude. The linkage between private housing and retention of cadres is significant: private rural housing is no longer seen as a concession to the peasant but rather as an inducement to stay in the village. While primarily intended for the labor-short Russian villages, and not for labor-rich Uzbek ones, the new benevolence cannot fail to benefit the private-initiative-oriented Uzbek village more than its Russian counterpart.

The presence of widespread private housing in urban areas is another characteristic feature of the Central Asian housing situation. All Central Asian republics have more private urban living space per capita than the RSFSR (see Table 8). In percent-

Table 8   **The Private Sector in Housing**

Republic	Privately owned urban housing, in % (1979)	Private housing construction as % of total (1979)	Private investment in housing, in rubles per capita (1979)
RSFSR	17.4	13.0	2.92
Ukraine	36.1	34.7	11.55
Belorussia	24.6	24.5	6.87
Lithuania	23.3	38.3	15.50
Latvia	19.1	21.5	4.74
Estonia	21.1	21.3	5.43
Moldavia	32.1	55.4	17.14
Georgia	39.7	34.6	11.90
Armenia	26.5	19.5	6.83
Azerbaidzhan	27.8	38.7	8.34
Kazakhstan	26.4	12.8	4.24
Uzbekistan	34.5	45.0	13.76
Tadzhikistan	26.8	51.1	11.79
Turkmenistan	27.7	57.7	17.33
Kirghizia	37.0	53.5	12.54

Source: Narodnoe khoziaistvo SSSR v 1979 g. Statisticheskii ezhegodnik (Moscow: Statistika, 1980).

ages of total living space per capita, the Central Asian republics are outdistanced only by Georgia and the Ukraine. If one begins to look into per family figures (either in square meters or in percentages), only Georgia, famous for its flourishing private initiative, can compete with Central Asia. Urban private housing adds as much to the attractiveness of this area as do the favorable climatic conditions.

In rural areas private property (or rather "personal property," as it is called in the USSR in order to exclude prohibited income-producing schemes) prevails in all of the Soviet Union. What is special in Central Asia is that collective farm members who live in their "personal" houses also earn a better than average proportion of their income from their "private plots"[24] (see Table 9).

This, in turn, increases the amount of uncontrolled funds available for further private housing. And it accounts for the visible presence of private initiative, something a visitor to Uzbekistan or Georgia almost feels in the air. Private initiative

Table 9   **Private Plot Agriculture in Uzbekistan**
(1978)

Commodity	% from private ownership	
	Uzbekistan	USSR as a whole
Livestock	52.9	20.2
including cows	68.1	30.9
sheep and goats	26.0	19.7
Production of		
grain	5	1
potatoes	35	61
fruits and berries	63	58
grapes	31	22
vegetables	49	29
meat	49	29
milk	62	29
eggs	41	34
wool	45	19
Private plots as %		
of all cultivated land	3.02	2.77

Sources: Narodnoe khoziaistvo SSSR v 1978 g. and *Narodnoe khoziaistvo Uzbekskoi SSR v 1978 g.*

in the USSR takes the form of private plots, collective farm markets, "second-hand goods" markets, privately contracted services, using state or collective facilities for one's own production, speculation with scarce commodities, and finally, outright theft of collective property or funds. In all these endeavors the Uzbek Republic is highly competitive.

7. *Welfare Colonialism*

Characterized by Martin Spechler as "welfare colonialism,"[25] Soviet economic policy in Central Asia (and here we have to exclude Northern Kazakhstan, which presents quite different problems) must be viewed in the light of three main considerations:

1. Moscow considers it politically imperative not to allow a serious gap to appear between Central Asian industrial development and that of the rest of the country. This gap is consistently filled by growing financial subsidies.

2. It is viewed politically prudent to let the local Muslim apparatchiki have their way in matters dealing with personal advancement:

    a. preferential hiring of local Muslims in most jobs, except in the enterprises of all-Union importance, is the rule (we are not speaking here of key party, government, and security control positions, which will be discussed elsewhere);

    b. tolerance of abuses of power or corruption by local Muslim officials, as long as such abuses are kept within "tolerable" limits. (This subject is also discussed in more detail elsewhere in this book.)

3. It is considered necessary to allow more private initiative in this area than elsewhere in the country (in housing, private plots, collective farm market trade, etc.), partly as a cure for potential unemployment in an area resistant to outmigration of surplus labor (a problem discussed in more detail in Chapter 5).

Soviet economic policy in Central Asia is neither one of traditional economic exploitation nor one of pure and selfless benevolence. It is rather a politically opportunistic attempt to combine three diverse elements: a genuine interethnic economic equalitarianism of Leninist inspiration, a social welfarism reminiscent of the American attitude toward its minorities, and a good deal of prudent tolerance for the increasingly numerous Muslim inhabitants in this politically sensitive geopolitical area.

CHAPTER FIVE

Population and Manpower

1. *The Demographic Background*

Tsarist colonial expansion into Asia, unlike English colonialism, never had to face the problem of very large numbers of natives to be subdued. By having Russian settlers follow its troops, Moscow was able to secure the areas it conquered. Central Asia, the last tsarist colonial conquest, was no exception. Its population, estimated at just over six million at the time of the annexation (not counting the so-called Steppe Region, already under Russian rule), grew very moderately, with high mortality, especially among infants, keeping numbers down. On the other hand, Russian and Ukrainian settlers, given all possible incentives to move into the area, increased rapidly in numbers (especially after the mid-1870s). Even their natural rate of increase compared favorably with that of the natives.

By the time of the Revolution, Slavic settlers accounted for 29.3 percent of the population of Kazakhstan and for 3.8 percent of Central Asia proper, within today's borders, for a total of over two million people. Muslims, predominantly Sunni, were about twelve million strong, including those living in the Russian protectorates of Bukhara and Khiva. Among the Muslims only five groups were numerically important: the Uzbeks (over three and a half million), the Kazakhs (over four and a half million), and the Kirghiz, Tadzhiks, and Turkmen (each under a million). The only significant non-Muslim minority remaining from before the Russian conquest was Bukharan Jews, numbering about 20,000 (see Table 10).[1]

Slavic migrants before the Revolution concentrated mostly in three areas they selected for natural conditions more appropriate to Russian colonization: north of the Steppe Region bor-

Table 10   **The Population of Central Asia before the Revolution**

	1897		1911	
	in 1,000s	in %	in 1,000s	in %
Steppe Region				
Muslims	1,905	77.3	2,176	58.5
Russians[1]	493	20	1,542	41.5
Others[2]	67	2.7	–	–
Turkestan				
Muslims	4,986	94.4	5,942	93.6
Russians[1]	199	3.8	407	6.4
Others[2]	95	1.8	–	–
Bukhara and Khiva				
Muslims	3,100	99.1	3,600	–
Russians[1]	28	0.9	?	–

Source: Aziatskaia Rossiia (St. Petersburg: Glavnoe Pereselencheskoe upravlenie, 1914), vol. 1.

[1] Including Ukrainians and Belorussians.

[2] Including nonindigenous Muslims, non-Russian Christians, and Jews.

dering on Siberia, in the black-soil lands of the Semireche, and in the Tashkent area. About half of the settlers were relative newcomers, having arrived after 1906, attracted by material inducements offered in Stolypin's "virgin land program."

After the October Revolution and during the early 1920s, Russian colonization of Central Asia was temporarily halted. After 1928, however, Slavic (mostly Russian and Ukrainian) colonization was resumed, and by 1936, 1.7 million new settlers had moved into the area: 786,000 into Uzbekistan; 156,000 into Turkmenistan; 290,000 into Khirghizia; 202,000 into Tadzhikistan (Kazakhstan not accounted for). By 1939 the Slavs constituted half of the population of the main city of the area, Tashkent.[2]

Although many newcomers were deportees exiled to Central Asia as persons politically or socially dangerous to the Soviet regime, they involuntarily found themselves in the role of promoters of Soviet Russia's colonial policy in Central Asia. The same was true for non-Russian newcomers, since natives often failed to make a distinction between the Russians and the other national groups of European origin. The latter, on the other hand, under the impact of local conditions, soon developed a kind of common "European solidarity" with the Russians vis-à-vis the Muslims.

Attempts made at that time by some native communist leaders to stop the waves of Russian migration had been unsuccessful. Nastrattulah Maksum, president of the Tadzhik Supreme Soviet, who tried to oppose Russian colonization in Tadzhikistan, was liquidated in 1933. Similar attempts by the Kazakh communists Sultanbekov, Dulatov, and Sasvokasov also ended in failure.[3]

In the Stalin era the influx of Russian settlers had a decisive bearing on the economic development of Central Asia. Before the large-scale Russian immigration, the region had faced several problems peculiar to underdeveloped areas in general, including the presence of large numbers of nomads reluctant to change their customary way of life, lack of industry, and consequently, the lack of a native proletariat.

The German invasion of Russia in 1941 brought another wave of newcomers: employees of evacuated enterprises and their families, refugees (many of them Jews) from German-occupied territories, and Polish citizens released from Soviet camps in Siberia.[4] As a result of industrialization, urbanization, and wartime population movements, some previously native cities became heavily Russified. For example, in the 1950s in the city of Samarkand, Uzbeks and Tadzhiks together accounted for only 39.5 percent of the population, while Russians, Ukrainians, and Belorussians accounted for 36.9 percent. Koreans constituted 1.4 percent; others (probably mostly Russian and Bukharan Jews, Armenians, Tatars, Volga Germans, etc.) were 22.2 percent.[5] By 1959 the proportion of Europeans in Kazakhastan had risen to about 65 percent, and in Central Asia proper to approximately 25 percent. Pre-World War II deportations of kulaks, "socially dangerous elements," and Koreans, as well as war-connected transplantations of "westerners" (from Poland and the Baltic states), Volga Germans, and other "unreliables," accounted for a large proportion of Europeans. In addition some wartime refugees were dissuaded from returning to the European area of the USSR.

The "virgin lands program" in Northern Kazakhstan in the early 1960s brought with it the last large-scale influx of Europeans into the area. In total, one and a half million Russians and other outsiders were transplanted into Kazakhstan and Central

Figure 1   **Growth of Population by Main National Groups**   Population
in millions

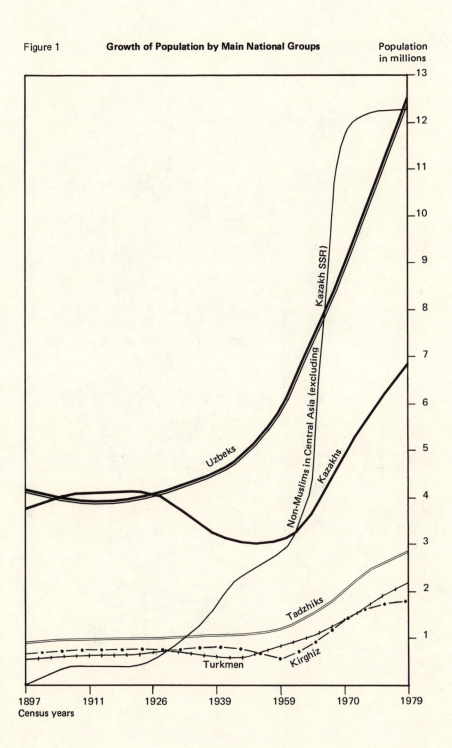

13

12

11

10

9

8

7

6

5

4

3

2

1

Kazakh SSR)

Non-Muslims in Central Asia (excluding

Uzbeks

Kazakhs

Tadzhiks

Turkmen

Kirghiz

1897   1911   1926   1939   1959   1970   1979
Census years

61

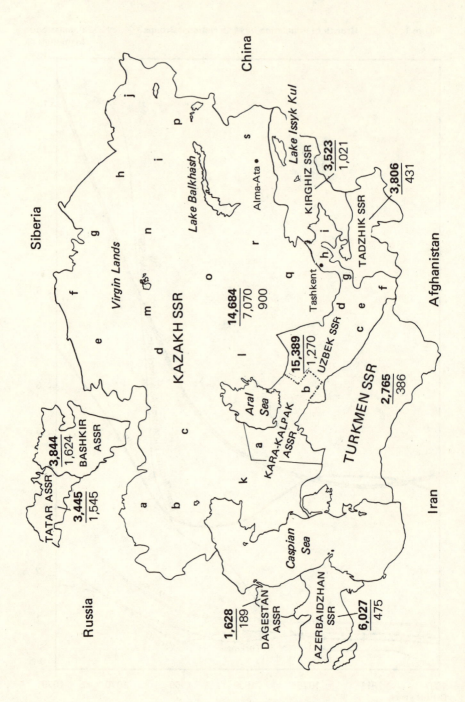

Siberia

Russia

China

Alma-Ata •

Lake Issyk Kul

3,523
 ──────
 1,021

KIRGHIZ SSR

3,806
 ─────
  431

TADZHIK SSR

Lake Balkhash

Virgin Lands

KAZAKH SSR

14,684
 ───────
  7,070

 900

Tashkent

15,389
 ───────
  1,270

UZBEK SSR

Aral
Sea

KARA-KALPAK
ASSR

TURKMEN SSR

2,765
 ─────
  386

Afghanistan

Iran

3,844
 ─────
 1,624

BASHKIR
ASSR

TATAR ASSR

3,445
 ─────
 1,545

Caspian
Sea

1,628
 ─────
  189

DAGESTAN
ASSR

AZERBAIDZHAN
SSR

6,027
 ─────
  475

Map 3: Political-Ethnic Map of Central Asia and Adjacent Muslim Republics (1979).

Figures show total population for each republic
(in thousands), broken down as follows:

000 —total population
00 —Slavs (Russians, Ukrainians, and Belorussians, where reported)
0 —Germans

Kazakh SSR regional breakdowns:

a: 585/256
b: 370/72
c: 630/233/30
d: 270/131
e: 943/637/95
f: 573/407/38
g: 616/327/76
h: 807/466/81
i: 773/323/44
j: 876/611
k: 253/109
l: 562/86
m: 809/476/103
n: 1,255/828/131
o: 449/311/24
p: 663/258/36
q: 1,565/335/51
r: 931/319/70
s: 850/305/60
Alma-Ata: **902**/605

Uzbek SSR (including Kara-Kalpak ASSR) regional breakdowns:

a: **905**/21
b: **747**/15
c: **1,267**/148
d: **1,399**/118
e: **1,124**/34
f: **897**/39
g: **512**/34
h: **1,793**/334
i: **4,502**/278 (includes the four regions of the Fergana Valley)
Tashkent: **1,759**/ca. 725/ca. 125 (other non-Muslims)

Asia between 1959 and 1970.[6] (See the ethnic map on pages 62-63 and Figure 1.)

But even such intensive immigration was unable to balance the decreasing Slavic and the rapidly increasing Muslim birthrates. By 1969, for example, the birthrate in the three Slavic republics of the USSR declined to 14.2—15.9 per 1,000, as compared to 16.8—18.1 in Western Europe and the United States, and 30.1—34.7 in the Muslim republics of Central Asia! The comparison of net rates of growth was even more ominous for the Slavs: 5.7 for the RSFSR versus 26.8 for the Uzbek Republic.[7] Between 1959 and 1970 the number of Central Asian Muslims grew by 50.4 percent (and of all Soviet Muslims by 41.8 percent), while the number of Eastern Slavs increased by only 12.3 percent. Between 1970 and 1979 the figures were 32 percent for the Central Asians (24.8 percent for all Muslims) as against 5.8 percent for the Slavs. The gap between Muslim and Slavic rates of growth had widened from 3.4 : 1 in 1970 in favor of the Muslims to 4.27 : 1 by 1979 (4.1 and 5.5 : 1 for these dates for Central Asian Muslims). (On the basis of yearly averages, the gap between Central Asian Muslims and Russians widened from 3.46 : 1 to 4.81 : 1.)[8]

According to the 1979 census, the proportion of non-Muslims fell to about 57 percent in Kazakhstan and to just under 18 percent in Central Asia proper (see Table 11). The 1979 census figures thus confirm the irreversibility of the ethnodemographic revolution taking place in today's Soviet Central Asia.

Table 11   **Percentage of Non-Muslims in Soviet Central Asia**
(rounded figures)

	1926	1939	1959	1970	1979
Kazakhstan	35	47	65	59	57
Uzbekistan	6	18	18	17	15
Turkmenistan	7	19	24	19	16
Kirghizia	19	34	44	40	34
Tadzhikistan	1	10	19	17	14

Sources: M. Rywkin, *Russia in Central Asia*, p. 79 (for 1926—59 data); complete 1970 census data for the 1970 census; preliminary 1979 census data from "Vsesoiuznaia perepis' naseleniia," *Vestnik statistiki*, 1980, no. 2.

---

2. *"La Vengeance des Berceaux"*

The sharp differences in birthrates in the various portions of the USSR are generating a profound shift in the ethnic balance of the Soviet population. The Slavic peoples of the Soviet Union, standing on the threshold of a consumer society, have opted for a better material existence at the expense of having children.[9] Even crash programs of apartment construction have failed to offset declines in birthrates among Russians, Ukrainians, and Belorussians. From 1958—59 to 1974—75 the gross reproduction rates in the RSFSR, the Ukraine, and Belorussia dropped

Figure 2   **Births by Ethnic Groups**

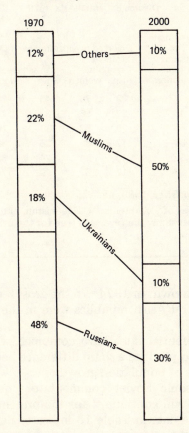

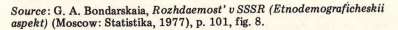
Source: G. A. Bondarskaia, *Rozhdaemost' v SSSR (Etnodemograficheskii aspekt)* (Moscow: Statistika, 1977), p. 101, fig. 8.

from figures in the range of 1.14—1.36 (1 = a roughly static population) to the exceptionally low range of only 0.98 for the RSFSR, 1.0 for the Ukraine, and 1.08 for Belorussia. By contrast, in Soviet Central Asia the Muslim majority—for the most part governed by different aspirations, life styles, and values—continues to look on large families as living proof of improved material conditions. Solomon Bruk, a leading Soviet demographer, stresses the survival of traditional marital-sexual habits (including community pressure against divorce and childless marriage) as a determining factor in this pattern.[10]

Table 12 **Divorce in Central Asia, 1979**

| Republic | Approximate % of Muslims in total population | Divorced or separated per 1,000. age 16 and above | | | | | |
| | | total per republic | | urban areas | | rural areas | |
		men	women	men	women	men	women
RSFSR	7	39	74	43	84	29	49
Kazakh SSR	43	27	56	33	71	18	33
Kirghiz SSR	66	25	52	30	75	21	33
Turkmen SSR	84	17	35	25	60	7	7
Uzbek SSR	85	16	34	24	58	9	14
Tadzhik SSR	86	17	37	29	74	9	12

Source: Vestnik Statistiki, 1980, no. 12.

Note: The rural areas of Turkmenistan, Uzbekistan, and Tadzhikistan contain very few non-Muslims; the reverse is true for the urban areas in all the republics.

The results are known: in 1974—75 the gross reproduction rates in the four Central Asian republics were in the range of 2.33—3.07.[11]

These differential rates have combined with other demographic factors to produce a sharp difference between the Slavic and Muslim rates of population growth.

Although some Soviet commentators question whether this momentum will continue,[12] for the present it seems likely to do so—as the data in Table 13 indicate. Between 1959 and 1970 the share of the youngest population group (ages 0 to 9 in the 1959 census and 0 to 10 in the 1970 census) of the five principal central Asian nationalities increased from 8.97 to 14.97

Table 13   Dynamics of the Ethnic Structure of the Soviet Population 1959—70
(in %)

	1959		1970		1979	
	Ages 0-9	(All ages)	Ages 0-10	(All ages)	Ages 0-10[1]	(All ages)
Total for main Muslim groups[2]	8.97	(7.67)	18.19	(9.91)	26.79	(12.16)
Uzbeks	4.23	(2.88)	7.10	(3.80)	9.91	(4.75)
Kazakhs	2.42	(1.73)	3.87	(2.19)	7.37	(2.50)
Kirghiz	0.69	(0.46)	1.13	(0.60)	2.06	(0.73)
Tadzhiks	0.97	(0.67)	1.70	(0.88)	2.58	(1.11)
Turkmen	0.66	(0.48)	1.17	(0.63)	1.80	(0.77)
Azeri Turks	1.94	(1.41)	3.22	(1.81)	3.07	(2.30)
Total for main Slavic groups	72.06	(76.28)	64.40	(73.97)	65.32	(72.19)
Russians	54.02	(54.65)	46.81	(53.37)	45.75	(52.42)
Ukrainians	14.56	(17.84)	14.12	(16.86)	16.26	(16.16)
Belorussians	3.48	(3.79)	3.47	(3.74)	3.31	(3.61)
All other groups	17.03	(16.05)	17.41	(16.12)	7.89	(15.65)

Source: Lubomir A. Hajda, "Age and Nationality in Soviet Population Change," an unpublished paper of the Russian Research Center, Harvard University, Cambridge, Mass., 1977, and "Vsesoiuznaia perepis' naseleniia," *Vestnik statistiki*, 1980, nos. 2 and 6.

[1] By republics (1979 data by nationalities not yet available).

[2] Titular nationalities of union republics only.

percent. The numerical advantage of Russians over Central Asians in this age group dropped from 6 : 1 to only 3 : 1 during this eleven-year period.

Between 1970 and 1979 the Soviet Muslims (for their population statistics see Table 14) gained as much in population as the four-times-more-numerous Russians (8,707,000 as against 8,381,000). And the next census will show the Russians further behind. True, Muslim rates of growth, especially outside Central Asia, tend to decelerate; but the Slavic ones go down even faster.[13]

The consequence of these developments is that by the 1980s, the rapidly growing Central Asian populations will be the major source of increments to the able-bodied population of working age, serving to offset net declines in other parts of the USSR. The critical issue is that these increments will become available in labor-surplus Central Asia, not in labor-deficit areas of the Soviet Union.

Table 14 — **Muslims in the USSR, by language groups, 1937–79 (in 1,000s, rounded figures)**

Nationalities by linguistic groups	1939	1959	1970	1979
Total	20,640	24,733	35,077	43,769
Turkic				
Uzbeks	4,844	6,015	9,195	12,456
Kazakhs	3,099	3,622	5,299	6,556
Tatars	4,300	4,968	5,931	6,317
Azeris	2,275	2,940	4,380	5,477
Turkmen	812	1,002	1,525	2,028
Kirghiz	884	969	1,452	1,906
Bashkirs	843	989	1,240	1,371
Kara-Kalpaks	186	173	236	303
Kumyks	95	135	189	228
Uigurs	109	95	173	211
Karachais	76	81	113	131
Balkars	43	42	60	66
Nogais	36	39	52	60
Turks	n.a.	35	n.a.	93
Iranian				
Tadzhiks	1,229	1,397	2,136	2,989
Ossetians[1]	354	413	488	542
Kurds	46	59	89	116
Iranians[2]	39	21	28	31
Baluchis	n.a.	8	13	19
Ibero-Caucasians				
Chechens	408	419	613	756
Kabardians	164	204	280	322
Ingush	92	106	158	186
Adygeis[3]	88	80	100	109
Abkhazians	59	65	83	91
Cherkess	—	30	40	46
Abazins	14	20	25	29
Peoples of Daghestan	519	771	1,124	1,369

Others				
Dungans	5	22	39	52
Afghans[4]	n.a.	2	4	n.a.
Arabs	22	8	n.a.	n.a.
Albanians	n.a.	5	4	n.a.

Sources: Consecutive censuses: 1939, 1959, 1970, 1979.

[1] Half of them are Christians.

[2] Mostly speaking a Turkic dialect; others recent Iranian refugees.

[3] In 1939 listed together with Cherkess.

[4] Those listed were of Pariah Indian origin.

Note: Many Tats are said to be Jewish. Muslim Tats called themselves Azeri Turks and are therefore not included in this table.

Here is a good example: Four Slavic cohorts aged 40—44 in 1970 will retire in the 1980s and will be replaced by four cohorts aged 0—4 in 1970. But according to Perevedentsev, the replacement will fall short by two million, a gap to be made up by the three-million surplus from the replacement cohorts in the Muslim republics. The latter will account for over a quarter of those entering the labor market, as opposed to fewer than one out of eight retiring![14] (See Table 15.)

It should be noted at this point that the population trends I am discussing will have an impact not only on the civilian economy but on the complexion of military manpower. It has been estimated that by the year 2000, some 35 percent of all recruits are expected to come from Central Asia and the Transcaucasus.[15] This trend may "employ," if temporarily, surplus Muslim youth in military occupations. However, it is unlikely that soldiers of Central Asian Muslim background would gravitate to labor-deficit areas upon demobilization as opposed to returning to their native republics. The anticipated change in the ethnic composition of the Soviet armed forces also has military and political significance, but these matters deserve consideration in their own right.

3. *Migration Prospects*

Soviet Muslims have shown little propensity to migrate out of their native republics let alone out of Central Asia. According to the 1979 census, half a million Kazakhs (or roughly 8 percent

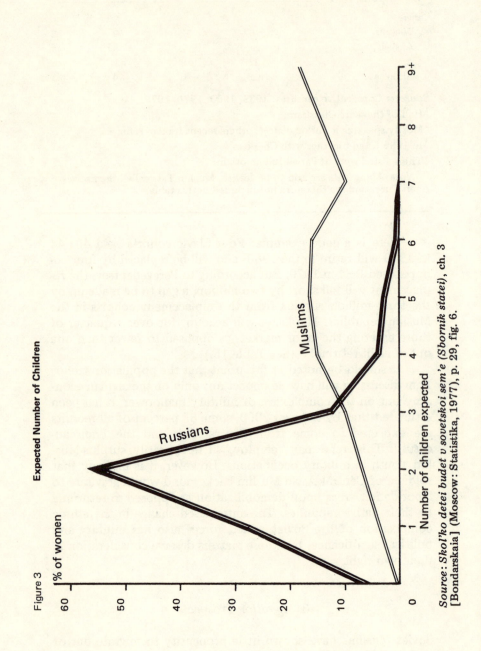

Figure 3

Expected Number of Children

% of women

Muslims

Russians

Number of children expected

*Source: Skol'ko detei budet v sovetskoi sem'e (Sbornik statei), ch. 3
[Bondarskaia] (Moscow: Statistika, 1977), p. 29, fig. 6.*

Table 15   **Soviet Manpower Prospects for the 1980s**

Cohorts coming from	age 0—4[1] (in %)	age 40—44[1] (in %)	0—4 in % of 40—44
Uzbekistan	9.18	3.28	302
Kazakhstan	7.53	4.47	182
Kirghizia	2.01	0.95	229
Tadzhikistan	2.40	0.81	322
Turkmenistan	1.70	0.61	301
Azerbaidzhan	3.63	1.52	257
All Muslim republics			
in %	26.45	11.64	245
in 1000s	5,424.6	2,212.0	+3,212.6 surplus
RSFSR	45.44	57.57	85
Ukraine	16.78	20.42	89
Belorussia	3.62	3.62	108
All Slavic republics			
in %	65.84	81.61	87
in 1000s	13,503.1	15,508.4	−2,005.3 deficit
All other republics			
in %	7.71	6.75	123
in 1000s	1,581.2	1,282.7	+298.5 surplus
Total USSR in 1000s	20,509.0	19,003.1	+1,505.9

Source: Calculated on the basis of V. I. Perevedentsev, "Sotsial'no-demo-graficheskaia situatsiia i vstuplenie molodezhi v trudovuiu zhizn'," *Rabochii klass i sovremennyi mir*, 1980, no. 3, p. 90.

[1] According to the 1970 census.

Note: The table illustrates the example of four age cohorts leaving and another four entering the labor market in the 1980s.

of that ethnic group) lived outside of Central Asia and Kazakhstan, mostly in contiguous areas of the RSFSR which Kazakh nomads formerly roamed.[16] Even fewer other Central Asian Muslims lived in portions of the Russian Federation exclusive of such border areas. Therefore migration would presumably have to be either encouraged by a combination of economic pressures and material incentives, or forced by the imposition of Stalinist methods of control and coercion.[17] Whether voluntary or not, such a migration might create more problems than it solves in terms of Muslim discontent or interethnic strife in Slavic cities and regions. "A potentially Wolverhampton situation at home and a Salisbury situation 'abroad' simultaneously," according to Besemeres.[18]

In 1970 V. Perevedentsev, a leading Soviet demographer, stirred up a controversy by linking the discussion of demographic trends with the possibility of migration of Central Asian Muslims to industrial areas of the RSFSR as a means of offsetting regional labor supply imbalances. Over the ensuing years there has been a considerable Soviet literature on this and other aspects of migration.[19] In assessing this debate and Soviet developments, Western scholars have arrived at two sharply opposing viewpoints concerning the probability of massive out-migration from labor-rich Central Asia to other portions of the Soviet Union.

The minority view anticipates heavy migration of Central Asian Muslims to other parts of the USSR and gives primacy to economic over sociopolitical and cultural considerations, i.e., they contend that like fellow Muslims elsewhere (e.g., in Turkey and Algeria), the Muslims of Central Asia—given the proper economic stimulus—will undergo the "universal experience" of migration to highly industrialized areas.

The minority view among Western scholars is expressed by Lewis, Rowland, and Clem, who see the possibility of widespread unemployment and welfare burdens in Central Asia if its labor surplus problem is not solved by one of the three options: (1) a crash program of economic development; (2) birth-control measures; or (3) emigration of surplus labor from the region.

Looking at the potential for accelerating economic development in Central Asia, Lewis and his colleagues argue that expansion of the rural economy cannot absorb more than half the surplus unless the Soviet leadership abandons further mechanization in favor of more labor-intensive agriculture or drastically enlarges the acreage under irrigation. The first flies in the face of decades of Soviet practice. As for irrigation, these scholars feel that Soviet plans to expand irrigated lands are insufficient to absorb the growing rural manpower.[20] Moreover, they viewed the targeted expansion of irrigated lands by 10 percent for 1971—75 (which has been fulfilled) as overly ambitious in light of past performance and the limited availability of land suitable for irrigation.[21]

Nor do Lewis and his fellow researchers believe local industry can absorb the surplus rural manpower. They say that for it to do so would require an industrial growth rate of between 9 and 13 percent a year, as compared with an average of 8 percent in the period 1965—70 (and lower in the 1970s). They note that over the period 1971—75, increases in per capita fixed capital investments in Central Asia were below the average for the USSR, and they attribute this to the area's limited endowment of natural resources required for large-scale heavy industry and its remoteness from the main Soviet industrial centers.[22]

Lewis, Rowland, and Clem further suggest that birth-control measures would probably not significantly reverse the Muslim population explosion before the 1990s.[23]

The only remaining option, they argue, is for the Central Asians to migrate abroad or to other areas of the USSR. The former is viewed as highly unrealistic, the Jewish emigration being seen as a special case not likely to be duplicated. As for internal migration, rural areas of the USSR are hardly likely to seek unskilled Muslim farmhands with alien life styles and language problems when what these areas need are technically trained young men capable of fitting productively into the local environment.

Consequently, Lewis, Rowland, and Clem see the only solution to be out-migration of rural Central Asian Muslims to distant urban areas in the RSFSR. They admit that poor Russian language training and lower educational and skill levels may impede the flow, but they argue that such factors will not be decisive "once local economic conditions begin to deteriorate."[24]

A contrary view (and one more widely held among Western experts) argues that the Muslims of Central Asia are more likely to stay in their native republics. In the words of Murray Feshbach,

> ... the overwhelming weight of the evidence—economic, demographic, and cultural, leads to the conclusion that there will not be a massive out-migration of labor from Central Asia to the labor-deficient areas of the USSR during the 1980's.[25]

In terms of economics, Feshbach points to current scattered symptoms of shortages of industrial manpower within Central Asia itself,[26] and he cites Soviet sources to indicate that Moscow has already resolved to bring new industry to Central Asia to absorb any surpluses of labor as they arise.[27] Moreover, he sees Muslims as unlikely to be attracted to other areas of the

USSR, where the cost of living is higher than in Central Asia. Demographically, he goes on, the burgeoning Central Asian population includes large numbers of children and many nonworking women raising large families (and thus unable to take jobs in distant parts of the USSR).[28] Finally, Feshbach stresses the linguistic and sociocultural impediments to large-scale out-migration. Even were Moscow able to bring about such a migration to solve manpower shortages elsewhere, Feshbach concludes, it would result in ghettoes and political friction in Russian cities and Soviet embarrassment before other Asian states because of the implicit admission of failure to solve Central Asia's unemployment problems on the spot.

Two additional aspects of the situation in Central Asia that have been neglected or insufficiently explored by all analysts are likely to have a significant impact on both migration and interethnic relations.

The first has to do with the place of the private sector in Central Asian life and related issues of the *real* (as opposed to *official*) standard of living there. Indeed, the combination of high levels of private activity and good climate which has made the Georgian republic so popular a place to live would seem to exist, to some extent, in Central Asia as well (see Chapter 4). These benefits come on top of a cost of living lower than in metropolitan Russia, and of average wages which exceed regional cost-of-living equalization figures.[29] Thus there is considerable economic incentive for Central Asians to stay put.

The second incentive to stay is a sociopolitical one. Natives of Central Asia do not suffer, at least not in their native republics, from the ethnic stratification caused by "hierarchic ranking of nationalities along socioeconomic lines," as some American scholars suppose. While nonnatives do occupy specific control positions in the party, government, and security apparatus, in the job market as a whole Muslims are given preference over Europeans, unless the latter are the only ones having indispensable skills (see the discussion in Chapters 8 and 9).

Modern Muslim national-religious feelings may conflict with Russian domination, but individual Muslims, including those responsive to such feelings, do not suffer from person-to-person discrimination. Consequently, for the average Muslim there is no inherent pressure of social inequality or deprivation driving him to pick up stakes and move to the cities of the RSFSR.

4. *Migration Mechanisms*

Examining the period 1959—70, a Soviet internal migration expert, A. V. Topilin discovered that of a yearly total migration of some twelve million people (5 percent of the total USSR population) only 10—12 percent occurred on an "organized" basis, i.e., in response to conscious government policy.[30] The bulk of migration was thus "unorganized." As Topilin observes, some of this migration (perhaps 10—12 percent of the total) happened to coincide with state interests and hence could be considered "rational." Still other movements were neutral in effect. However, over 50 percent of all migration was unorganized *and* irrational. Thus Topilin distinguished seventy separate migration streams into and out of Central Asia and Kazakhstan alone, and of these thirty-four were "irrational," while only thirteen could be classified as "rational" from the perspective of government interests. An obvious example of the "irrational" category would be migration from labor-deficit Siberia to labor-surplus Central Asia.[31]

Topilin examines the many factors—economic, environmental and climatic, ethnic, demographic, and moral-psychological—that contribute to or impede migration. He specifically notes the low inclination of Central Asia's rural Muslim population to move to the cities, let alone to other parts of the Soviet Union, and the resulting build-up of surpluses of actual or potential labor in the Central Asian countryside.[32] He attributes this low mobility to such factors as attachment to the native village, weak knowledge of Russian, peculiarities of the local cultural and religious patterns, and insufficient skill levels to compete.[33]

The irrational and unsatisfactory nature of much of Soviet population migration leads Topilin to advocate a more active migration policy, combining both "carrot" and "stick." He calls for an increase in the proportion of organized migration (to be planned and organized through the All-Union State Planning Committee—Gosplan), resettlement to more distant sites, and measures to bind the migrants to their new places of settlement and employment. Among incentives to "rational" voluntary migration, he lists the standard measures of offering better housing, more social services, higher wages, and better educational opportunities to offset climatic disparities.[34]

In discussing the possibilities of altering regional standards of living to achieve optimal migration patterns, Topilin does not rule out the artificial *lowering* of living standards in labor-surplus areas. Other Soviet specialists have openly discussed such an approach. For example, a 1978 article proposed to spur village-to-city migration by ending all privileges——relating to taxation, procurement prices, differential economic development, and social welfare assistance——still enjoyed by rural areas in formerly backward regions.[35] Central Asia clearly fits the definition.

The same article articulates another dimension of Soviet thinking concerning the manpower issue:

> . . . the state is preoccupied not only with the number but with the quality of its citizens. It is not indifferent to the kind of population, to the kind of labor force in question——whether highly or poorly trained, mobile or burdened with such circumstances as large family, language impediment, and attachment to a specific area.

Specifically, the article proposes limiting child allowances to second and third children, since existing benefits for larger families have the effect of favoring births among what the author clearly views as "overfertile" ethnic groups. Similarly, at a 1975 meeting on the socioeconomic aspects of population problems held under the auspices of the USSR Academy of Sciences, there were calls for an "active demographic policy" designed to achieve "optimal birthrates" that would allow Soviet women (presumably of all nationalities) to combine motherhood with outside employment.[36] Some voices openly lament the lack of coincidence between "quantitative" and "qualitative" factors in the reproduction process. Hoping for a fall in Central Asian birthrates (and an increase in Russian), they worry that "those who are best equipped to educate the new generation" fail to have more than two children.

What is needed, they say, is more children equipped with a "quality of socialization."[37] Whatever this mysterious "quality" portends, Muslim children, if one follows the author's thoughts, seem somehow short of it. At the Twenty-sixth Party Congress, Leonid Brezhnev endorsed the need for an "effective demographic policy," but it is still unclear whether such a policy will lead to an effective "regionally variable" family legislation.[38]

5. *Possibilities of Reemigration*

While many have debated the chances for Muslim out-migration,

Table 16

Muslims and Non-Muslims in Kazakhstan and Central Asia, 1979

	Total 1979 population (thousands)	Percent of all Muslim groups in republic population	Percent of titular Muslim group in population	Percent of titular group in population aged 0–10 (1970)	Percent of all non-Muslim groups in population		Percent of Eastern Slavs in 1979 population
					1970	1979	
Kazakhstan	14,685	43	36.2	43.8	59	57	48.1
Kirghizia	3,529	66	47.2	53.3	40	34	29.2
Tadzhikistan	3,801	86	58.8	62.7	17	14	11.4
Turkmenistan	2,759	84	68.4	74.7	19	16	14.0
Uzbekistan	15,391	85	68.7	73.6	18	15	11.6

Sources: "Vsesoiuznaia perepis' naseleniia," *Vestnik statistiki* (1980, no. 2), and Michael Rywkin, "Central Asia and Soviet Manpower," *Problems of Communism*, January/February 1979.

there is little mention in Soviet or Western literature about the possibility that the non-Muslim, largely European settlers in Central Asia might migrate back to their home areas, thereby easing labor shortages in the latter areas and opening new opportunities locally for Central Asia's growing rural Muslim population.

There are, to be sure, a number of reasons why one might not anticipate such a reemigration. For one, these nonnative settlers—who account for almost every fifth person in Tadzhikistan, Turkmenistan, and Uzbekistan, and every second person in Kazakhstan and Kirghizia (see Table 16)—are said to possess the necessary qualifications for running the economy of the area. Their mass departure is viewed as potentially disastrous economically (the argument used by A. I. Mikoyan to reject pleas of the Volga Germans in the 1960s that they be allowed to return to their home areas).[39] Second, Moscow is said to shy away from letting the numerical ratio between European settlers and native Muslims deteriorate too much. In this century the proportion of Europeans in Central Asia grew with every consecutive census (from 1897 to 1959) until 1970, when it first became evident that growth in the Muslim birthrate combined with successful equalization of the mortality rates for Soviet citizens of European and Muslim nationalities was offsetting the effects of in-migration by Russians and other European groups. (On the migration balances of the Central Asian republics for 1961–70, see Table 17.) Moscow may be leery of seeing the Muslim "reconquest" of Central Asia accelerated by non-

Table 17	Migration Balances for Selected Soviet Republics, 1961–70 (immigrants minus emigrants)	
	1961–65	1966–70
Kazakhstan	602,000	90,000
Kirghizia	105,000	25,000
Tadzhikistan	120,000	18,000
Turkmenistan	negligible	18,000
Uzbekistan	77,000	69,000
RSFSR	−861,000	−1,567,000
Ukraine	150,000	399,000

Source: V. A. Shpiliuk, *Mezhrespublikanskaia migratsiia i sblizhenie natsii v SSSR* (L'vov: Vishcha Shkola, 1975), p. 76.

Muslim out-migration. And finally, there are the obvious incentives of good climate and opportunities for better jobs and housing which spur voluntary migration to the Central Asian sun belt. It is contended that on the job market these settlers will continue to compete successfully with less-qualified rural Muslims.[40]

Despite such arguments, one can also make a strong case for the eventual out-migration of European settlers from Central Asia. In the first place, many inhabitants of Central Asia and Kazakhstan belong to deported national groups and may be presumed anxious to return to more familiar surroundings. Among such groups one would number a million Germans (mostly from the Volga), including some 900,000 in Kazakhstan, 38,000 in Tadzhikistan, and 90,000 in Kirghizia (1970 census data), some of whom are not only returning to the European part of the USSR[41] but to West Germany as well (56,000 between 1971 and 1979, many of them from Kazakhstan).[42] Also important are the roughly 300,000 Crimean Tatars (not listed separately from other Tatars in the 1970 or 1979 censuses); various Poles, Lithuanians, and other former inhabitants of "western" regions acquired by the USSR in 1939, including some 75,000 living in Kazakhstan; and more than 170,000 Koreans (deported from the Far East in the late 1930s).[43]

Moreover, many of the Slavs who inhabit Central Asia and Kazakhstan are themselves sons and daughters of deportees of the late 1930s, i.e., of involuntary migrants. Residual thoughts of returning to more familiar surroundings may be reinforced by the increasingly nationalistic spirit of the local Muslim majority.

Second, a good number of Muslims have acquired, or are in the process of acquiring, the necessary qualifications to function in an urban industrial society as a result of considerable Soviet efforts to raise native skill levels. This makes European reemigration from Central Asia and concomitant *korenizatsiia* (replacement of outsiders by natives) more feasible economically,[44] i.e., the local economy becomes increasingly less likely to fall apart should the Europeans leave.

There are already signs that Central Asia's European settlers are beginning to emigrate to other parts of the USSR. The 1970 census showed small positive balances for the RSFSR in its population exchanges with Kazakhstan and the four Central Asian republics (based on counts of new arrivals who had resided in the respective republics fewer than two years at the time of the census). The surplus in the Russian Federation's exchange with Kazakhstan was 36,000; with Kirghizia, 7,000; with Tadzhikistan, 11,000; with Turkmenistan, 7,000; and with Uzbekistan, 44,000 (see Table 17).

Furthermore, the number of immigrants who came from Central Asia and Kazakhstan to other republics during the two years preceding the 1970 census is double the number of Central Asians registered there during the 1970 census (and even the latter cannot possibly be counted as having arrived only between 1968 and 1970).[45] Thus the most logical conclusion is that (a) the population exchanges between Central Asia and the rest of the country involve mostly Russians and other nonnatives, and (b) among those leaving Central Asia and Kazakhstan, Europeans are in the great majority (see Table 18).

Other data tend to confirm the impression that it is predominantly non-Muslims who are migrating out of Central Asia. For example, in 1967, among those leaving Central Asia for the city of Kiev in the Ukraine, only 7-10 percent were Muslims; another 20-30 percent were Ukrainians; and the remainder were presumably also Europeans (Russians, Jews, Germans, etc.[46] In addition, according to one source, 7.3 percent of all immigrants to the Soviet Far East in the 1960s came from Central Asia, Kazakhstan, and the Transcaucasus; yet the 1970 census showed very few Muslims residing in the Far East.[47] Between 1970 and 1979 the number of Central Asian Muslims residing in the RSFSR (and of students, draftees, etc., among them) rose so insignificantly that except for a very minor movement of few Kirghiz, it amounts to many fewer than what would have normally resulted from a natural increase in the given national group based on all-Union data (compare Tables 18 and 19).

Even taking into account lower fertility rates for Muslims residing outside their own area, the conclusion is clear: there was no out-migration of Muslims from Central Asia and Kazakhstan between the 1970 and 1979 censuses, not even on a very limited scale.

6. *Future Prospects*

For decades to come, the numerical balance between the major ethnic groups in the USSR will continue shifting in the Muslims' favor. By the beginning of the twenty-first century it will project the Muslims into direct numerical competition with the

Table 18

Out-migration from Central Asia and Kazakhstan, 1968-70
(in thousands)

	Total Central Asia and Kazakhstan		Uzbekistan		Kazakhstan		Kirghizia		Tadzhikistan		Turkmenistan	
	came from above[1]	Central Asians living in republics below[2]	came from above[1]	Uzbeks living in republics below[2]	came from above[1]	Kazakhs living in republics below[2]	came from above[1]	Kirghiz living in republics below[2]	came from above[1]	Tadzhiks living in republics below[2]	came from above[1]	Turkmen living in republics below[2]
RSFSR	455.6	233.6[3]	108.3	61.6	252.4[3]	118.8[3]	43.6	9.1	29.6	14.1	21.7	20.0
Ukraine	97.6	23.3	18.4	10.6	65.7	7.6	5.2	1.6	4.7	2.5	3.6	1.0
Belorussia	23.4	3.3	2.7	1.6	18.7	1.1	0.6	0.1	0.5	0.3	0.9	0.2
Lithuania	2.2	0.6	0.3	0.3	1.6	0.2	0.1	0.01	0.1	0.03	0.1	0.03
Latvia	3.6	1.1	0.6	0.4	2.4	0.5	0.3	0.03	0.2	0.08	0.1	0.1
Estonia	5.8	0.6	1.2	0.2	2.5	0.2	0.8	0.05	1.4	0.04	0.03	0.1
Moldavia	6.1	0.8	0.7	0.4	4.6	0.2	0.2	0.02	0.5	0.09	0.1	0.05
Total, USSR	593.9	253.2	132.2	75.1	347.9[3]	128.6[3]	50.8	10.9	37.0	17.1	26.5	21.5

Source: Itogi vsesoiuznoi perepisi naseleniia 1970 goda (Moscow: Statistika, 1973-74), vols. 4 and 5.

[1] Arrived two years or fewer before the 1970 Census.

[2] Total by the time of the 1970 Census, regardless of date of arrival.

[3] Excluding Astrakhan Orenburg, Omsk, Saratov, Volgograd, and Cheliabinsk regions with their historical Kazakh minorities.

Table 19

Main Central Asian Nationalities Living in the RSFSR

Nationality	1970		1979		Total numerical increase	1970-79 % increase of given nationality	
	Numbers	% of totals of given nationality	Numbers	% of totals of given nationality		In RSFSR	Total USSR
Kazakhs	477,820	9.02	518,060	7.90	40,240	8.42	20.62
Uzbeks	61,588	0.67	72,385	0.58	10,797	17.53	33.48
Turkmen	20,040	1.31	22,979	1.13	2,939	14.67	31.21
Kirghiz	9,107	0.63	15,011	0.78	5,904	64.81	28.47
Tadzhiks	14,108	0.66	17,863	0.62	3,755	26.62	32.69

Source: 1970 and 1979 censuses.

Russians, Ukrainians, and Belorussians, the numbers of Muslim children matching those of the Slavic ones. In the meantime, Moscow will not solve its manpower problems through massive out-migration of Central Asian Muslims to the existing industrial centers of the RSFSR. Some Muslims will be drafted for specific industrial projects, but this will be through temporary *orgnabor* (organized recruitment), with the draftees returning home after acquiring improved labor experience.[48] The problem of surplus rural Muslim labor will be attacked in Central Asia largely through increased village-to-city migration (Muslims will compete for all but the thinnest veneer of security and control jobs reserved for Europeans), a policy of importing labor-intensive light industry, some sort of restrictions on the migration of competing Siberian workers to the sun belt, and faster development of irrigation. To the extent that Central Asian Muslims move from their native areas at all, it will probably be to southern Kazakhstan. In turn, Kazakhs may be expected to peacefully "reconquer" Russian-populated areas in northern Kazakhstan or adjacent portions of the RSFSR.[49]

It is not the Muslims but the European settlers who can be expected to migrate from Central Asia in significant numbers.[50] They will do so in response, on the one hand, to increased competition from trained native workers and the "Muslimization" of urban life in Central Asia and, on the other hand, to a wide range of incentive measures designed to attract fresh manpower to labor-deficit parts of Russia proper.

Although this migration out of Central Asia by citizens of European nationalities can be expected to alleviate manpower shortages in the RSFSR, it will not be of sufficient dimensions to solve them. Thus the Soviet government will need to increase labor productivity at a still more rapid pace if there is not to be a deceleration of production growth. The need will be even greater to the extent that the share of total Soviet investment going to Central Asia is increased, since this region has traditionally shown lower labor productivity than other parts of the USSR. Consequently there will be objective pressures on the Soviet government to consider liberalization of managerial practices and of the general socioeconomic framework of its society.[51]

In Central Asia, Muslims show a reluctance, and European settlers display a mounting inclination, to emigrate from the area; the widespread *korenizatsiia* of the Central Asian republics, which is already occurring as a result of Muslim fertility, can only accelerate. It would be utterly naive to think that this can possibly occur without triggering increasing demands for more political power from the growing Muslim elite, well conscious of its rapidly mushrooming power base.

CHAPTER SIX

The National-Religious Symbiosis

Islam, which bears on the identity, behavior, attitudes, and way of life of the peoples of Soviet Central Asia, permeates all the social, political, and economic aspects of their lives. Even when one discusses each aspect of these lives separately, as I am doing in this book, religion remains an indispensable ingredient.

There is hardly a problem in Soviet Central Asia devoid of a Muslim component. The demographic explosion would not have occurred without the influence of Muslim tradition on family life. Similarly, Islam divides the natives from the Russian settlers, has an impact on the division of labor along national-religious lines, curtails social contacts between the two communities, and inhibits the Muslims from migrating outside their areas.

Thus it is hard to discuss Central Asian Islam as a subject in its own right. One either falls into a narrow study of mosque attendance and observance of rituals or, on the other hand, merely reviews all possible social, economic, and political issues and repeats what has been already been said elsewhere. Even the term "Muslim" used throughout this book (and by other authors as well) is not a perfect label; it is just the best possible common denominator for the various Central Asian nationalities.

From all this stems a national-religious symbiosis within the Muslim *umma* (community), a merging or overlapping of ethnic and religious sentiments and loyalties that reappears in all aspects of Central Asian existence. It is this symbiosis that so frustrates Moscow in its attempts to integrate the growing Central Asian masses into a common mold as part of the "Soviet people." Conquered over a century ago, Sovietized for six decades, modernized, educated, and indoctrinated by a succession of regimes, Central Asian Muslims seem just as remote from Russian reality and intentions as at the outset of Soviet rule.

The obvious reason for this disjunction lies in the Muslim-based, modern, nationalist spirit emerging in the area. It is an unplanned by-product of Soviet nationality policies and a direct result of Soviet socioeconomic achievements in the area. Moscow is learning that progress fosters nationalism instead of curtailing it. This nationalism refuses to be channeled into a national cultural form modeled to house a Russian-prepared socialist content. On the contrary, it provides a Muslim nationalist content dressed in a Moscow-made socialist form. To the communist "national in form, socialist in content" policy it offers a "socialist in form, nationalist in content" alternative. The Islamic tradition, while losing many of its ritualistic aspects, provides the essential ingredients for this new nationalism.

1. *The Spirit of Islam*

Irish or Polish nationalism has been traditionally Catholic, Arab nationalism Muslim, while World War II Italian or German nationalism, despite its intensity, was rather indifferent to religion. History teaches that "when conflicting nationalities were of different religions, religion often played a large part in the defense mechanism of the weaker nationality."[1] It is therefore quite normal that for the Muslim peoples of Central Asia, group identity vis-à-vis the non-Muslim, mostly Russian, settlers has been based on feelings of Muslim religious identity. As put by a leading Soviet ethnogeographer, Lev Gumilev, "Religious differences deepen their dissimilarity to the Russians."[2]

Moreover, until recently, in the eyes of the native Muslims there was little difference among most settlers found in the area. Russians, Ukrainians, Belorussians, Georgians, and Armenians, or even wartime immigrants like Poles, Volga Germans, and Russian Jews, appeared as Europeans with a European way of life. On the other hand, Central Asian Muslims had their own "Oriental" life style, quite different from that of the settlers. Therefore, within the Central Asian context, terms like "outsider," "nonnative," Russian, Slavic, European, etc., label similar categories, while terms like "native," Muslim, Turkic, Turkestani, and Central Asian define the opposite group. The word "Muslim" thus does not necessarily indicate a religious person, but rather somebody identified as a native of Central Asia (not a settler or a Bukharan Jew). This usage in turn demonstrates a connection, a symbiosis between the national and the religious that is accepted as a fact by both Muslims and settlers.[3]

The gap between the European and Muslim communities that is expressed on both the national and religious levels reinforces their conflicting sets of values[4] and restricts mutual contacts between them. Thus social intercourse between Muslims and Russians outside the workplace is rather limited. Intermarriage is rare, and that involving Muslim girls almost nonexistent; obedience to the Shariat prohibition against such alliances is clearly far from outmoded. Moreover, in most mixed marriages between Muslim men and Russian women, children overwhelmingly tend to select their father's nationality, with all that entails. This follows the universal rule according to which "children are affiliated with the racial group of the lower-ranking parent" (i.e., of the Central Asian Muslim parent as viewed by the politically dominant Russian society). In addition, such children tend to inherit the national consciousness of the parent whose nationality they have adopted, neutralizing the gap-bridging impact of these rare interethnic marriages.[5]

The national-religious relationship thus comes full circle: Islamic tradition inhibits acculturation, and the resulting separateness of the Muslim milieu reinforces the influence of Islam, which in turn increases resistance to acculturation, and so on.

A Soviet brochure describing the ideological content of present-day Muslim preaching in the USSR deplores its tendency to place Muslim solidarity above all-Soviet unity, as exemplified by this statement:

> A Muslim is a friend and a brother of [another] Muslim, whatever his nationality or country of origin; a Muslim should never suffer loss or harm from his brother's hand (from a 1976 sermon in the Ufa mosque in the Volga Tatar ASSR).[6]

This is an open acceptance of the concept of *Dar-ul-Islam* (Land of Religion). Bennigsen explains:

> Islam . . . is a collectivist religion, authoritarian: one whose doctrine is binding on the mass of believers and which tends to deploy its directions and its judgments over the whole field of life, corporate and individual alike. In Islam, no distinction is drawn between the temporal and the spiritual; there is a traditional fusion of the two which endows life, public and private, and all its manifestations, with a sacred character.[7]

According to Maxime Rodinson, the eminent French student of Islam, communism and Islam are both movements of a militant type that share a number of common characteristics: a "utopian" ideology, a "lay" program geared to practical application of ideological principles, a structured organizational setup, often with a charismatic leader, as well as practices, rites, and symbols showing adherence to the movement. Like Islam, communism also displays several characteristics of an established church: its own credo, councils, excommunications, fidelity of adherents, etc. Both the Islamic *umma* (community) and the communist "international" started, according to Rodinson, as *Vereine* (associations), but the *umma* evolved into an *Anstalt* (establishment) whose membership is determined by birth and not by association.[8] Obviously, the latter movement tends to be even more exclusive than the former, while both consider control over people's minds crucial to their existence. If one accepts the classical definition that a nationality is "a state of mind corresponding to a political fact,"[9] then in Soviet Central Asia the state of mind of the Muslim population is cemented by feelings of Islamic community standing in opposition to the political fact of Western, European, Russian, Soviet (used interchangeably) domination. Thus the religious and national feelings of the natives on the one side, and the antireligious and antinationalist actions of Moscow on the other, tend to become not only interrelated but also interdependent.[10]

2. Soviet Attitudes

The Soviet regime, from the very beginning, adopted a position favorable to Islam's equalitarian principles but hostile to its allegedly "reactionary" social content. Campaigns against Islam have been part of a permanent struggle conducted by the Soviets against all religious faiths; but considerations of local political opportunism have not been disregarded, and the religious issue has not always been pressed with the same determination. Religious toleration existed from 1917 to 1920 and, in somewhat curtailed form, lasted until 1928, when religious schools were finally closed. The beginning of collectivization was accompanied by strong antireligious activity, which lasted through the purges of the 1930s. The extent of Soviet measures is also reflected in the reduction of the number of mosques in the

USSR from 26,279 in 1912 to 1,312 in 1942, and to only about 450 in 1976.

After 1938 antireligious activity underwent visible relaxation, especially after the German invasion, when atheistic propaganda was, in its turn, curtailed for fear of its possible ill effects on the war effort.[11] Thus the Mir-Arab *medraseh* (religious school) was reopened in Bukhara for 1945/46 (with fifty students); another school opened much later (in 1971) in Tashkent with thirty. A journal, entitled *Muslims of the Soviet East*, has been issued since 1968 in Uzbek (but in Arabic script), Persian, Arabic, English, and French, although mostly for foreign consumption, by Muslim religious authorities in Tashkent.

Following Catherine the Great's practice, Islam under Soviet rule has been divided into territorial Sunni Muslim directorates (Tashkent, Ufa, Baku, Makhach-Kala). At the same time, Soviet Islam has also been split into an official religion, represented by sanctioned and cooperative administrations, and an unofficial one grouped around the *Tarikats* (militantly religious fraternities). *Tarikats* are said to flourish in the Northern Caucasus and in Azerbaidzhan; they also exist, to a much more limited extent, in Central Asia. While the existence of *tarikats* is confirmed by Soviet press complaints about their activity, their numerical importance is hard to verify given the scarcity of other reliable data on the subject.

Present-day Soviet antireligious propaganda handles Islam with obvious care. While it rejects Muslim clerics' claims to being instrumental in "solving the nationality question" in the USSR[12] (a prerogative only the party is supposed to claim), it maintains an otherwise restrained tone, unlike the one used in castigating Catholicism or Judaism. The popular Soviet organ of antireligious propaganda, *Science and Religion*, admits the close relationship between the national and the religious elements in Muslim identity and agrees that the matter should be handled cautiously. "In some customs and traditions the national and the religious are closely interconnected. Their delimitation is a very delicate and complex business," warns the journal.[13] The more scholarly *Problems of Scientific Atheism* goes even further by speaking of a "symbiosis" between the Islamic religion and the common ethnic values of Soviet Muslims. Even the survival of the authority of the mullah in matters of "nationality interests" (*interesov natsii*), where the mullah explains "what is good and what is bad," is no longer denied.[14] Attempts are even made to adapt "new customs and rituals" of a Soviet character to

Muslim ritual tradition in order to compete with the latter.[15]

Thus a mutually acceptable *modus vivendi* between communism and Islam is being sought and promoted by both sides, however uneasy such a truce may be for either of the partners. But despite its formal cooperation with the atheist authorities, official Soviet Islam has "never been accused by anyone—friends or adversaries—of heresy (*shirq*), infidelity (*kufr*), or even innovation (*bida*)."[16] Obviously, both parties are aware of the limits official Islam cannot possibly overstep without running the risk of losing all its prestige and being overshadowed by the infinitely less cooperative and more intensely nationalist unofficial counterpart.

3. *Observance of Islam*

Islam is not only a religion but a part of personal identity: one cannot simply call oneself an Uzbek or a Tadzhik and, at the same time, reject Islam. This not only strengthens the Islamic tradition but makes it part and parcel of the ethnic one. And ethnic traditions, even apparently much weaker ones, are highly resistant to change or erosion. As explained by Lev Gumilev:

> As long as inertia [i.e., tradition] does not dry up, people belong to a given ethnos and consider themselves part of it. And it makes no difference whether they speak the language of their ancestors, observe rituals, honor their ancestors, or live on the land which gave birth to their nation.[17]

This description clearly applies to such national groups as Soviet Jews, Volga Germans, or Crimean Tatars. For the Muslims of Soviet Central Asia, who have not been deprived of their territory and native languages, and who observe their rituals more faithfully than the others, now that their biological and numerical strength has been asserted, no loss of national-religious tradition can be contemplated—unless in the long "historical perspective."

But while this tradition appears permanent, not all Islamic religious rituals are being either followed or observed by the bulk of the population. (Keep in mind that according to Gumilev, this "makes no difference" anyway.) Of the five pillars of Islam—the religious pilgrimage (*hadj*), almsgiving (*zakat*), the required five daily prayers (*salat*), the Ramadan fast (*muhazzad*), and the affirmation of faith (*sharaghad*)—only the last is universally observed, especially through circumcision. Estimates for the actual recitation of daily prayers vary between 20 and 40 percent of the total adult population (non-Soviet estimates) to 30 percent of older people (Soviet estimates). The same holds for fasting. Non-Soviet scholars speak of every second person observing the fast (but for only three days in the cities), and Soviet experts indicate that 40 percent of older people do so, while those between the ages of 16 and 59 fast for only three days.[18] Friday sabbaths cannot be practically respected by those working normal hours, but at least the open-air Tashkent *tolkuchka* (black market) is almost empty on Fridays, if one can judge by weekday and Friday pictures of crowds taken by Western travelers.

But customs that *can* be practiced under modern living conditions without much difficulty are well observed. Among them are universally practiced circumcision, marriage, divorce, and burial rituals, avoidance of public places and ceremonies during Ramadan, Muslim dietary prohibitions against pork, wearing a *tubiteika* (skullcap), and the *chaikhana* (teahouse) style of "cafe life."

Social restrictions for women have to a large extent vanished, but not Islamic morality in family matters. Women are no longer secluded, wear no veils, and attend schools and even work outside the home. But they still marry young (average age 16-17), respect the tradition of *kalym* (reverse dowery), albeit generally without the old wife-buying implications, and are held to strict morality in sexual conduct. Open polygamy is dead, but individual cases of second wives passed off as relatives living with the family still surface from time to time.

The norms of the Shariat are part of accepted national usage, especially in all family matters. But one must keep in mind that family plays a much larger role among the Muslims than among the Russians. An average Muslim is said to spend two and a half times more of his own free time with his family and relatives than does an average Russian.[19] Thus the Muslim family constitutes the basic element in the religious, ethnic, and social coherence of the Muslim milieu.

4. *Modern Islam*

The demographic explosion among Soviet Muslims, as contrasted to the demographic stagnation among the Slavs, in itself threatens Slavic domination over Soviet Central Asia. But it is the growing Islam-based modern nationalist spirit *combined* with this demographic explosion that is the most important threat to Moscow.[20]

Rapid modernization (education, urbanization, technical progress, etc.), however, has not brought with it the acculturation desired by the Soviets. An educated Uzbek manager and party member may speak Russian, ride to work in an automobile, and dress in Western style; but this has no bearing on his national-religious feelings. On the contrary, "his" Islam is even more dangerous to Moscow. It is not a faith of "superstitions" or of *perezhitki* (survivals from the past), something a skillful agitator might at least try to demolish at the next public meeting. Rather, it is the basis of his national-religious identity and consciousness.

This symbiosis thrives best under outside attack. As early as 1922, a leading proponent of modern Soviet Islam, the Tatar revolutionary Sultan Galiev, had warned that the majority of Muslims view antireligious propaganda as a political, not a religious act. Consequently, such propaganda should be conducted only by Muslims, against certain backward religious practices, and never against the sociopolitical content of Islam.[21]

Even Soviet propagandists understand the reality of the religious-national symbiosis:

> To explain today how the Koran interprets the creation of the world is . . . not very appropriate. But if we want to oppose Muslim preaching, we must know what it says about . . . the national question.[22]

Of the two dogmas, the communist and the Islamic—both collectivist and authoritarian, both encompassing the temporal as well as the spiritual, both competing for Soviet Muslims' allegiance—the communist one, being a Russian import, appears to be the weaker. In the nationalist—Muslim—communist triad, therefore, the communist element seems the only one potentially discardable.

The fact that both communism and Islamic nationalism are mutually exclusive ideologies with strong totalitarian tendencies does not facilitate their coexistence. Rodinson argues that communism has been moving from a nontotalitarian origin to totalitarian grounds, while Islam took the opposite road; but he still considers future coexistence between the two probable, from sheer historical necessity.[23] Others view the differences between the two doctrines as fundamental and not conducive to a Marxist "thesis, antithesis, synthesis" conclusion, especially with the Russian chauvinist element present in the communist formula. Original Muslim nationalist-communists like Sultan Galiev, Khodzhaev, Safarov, Narimanov, Hanafi Muzzafar, and others failed in their attempts to amalgamate the two ideologies. Such amalgamation could succeed only if communism presented a national Islamic image, not a European-dominated and European-imposed one. For the time being, Moscow seems much too conservative to attempt such an experiment within its own borders.

CHAPTER SEVEN

Culture

1. *From Arabic to Cyrillic*

The alphabets of Soviet Central Asia have been changed twice by the Soviet regime. At first the modified Arabic alphabet, in use since 1922, was discarded in favor of the Latin alphabet; then the Latin alphabet was dropped and replaced by the Cyrillic alphabet. Moscow justified the first reform on the gounds that the Arabic alphabet, even in its modified (phonetic) version, was too difficult to learn and was too easily identified with what was then called "the reactionary philosophy" of Islam. The Latin alphabet, on the other hand, being universal, would more effectively combat illiteracy. It would, moreover, facilitate the study of Central Asian languages as well as the translation of foreign books into these languages. Moscow also assumed that by adopting the Latin alphabet it could more easily control publications printed in local languages[1] and create a barrier between the new national literatures of the Central Asian republics and their common Chaghatai source.[2] (Chaghatai is the medieval literary language of all the Turkic peoples of Central Asia.)

Prior to 1926 the change to the Latin alphabet was pursued only by persuasion. In 1926 the principle of reform was adopted by the Turkological Congress in Baku. Subsequently, the Latin alphabet and a unified mode of transcription were implanted in most regions formerly using the Arabic script, but not until 1935 did the implantation become complete.[3]

The second reform, introduction of the Cyrillic (Russian) alphabet, began in 1935 but made no serious progress until 1939. The Soviets pointed out that the Latin alphabet was useful in conquering illiteracy, but that the Cyrillic was better adapted for the transcription of Turkic sounds because it contained more letters than did the Latin. There are, for example, thirty-eight sounds in the Uzbek languages and thirty-two letters in the Cyrillic alphabet, but only twenty-six letters in the Latin alphabet. The Cyrillic alphabet would facilitate both the penetration of national tongues by the Russian language and the study of the Russian language by the natives.

These expectations were fulfilled. According to Western studies, the percentage of words of Russian (or Russified French) origin in the Uzbek language rose from 2 in 1923 to 15 in 1940. During the same time the percentage of words of Arabic or Persian origin used in the Uzbek language fell from 37 to 25.[4] Many of the Russian loan words that entered the Uzbek language (as well as the other languages of Central Asia) are technical and political terms or modern Soviet and international abbreviations and expressions.[5] They usually maintained their original Russian transcription but acquired an Uzbek ending when appropriate. In the 1950s Uzbek endings were often dropped, and loan words appeared in the original transcription (example: the plural of *kommunist* became *kommunisty*, with a Russian plural ending, instead of *kommunistlar*). At the same time, a number of existing terms of Turkic origin were replaced by Russian ones. Russian words like *obed, obida,* and *obzor* entered the Uzbek language in their Russian phonetic form— *abed, abida,* and *abzor*—taking the place of the corresponding Turkic words.[6] Simultaneously, the uniformity in the writing of the Turkic languages of the USSR was broken by the modification of the official Uzbek literary language. The dialect of the town of Turkestan (Kazakh SSR) was replaced in 1937 as the official Uzbek literary language by the urban dialect of Tashkent, which was less intelligible to other Turkic peoples of the area.[7]

Whereas the first reform of the alphabet seems to have been motivated by both political and practical factors, the second was caused solely by political considerations. It was probably felt by Moscow that the introduction of the Russian alphabet in Central Asia would re-create a cultural barrier between the Turkic subjects of Russia and Turkey, who, following the first Soviet reform, also opted for the Latin script. On the other hand, it would also consolidate the cultural unity between Russia proper and her Central Asian possessions.

The adoption of the Russian alphabet made obsolete millions of books already printed in Latin characters and drove thousands of natives back to semiliteracy. At the same time, it enhanced the prestige of the Russian language, which, according to the Soviet point of view, was to become "the second mother tongue of the non-Russian intelligentsia, . . . the language of international intercourse between various national groups of the Union."[8]

It is worth noting, however, that voices are now being heard advocating the study of Arabic script in local schools as a necessary tool for access to prerevolutionary literature written in that script. As explained by a Kazakh intellectual:

> A basic cause of our sometimes being ignorant of the history and culture of the peoples who have been related to us since time immemorial, who come from the same roots, who have the same interests—the Kirghiz, Uzbeks, Turkmen, Bashkirs, and Tadjiks—is connected with the fact that our knowledge of the ancient written heritage is extremely inadequate.[9]

On another occasion an article praising the Russian-language contribution to Uzbek referred to Uzbek as the "state language" of the republic, something the Uzbeks, unlike the Georgians or the Armenians, did not fight to have included in their constitution.[10]

2. *Russian as the "Lingua Franca"*

Russian functions not only as a convenient common language in the USSR but, in practice, as the official language of the entire country. Some union republic constitutions mention their own languages as official languages within the republics. In 1978 Georgians and Armenians fought the threat of having such mention deleted from their new constitutions, and Moscow backed down.[11] But Russian is the language of all three branches of the USSR's union-wide power structure (party, government, and soviet), of the army, diplomacy, federal law, the post office, filing cabinets, accounting, and so on. No important career can be pursued, no technical breakthrough recorded, no important decision implemented in another language. All other languages play only limited political and social roles and approximate the importance of Russian only in cultural and social fields, and this within the borders of their respective union republics and never throughout the USSR.

In the field of education the Russian language is obligatory for all pupils in schools of non-Russian republics. But reciprocity no longer exists, and Russian pupils attending Soviet schools outside the RSFSR are not required to study local languages, something even Stalin felt it necessary to require.

The much heralded Tashkent conference of May 1979, devoted to the teaching of Russian to non-Russians, recommended that the Russian language be taught to non-Russian children from the age of five (kindergarten) on and be used, at least to some extent, in the teaching of other subjects in non-Russian schools. Technical schools were advised to switch some of their courses into Russian starting with the second year of study. Other recommendations pertain to practical means of achieving the basic aim of fostering "Russian as a Second Language" (RSL, as opposed to our American ESL: "English as a Second Language"). This was supposed to be done in the name of "fraternal unification" of Soviet peoples.

Measures to implement the bulk of the Tashkent Conference suggestions are gradually being put into effect. Russian is already being taught to Uzbek children starting with the first grade.[12]

Can these factors be seen as features of a *policy* of Russification, as were most of the changes imposed on Central Asian alphabets?

Unlike the imposition of the Cyrillic alphabet, the bulk of post-Stalin Soviet linguistic policies cannot be viewed as purely political maneuvers. Of course, there are political motives in keeping "Moldavian" away from Romanian (to justify Soviet annexation of Bessarabia), making exiled Crimean Tatars speak Uzbek (to make them forget their Crimean homeland from which they were expelled by Stalin in 1944), or attempting to Russify Volga Germans in Kazakhstan (to keep them from following the road taken by the Russian Jews). But in most other cases, whatever evolution has taken place was caused primarily by objective factors that stem from the existence of a multilingual community of nations of diverse historical heritages and highly varied cultural, socioeconomic, and political backgrounds.

The juxtaposition of the non-Russian languages and the Russian lingua franca (since no other language could objectively assume that function) would have created numerous problems regardless of Moscow's best or worst intentions or total inaction. The disappearance of Yiddish, the weakening of Belorussian, or the flowering of Uzbek or Georgian, as well as growing bilingualism throughout the USSR, are natural developments caused by a multitude of objective factors operating in a modern multilingual society. They are *not* the result of Machiavellian policies concocted in Moscow.

Every imperial structure of the past had a master language. Russian was the master language of the Romanov Empire in a more predominant form than it is today in the USSR. But one cannot attribute the dominant position of a master tongue solely or even mainly to forceful imposition, especially in our age of technology, mass media, fast travel, and ever present bureaucracy. The dominance of Russian in the USSR, like that of English in the United States, results mostly from voluntary and/or natural reasons, such as the obvious attraction of a widely spoken and internationally accepted idiom. In addition, one must consider the convenience of mastering a language which gives its speakers professional, geographic, and social mobility within the borders of the multiethnic country they inhabit.

Nevertheless, neither mastering Russian as a second language nor linguistic Russification (Russian replacing the mother tongue) results in a loss of the feeling of ethnic identity by the individual (notice the Jewish example) or in diminished resentment against Russian dominance (the Baltic example).

The Muslims of Soviet Central Asia are no different.

Among the principal Central Asian nationalities, the proportion of those who declared themselves "fluent in Russian" in the 1979 census varies between every fourth Turkmen, every second Kazakh, Uzbek, and Kara-Kalpak, and every third Kirghiz and Tadzhik. These data, however, are difficult to assess, since fluency in Russian as a second language is recorded as respondents themselves prefer. Thus while between 1970 and 1979 the proportion of Uzbeks fluent in Russian officially rose from 14.5 to 49.8 percent, the percentage of Estonians officially fluent in Russian declined from 29.0 to 24.2.[13] It is quite possible that demographically vigorous Uzbeks, feeling ethnically secure, tend to exaggerate their own knowledge of Russian, while the numerically stagnant Estonians defensively understate their own linguistic abilities in their "big brother's" tongue (see Table 20). This is especially so since the percentage of those declaring Russian as their *native* tongue is insignificant: less than 2 percent in both Kazakhstan and Central Asia.

The European settlers, for their part, show no interest whatsoever in learning local languages and, consequently, in getting acquainted with local cultures, and this despite the presence of those languages (as electives since Khrushchev, as re-

Table 20   **Russian Fluency among Principal Central Asian Nationalities**

| | Russian as first language | | | | "Good knowledge" of Russian | |
| | 1970 | | 1979 | | | |
Nationality	in 1000s	in %	in 1000s	in %	1970, in %	1979, in %
Uzbeks	49 (42)	0.53 (0.47)	78 (67)	0.63 (0.54)	14.5	49.3
Kazakhs	87 (56)	1.64 (1.17)	131 (87)	2.0 (1.44)	41.8	52.3
Tadzhiks	13	0.62	23 (20)	0.78 (0.69)	15.4	29.6
Turkmen	12 (11)	0.81 (0.73)	19 (17)	0.96 (0.84)	15.4	25.4
Kirghiz	5 —	0.33 —	9 (8)	0.49 (0.42)	19.1	29.4

Source: 1970 and 1979 censuses.

Note: The figures in parentheses show the relevant numbers and percentages of each nationality living outside the RSFSR. For populations of Central Asians living in the RSFSR, see Table 19.

quired subjects before) in school curricula. Those few settlers who do learn tend to live among the natives. It is characteristic that the percentage of Russian settlers speaking Uzbek (5.8) is nine times higher than those speaking Kazakh (0.66) (see Table 21). This is because settlers in Kazakhstan, especially in its heavily Russian northern provinces, have much less contact with the natives than their counterparts in Uzbekistan (conversely, Kazakhs have a better mastery of Russian than do Uzbeks).

What factors, in the opinion of Western scholars, might affect the delicate balance between the Russian language and the national languages of the larger non-Russian nationalities? Hélène Carrère d'Encausse considers cultural strength derived from the rich historical heritage of the Central Asian Muslim groups to be the key element shielding their national languages from Russian linguistic competition. Brian Silver emphasizes religious difference as well as the demographic vitality of the group in question as essential protective factors. Richard Pipes sees dangers of linguistic Russification in areas subjected to Russian numerical and administrative preponderance, while Alexandre Bennigsen dismisses all danger of linguistic assimilation for

Table 21   **European Settlers Speaking Local Languages, 1970-79**

Nationality		Total number in the republic	Consider the language of the republic native		Speak the language of the republic	
			number	%	number	%
In Uzbekistan						
Russians	1970	1,473,465	514	0.035	55,498	3.766
	1979	1,665,658	465	0.028	97,652	5.863
Ukrainians	1970	111,676	95	0.085	3,203	2.868
	1979	113,826	113	0.099	3,732	3.279
Jews	1970	102,855	332	0.323	6,788	6.6
	1979	99,908	212	0.212	4,811	4.815
In Kazakhstan						
Russians	1970	5,521,917	281	0.005	55,118	0.998
	1979	5,991,205	353	0.006	39,837	0.66
Ukrainians	1970	933,461	83	0.009	4,502	0.482
	1979	897,964	95	0.01	3,391	0.378
Germans	1970	858,077	299	0.035	4,228	0.493
	1979	900,207	422	0.047	4,141	0.46

Source: 1970 and 1979 censuses.

Soviet Muslims. Connections between bilingualism and linguistic Russification are thus rejected by most experts.[14]

Their views are supported by certain patterns in language use in Central Asia. For instance, the circulation of native language newspapers, periodicals, and books increased sharply throughout the 1960s and 1970s, outpacing similar increases in Russian-language publications.[15] Finally, reversing the trend of the 1930s and 1940s, Russian loan words are being purged from local languages. A genuine linguistic de-Russification "has become overt and official."[16] The conclusion is clear: better educated Muslims do learn Russian as an indispensable tool for their own advancement, but linguistic Russification has not taken place, and local Turkic languages are undergoing a real revival.

3. *History Reinterpreted*

Prior to the mid-1930s the theory of "absolute evil" (developed by the leading Soviet scholar M. N. Pokrovskii, a prerevolutionary Marxist historian) was in force. It condemned all colonial conquests, whether English, French, or tsarist Russian, and glorified all national-liberation movements against Great Russian oppression. Thus Turkestan's prerevolutionary struggle against tsarist colonization was officially lauded as part of the general revolutionary movement of the peoples of Russia. Native communists who supported this point of view (Khodzhaev, Ikramov, Ryskulov, and their allies) were dominant in the cultural field. This period ended with their liquidation in the purges of the late 1930s, during which prominent Turkestani literary figures such as Cholpan, Abdurauf Fitrat, and Münevver Quari perished, among others. It coincided with the official condemnation of the historical school of Pokrovskii on August 28, 1937.

During the next period, between 1937 and the end of the 1940s, a new historical theory was established: that of "lesser evil." According to the new theory, Russian conquests, although colonial, were lesser calamities than Turkish, Iranian, or British domination. Nationalist struggle against the tsarist regime was still lauded, but a "chauvinistic" (i.e., nationalist) outlook on their own national past was no longer tolerated from native historians.

During the war against Germany, when Soviet victory depended on the strong fighting spirit and patriotism of the Russian people, the "big brother" role of Russia with respect to other nationalities of the USSR began to receive strong emphasis. After the war the situation did not change.

In 1951 the "lesser evil" theory received its final seal of approval from the official mouthpiece of Soviet historical science, M. V. Nechkina, and was gradually drawn closer to the newest Soviet historical theory of "absolute good." According to the new line, the national struggle against tsarist colonization was condemned, while the virtues of union with Russia were extolled. The progressive character of tsarist conquest, which carried along with it "the more advanced Russian culture," began to be presented as a positive event, since it was a way of getting under the protection and "the benevolent influence of the Great Russian people and its culture."[17] Kazakh historians were reminded that their native chieftains, in opposing tsarist armies, had not been patriots but "reactionary feudals." In 1950 Shamil, the famous Caucasian Muslim nationalist leader of the nineteenth century (cited as a "great democrat" by Marx), received a similar label. The Kirghiz national epic *Manas*, pride of

Soviet Kirghizstan but untimely in being anti-Chinese, was suddenly condemned as "Pan-Islamic" and "feudal" (this stand was reversed when China dropped out of favor). *Alpamysh*, a part of Uzbek literary heritage, the Turkestani epic poem describing the struggle of Turkestani Muslims against the Buddhist Kalmuks, was condemned in 1952 as a work inspired by Muslim fanaticism and chauvinism. Native scholars were compelled to condemn their own previously held views and to adjust their "new opinions" accordingly. Some refused to comply, but they were reduced to silence after the 1951—52 purge of the Caucasian and Kazakh intellectuals and the faculties of Samarkand and Stalinabad universities. The theory of "absolute good" finally triumphed.

After Stalin's death, however, the cultural pressure on Soviet Muslims was somewhat reduced. National epics were rehabilitated. Bagirov, prime minister of Azerbaidzhan, who initiated the 1950 anti-Shamil campaign, was demoted and later liquidated as Beria's agent. The question was reopened, and the 1956 discussion showed a division among Soviet historians. It was again possible to say that the Russian conquest was not always enthusiastically accepted. However, the basic tenets of the theory of "absolute good" of the Russian conquest of the Caucasus and of Central Asia were not rejected, and no return to Pokrovskii's theory of "absolute evil" of colonial conquest seemed in sight, although Pokrovskii had been favorably mentioned again in the Soviet press.[18]

The 1960s were marked by a growing interest among the Central Asian Muslim intelligentsia in their own national past. Western Mediterranean-oriented historians (used as substitute whipping boys for their Russian counterparts) were criticized in Central Asia for undervaluing the Central Asian contribution to world culture. Conferences were held about "language culture" aimed at purifying local languages of unnecessary Russian loan words and at preserving and enriching the native "culture" and "heritage" and restoring the purity of national traditions.[19]

The 1970s saw a "blossoming" of historical novels. In Uzbekistan alone, such works as Abil Yaqubov's *The Treasure of Ulugbek*, Mirmushin's *The Architect*, Pirimqul Qairov's *Starry Nights*, and the first two volumes of Mirzäkälan Ismaily's *Fergana before the Dawn* not only addressed themselves to the area's rich historical past but also reintroduced Chaghatai expressions.[20] In Kazakhstan voices have been heard contradicting the "barbarian image" attributed in old Russian literature to

Asian invaders (even the *Igor Tale* has not been spared).[21]

In Tadzhikistan the traditional wealth of Tadzhik-Farsi po-
etry has been used to glorify its historical past at the exclusion
of foreign implantations. The best poems by Mirza Tursunzdad,
the former chairman of the Tadzhik Writers Union, are devoted
to his own *vatan* (homeland). Another poet, Laiq, writes about
"the thieves who stole not only the property but the heritage of
our ancestors."[22] In the field of history a kind of compromise
has been reached. The Muslims have been allowed to extol practically anyone from their prerevolutionary past, while Russian
historians have been given a freer hand in "rehabilitating" the
tsarist generals who conquered the area.

Interest in the Central Asian past has led to closer acquaint-
ance with Oriental cultures and literatures in general, circumstances spurred by the Soviet use of Tashkent as headquarters
for cultural contacts with neighboring Asian countries. Here the
fundamental dual predicament of all Soviet endeavors in Central
Asia has surfaced again: how to use Tashkent as "the lighthouse
of the East" without allowing it in turn to be influenced by its
own non-Soviet Muslim neighbors. While on many occasions
Moscow managed this quite well, the events in Afghanistan
seem to have changed the situation. The long-planned September
1980 Tashkent conference on the role of Islam in the past fourteen centuries and present-day "peace and friendship" between
nations (eternal *mir i druzhba*) ended in disarray. Many Islamic
countries refused to attend. Those that did attend clearly said
things not to Moscow's liking, since after the conference three
of the four Soviet muftis (excluding only Zinautdin ibn Ishan
Babakhan of Tashkent) were dismissed for their inability to
turn the conference in Moscow's favor.[23]

There is an obvious degree of self-imposed restraint in the
exercise of this kind of ethnocentrism in a multiethnic community such as the USSR. Yet now, against Lenin's warnings and
contrary to the situation in the 1920s and 1930s, outbreaks of
Russian chauvinism are usually tolerated. For instance, in 1973
the head of the USSR's Central Committee propaganda department lost his job merely for his overzealous attempts to silence
the extreme Russian ethnocentrists who published articles directly glorifying tsarist generals involved a century earlier in the
colonial conquest of Central Asia.[24]

In the 1970s, the newspaper *Soviet Russia* (Sovetskaia
Rossiia) and the journal *Our Contemporary* (Nash sovremennik)
became rallying points for so-called "village prose," which is de-

voted to the "eternal" values and patterns of Russian rural life and is cool to other Soviet nationalities. It is rumored that such men as Ivan Kapitonov (secretary and head of the CPSU Central Committee's Department of Party Organs) and Iurii Solomentsev (a Politburo candidate) are behind this isolationist trend.

Now only Alexander Solzhenitsyn's style of Russian ethnocentrism, advocating, among other things, a physical and spiritual return to old Muscovy and the abandonment of imperial ambitions in line with ideas of the Old Believers of the past, is suppressed. St. Petersburg's imperial ethnocentrism has become the source of Soviet Russian patriotism, with practical distinctions between "Soviet" and "Russian" being blurred. It is considered an inherent Russian right to be patriotic, a right, at least in part, denied to other Soviet ethnic groups, whose history is respected until the moment it conflicts with Russia's, but never beyond.

A present-day Russian political pamphleteer felt proud of Russia's "burden" and declared:

> There is no, there was no, and there will probably be no other nation [ethnic group] in the world that, like the Russian people, labored and labors for all the people of the USSR, and not only of the USSR.[25]

Among the ethnic groups of the Soviet Union, the Russian is the only one officially entitled to be called great (*velikii*), an adjective also reserved for powerful foreign nations such as the United States and China; it is also the only one so labeled in the Soviet anthem. On the occasion of the fiftieth anniversary of the formation of the USSR, Brezhnev called the RSFSR first among equals among the other constituent Soviet republics.[26] Thus he openly stressed, if not its privileged status within the USSR, at least its special historical position as the legitimate heir to the Romanov empire.

4. Education

During the years of the Soviet regime, political considerations notwithstanding, achievements in education in Central Asia have been impressive. Equal opportunities have been provided to Russian and Muslim children. The development of the school system and of literacy has been remarkable, although not as great as the Soviet figures indicate. The number of native pupils in elementary schools in Russian Turkestan and in religious schools in Bukhara and Khiva together amounted to fewer than the number of Uzbek students in Soviet institutions of higher learning alone in 1969/70.

The high percentage of literacy achieved in Central Asia three decades ago was due to the strongly developed compulsory school system and to the mass campaigns launched against adult illiteracy. By the 1950s the percentage of literacy in Central Asia was much higher than elsewhere in the Muslim Middle and Near East. Many experts, however, considered Soviet prewar literacy claims highly exaggerated. Dubicki, a Polish émigré who lived in that area, estimated the proportion of literate natives in the 1940s at 30 percent and adult literacy at only 7 or 10 percent. The English expert, Lieutenant Colonel G. E. Wheeler, considered literacy to be around 50 percent (in the early 1950s). The explanation presumably lies in the fact that the official literacy statistics obviously included semiliterate people who were barely able to sign their names or spell more than a few words. In Stalin's time this group may have accounted for one half of the total "literate" people.[27]

Elementary-school attendance in Central Asia in the 1940s was more or less the same among European and native boys. However, thousands of Muslim school-age children in rural areas did not attend schools, and among secondary-school, college, and university students, natives were strongly underrepresented, a sign of the still existing gap in cultural levels between Russian and native communities. As a result, Uzbek students amounted to only 32.5 percent of the total enrollment at the University of Central Asia in Tashkent (SAGU) in 1940, and Kazakh students only 30 percent of the total at the University of Alma-Ata. Among 2,200 students who graduated from high schools in Uzbekistan in 1943, only 500 were of Uzbek nationality[28]

By the 1969/70 school year, the proportion of Muslim students attending such institutions had become more or less equal to the proportion of Muslims in the total population of the republic (better than that in Kazakhstan, Kirghizia, and Turkmenistan, slightly worse in Uzbekistan and Tadzhikistan).[29] True, some Russian settlers attend out-of-state schools (as do some Muslims), and educational standards in many institutions with local languages of instruction are still quite low; but at least numerical parity has been achieved.

Soviet education statistics are especially impressive with regard to Muslim women, who before the Revolution took no part in public life. Until World War II, attendance by Muslim girls in secondary schools and universities had been poor (between 5 and 8 percent of the USSR average in 1939).[30] Only in 1959 did Muslim girls finally cross the 50 percent barrier as compared with the rest of the country.[31] Thus, while by 1939, among women of titular nationalities in the Central Asian republics, only between 3 and 6 per 1,000 completed a junior high school education, as against 71 for the USSR as a whole, by 1959 the situation had drastically improved, with between 133 and 165 reaching that level (205 in Turkmenistan), as against the USSR average of 271.

But even in the 1970s, Muslim women still failed to reap the fruits of their education. Fewer than 10 percent of rural Muslim women in Uzbekistan and Turkmenistan were employed in agricultural occupations demanding intellectual effort (compared with one third in Russia proper and 50 percent in Estonia).[32] Thus for Muslim women educational opportunities have not led to on-the-job equality, at least not for the time being.

The creation of a native Muslim technical and scientific elite can be counted as another achievement of the regime. Strong incentives for native students, including outright privileges (easier admissions, more available scholarships, and more lenient grading) began to bear fruit. By 1975 Muslim technical and scientific cadres in Uzbekistan had reached 57.6 percent of the total, quadrupling in number since 1960.[33]

The Soviet educational record in Central Asia is as good as humanly possible given the objective circumstances and the low starting points. The only serious weaknesses are in the qualitative gaps prevailing between Russian-speaking schools (or courses) and their graduates, on the one hand, and the native ones on the other. But such shortcomings are inevitable and need time to be alleviated.

While Moscow's eagerness to spread education among Central Asian Muslims has not been totally selfless (improved labor efficiency and increased political conformity being very much on Moscow's mind), the results must be accepted as one of the most positive achievements of the so much derided (often with good cause) Soviet nationality policy.

5. *Assimilation or Acculturation?*

"Russians have always been a missionary people," states Mobin

Shorish.[34] Whether in spreading their version of orthodoxy or of Marxism, in making people cross themselves with three fingers instead of two (the Nikon reform as against the Old Believers), or in instructing "the younger brothers" to follow the path of the "elder Russian brother," the Russians demonstrate the same stubborn proselytizing spirit. A deep belief in their own righteousness, combined with an innate inability to compromise, has historically made the Russians' missionary spirit uncomfortable for their weaker neighbors.

Yet Russian missionary ardor inevitably provokes backlashes among those who are to be converted. For example, the very fact that Russia promoted socialism in Poland makes that doctrine subjectively unpopular there. Had the same ideology been spread by the English or French, it might well have been much more objectively regarded. Similarly, for the Muslims of Central Asia, the Soviet image is clearly dressed in Russian cloth. "The attributes of the Soviet Man as emphasised by the schools are those outlining a Russian," continues Shorish.[35] This in itself alienates young Muslims from the officially promoted model.

Hélène Carrère d'Encausse insists that in their total opposition to *Homo sovieticus*, Central Asian Muslims, the most unassimilable element in modern Soviet society, ought to be regarded as genuine *Homo islamicus*.[36] But there is no neat division between the two species. The Soviet *Homo islamicus* does in fact display some characteristics of his Russian counterpart, unless he is among the minority who live in the most remote villages with no contacts with the Russians and practice Islam in the most traditional way, with all its rituals. For the bulk of Soviet Muslims, it is impossible to remain totally unaffected by Soviet *Russian* reality, and this results in multiple social identities. Thus, for example, an Uzbek may view himself as Uzbek, as Turkestani, as Muslim, and as Soviet depending on circumstances and the person (or persons) with whom he deals or converses.

It is even conceivable that such an Uzbek, while traveling to a place like New York City, in order to explain and simplify his identity to an unsophisticated American, might introduce himself as a Russian (while presenting himself to Russian émigrés as Uzbek, Turkestani, or Muslim). The same person in contact with a Kazakh both perceives himself and is perceived as an Uzbek; with a Tatar he becomes a Turkestani; and with a Volga German co-worker in Central Asia—a Muslim, and so on.[37]

We must accept the fact that despite regional differences, enhanced by ethnic factors, the Soviet way of life could not have failed to influence all but the most culturally isolated individuals. The resulting acculturation (as well as the bilingualism that is part of it) does not necessarily lead to assimilation. On the contrary, a certain degree of acculturation may increase one's resistance to assimilation. Thus smoking instead of chewing tobacco, learning to drink some vodka, or wearing European clothes in an office has even less assimilative effect than learning Russian as a second language.

The Soviet Central Asian is, of course, also not simply a mirror image of his across-the-border coreligionists. He has acquired enough Soviet traits and Russian habits to make him distinctive. It is only in his opposition to the Russian *Homo sovieticus* that he can be viewed as Carrére d'Encausse's *Homo islamicus*.

CHAPTER EIGHT

The Sociopolitical
Setting

1. The Formative Years of the Party

In 1921 Stalin gave a clever definition of the Soviet system:

> In our Soviet country we must evolve a system of government
> which will permit us with certainty to anticipate all changes, to per-
> ceive everything that is going on among peasants, the non-Russian
> nationals and the Russians; the system of barometers which will anti-
> cipate every change, register and forestall a Basmachi movement,
> Kronstadt, and all possible storms and ill-fortune.[1]

The system envisaged by Stalin developed itself along four
principal channels of command and control: the party organization, the government bureaucracy, the armed forces, and the
police apparatus. The party was designed to be the vanguard,
and the driving force of the system; the bureaucracy, its executive arm; the army, its shield against an outside menace; the police apparatus, its sword against the internal enemies of the
regime.

The main driving force of this system, the Communist
Party, was, during the years of Stalin's rule, deprived of its
leading position and reduced to the function of another executive arm, parallel to that of the governmental bureaucracy. The
"cult of personality" (that is, the complete subservience to the
person in command) dominant in the party exerted a paralyzing
effect on the party membership, as well as on the party apparatus, and resulted in the bureaucratization and stratification of
the entire structure. Party officials were afraid of responsibility,
of possible errors, and consequently lacked initiative. The purge
became the only way to renovate the party cadres and inject

fresh forces into its otherwise stratified body. The medicine was, however, defective in itself: the fear of the purge reduced party officials to the very state of immobility against which the purge had initially been brought into action. The best party men often fell victim to such indiscriminate purges, while those who should have been removed managed to survive. This state of affairs worked against the ideal theoretical concept of the party as the association of the "best people" in Soviet society.[2]

The party was presumed to select its members from among the most "revolutionarily conscious" workers, ideally those with proven leadership abilities. This may well have been the case in the early days of the Revolution. It was not so in Central Asia, where the communist parties of all the five republics were in a shaky condition, most of their vitality having been sapped by the purges of the 1930s.

From 1930 to 1938 seven successive purges destroyed almost all the fragile local Communist Party cadres in all the Central Asian republics. In the purge of 1937, 55.7 percent of the party officials in primary party organizations and 70.8 percent in district party committees were replaced by new people.[3]

Faizullah Khodzhaev, former head of the government of the People's Republic of Bukhara (1922—24) and chairman of the Council of People's Commissars of Uzbekistan (1924—37), "confessed" that he had joined the Right Opposition (Bukharin and his friends) because the latter would guarantee the independence of the Uzbek Republic. He was then forced to declare:

> ... even if it would become possible at the price of black treachery, at the price of treason to the fatherland ... it goes without saying that this fictitious independence would have been a new disaster to the peoples of Uzbekistan.[4]

At the Uzbek government level, after the removal of Khodzhaev (July 1937) three successive Uzbek premiers were ousted in less than a year. Abdulla Karimov lasted two weeks, Torabekov a few weeks, and Soltan Segisbaev half a year. All were liquidated as enemies of the people, while at the same time thousands of their followers were purged. In Kazakhstan every member of its first Politburo was shot, while Turkmenistan remained for several months without a Politburo for lack of a quorum among members not yet arrested.[5]

The potential or imaginary danger of national communism was thus eliminated, but the cost for the party was a heavy one:

native party cadres, after the storm of 1937—38, became weaker and less efficient than ever and, consequently, more dependent on outside (Russian) guardianship. The process of rebuilding the native cadres, in progress in 1938—40, had not yet reached completion when the Soviet Union found itself at war with Germany.

Between 1936 and 1941 a policy of recruiting party candidates from among the upper crust of Soviet society prevailed. During these years the workers were gradually forced into a position of inferior status within party ranks, and the so-called party-economic elite became the real party within the party. Then, with the beginning of World War II, a new policy of "mass wartime recruitment had the net result of giving the Party firmer roots in the lower reaches of the Soviet society."[6] Such recruitment was generally conducted in the army units, but a large number of native Central Asian draftees, because of their known lack of enthusiasm, were sent to labor units, where no mass party recruitment took place.[7]

In Uzbekistan the proportion of factory workers within the party remained small. Even in highly industrialized Tashkent, only one fourth of the new party candidates admitted in 1946 were workers. The more able elements among these recruits were soon incorporated into the managerial elite, thus eliminating the danger of a competing proletarian elite arising from within the party, which remained a managerial party with weak working-class connections.

Already under Stalin the most powerful group within the party elite was the so-called "designated workers" (*nomenklaturnye rabotniki*), whose names are on the lists specially kept by district or regional party committees to supply a pool of reliable party members qualified for future managerial openings. First in line for promotion, they enjoy a variety of special privileges: access to consumer goods in short supply, priority in getting new apartments, travel privileges, and what is most important, a kind of "party tenure." They cannot be fired without a party committee's consent granted after a proper hearing. Even those who have performed poorly at a given job are often simply shuffled to another managerial post, their political reliability being too important an asset to forego. The privileged status and power of *nomenklatura* have thus remained unchallenged since Stalin's time.

The party in the villages had even weaker popular roots than in the city. Many collective farms had no party primary organizations. On many smaller farms the chairman was the only party member. On larger collective farms, where the number of party members was higher, the party membership remained limited to the managerial personnel, and party cards were seldom held by average farmers. Hence the party in the villages became representative of the new rural socioeconomic elite (those people deriving their higher status from the collective farm policy imposed by the communist regime), a situation which became a permanent legacy of the Stalin era.[8]

Nor was the situation on state farms and MTS (Machine-Tractor Stations, later abolished under Khrushchev) any different. Party membership was limited to the managing personnel, while the rank-and-file employees remained outside the party.

Several chains of control were established in the village in order to insure proper functioning of the collective farm system. The work of the collective farm board and of its chairman was supervised by the collective farm party organization, and the latter was supervised by the party organization of the local MTS, which was responsible for several farms in the neighborhood. The district departments of agriculture controlled the collective farms both directly and through the local MTS, in whose hands was placed, the indispensable farm machinery.[9] The executive committee of the district soviet exercised its control through village soviets. The district party committee supervised the work of all the above-listed organizations, allocated grain delivery quotas among the collective farms, and kept itself busy interfering directly in most other matters. The turnover of collective farm chairmen was high. But following the *nomenklatura* precedent, a chairman who failed in his job was often transferred —to the chairmanship of another farm! However, a case of extreme failure usually ended in court.[10]

The party had to content itself with the available human material. Better-qualified men were scarce in the local officialdom, and economic conditions, especially in wartime, were such that even able people deteriorated quickly under the impact of pressures, demands, threats, shortages, inefficiency, and inflation.

2. *Coopting the Muslim Elite*

Stalin, in order to make the Central Asian republics "national in form, but socialist in content," proclaimed a line to be followed by the Soviet regime in that area:

> 1. To create industrial centers . . . as bases on which peasants can be rallied around the working-class. . . .
> 2. To advance agriculture and above all irrigation.
> 3. To improve and advance co-operative organization among the broad masses of the peasants and handicraftsmen as the most reliable way of bringing the Soviet Republics of the East into the general system of Soviet economic development.
> 4. To bring the Soviets into close touch with the masses; to make them national in composition, and in this way to implant a national Soviet state organization that will be close and comprehensive to the toiling masses.
> 5. To develop national culture; to build up a wide system of courses and schools for both general education, and vocational and technical training in native languages, with the purpose of training Soviet party, trade union, and economic cadres among the native people.[11]

In order to achieve these goals, an understanding of nationalist aspirations was, according to Stalin, essential:

> Russian Communists cannot combat Tatar, Georgian, or Bashkir chauvinism [read: "nationalism"], for if the Russian Communists were to undertake this difficult task . . . it would be regarded as a fight of a Great Russian chauvinism against the Tatars or the Georgians. This would confuse the whole issue. . . . Only Georgian Communists can successfully combat Georgian nationalism.[12]

Native communists were bound, moreover, to remember that ideological and political conformity with Moscow's orders had to be observed. In 1929 one of the Soviet leaders, Mikhail Kalinin, trying to put the objectives of the Soviet policy in Central Asia into simple words, said that its aim was "teaching the people of the Kirgiz Steppe, the small Uzbek cotton grower, and the Turkmenian gardener the ideals of the Leningrad worker."[13]

Between that time and the beginning of World War II, a social revolution along Stalin's lines took place in Central Asia with the collectivization of agriculture, three five-year plans, a large Russian immigration, small purges, the "Great Purge," antireligious campaigns, campaigns against "local nationalism," campaigns for the "liberation of women," campaigns for eradication of illiteracy, reforms of alphabets, reforms of local administration, constitutional changes, and a number of other changes, campaigns, reforms, and plans too numerous and too varied to be listed.

The "small Uzbek cotton grower" was forced to join a collective farm, his son went to work in the city, his daughter took off the veil, and one or two among his more opportunistic relatives joined the ruling party.

Throughout the Stalinist era, the party elite of each community was given the responsibility of insuring the political conformity of its own people. In addition, the Russian party elite had the task of helping its less experienced native counterpart and of keeping an eye on native nationalist elements, whether of Basmachi or of national-communist origin. The natives, aware of the situation, felt no hostility toward the native party members. On the contrary, they regarded them as allies against the Russians and protectors against the hardships imposed by the regime. Native Muslim confidence in Muslim communists was, however, an advantage to the Soviet regime itself. For the party was thus able to use the native communists more effectively. It would have been very difficult indeed to administer the area properly had the native communists been regarded by their own people as Russian puppets, thereby making the reality of Soviet Russian rule visible to everyone.

Most of the native Muslims who joined the party after the Great Purge were members of the socioeconomic elite. They were chairmen of collective farms, brigadiers, factory directors, office managers, local party officials, administrators, and people of similar status. These people had living standards far higher than the average and enjoyed priorities and advantages commensurate with their position. No idealists, they had a vested interest in the smooth functioning of the regime, both in the fulfillment of its production plans and in the success of its propaganda campaigns. They owed the positions they occupied to the regime in power.

Here the question may be asked whether the native party members were recruited from the socioeconomic elite or promoted into it only after having joined the party. Actually, the party picked its recruits from among those natives who showed a readiness to obey and to execute party orders, who possessed an ability to command, an eagerness to learn from the Russians the more advanced "Western" methods of organization, a better than average intelligence and a lack of scruples, all connected with a strong inner drive to succeed. Although better-educated people were eagerly sought, lack of education was not an obstacle to a party career.[14] Those selected were, following their admission into the party, speedily promoted to positions of responsibility.

New members recruited from among those in managerial positions were first in line for promotion. The new party member had no choice but to show his zeal for his job and for the party, which gave him his promotion. Bad will or obvious failures could lead to serious troubles, including demotion or even ejection from the party. A person expelled from the party was in a worse position than one who had never applied for admission. But the party could not be too demanding either, since the number of natives who survived the purges and still possessed the minimum qualifications for party membership was so small.

Consequently, the native party members who had joined the party after the demise of the old members knew little about communism and cared even less. In any case, they valued leadership for its own sake and enjoyed the pleasure of command in a truly Oriental way.[15]

What is striking is that forty years later, the much better educated modern Muslim party cadres have inherited the same indifference to dogma, the same opportunism, and the same nationalist feelings that affected their predecessors. The gap between the theory and the practice of communist ideology, so marked in Moscow, remained most pronounced in the Muslim republics.

In the West, for instance, becoming a member of the Communist Party is either a sign of acceptance of Marxist ideology or a protest against the injustices of the capitalist way of life. For a Russian it is most often a morally difficult decision made for the sake of career advancement. Even more so for an Estonian, it is often a painful choice between national pride and personal advantage. But for an Uzbek it is an opportunistic step taken with neither conviction nor remorse. Some candidates among store managers are even ready to bribe their way into the party.[16] It is like joining an insiders' club that opens the doors to power, protection, and money, but whose ideology is either nonexistent or totally irrelevant. Marxist-Leninist terminology is memorized and recited by Muslim party members like incomprehensible prayers in Arabic. But while prayers evoke a warm feeling of group belonging and symbolize tradition and identity, party meetings evoke no emotion whatsoever. They are just prerequisites for privileged membership.

A Muslim party member may therefore be considered an

"ideal" recruit. He has no ideology, no beliefs, and no illusions whatsoever—only self-interest.

3. *Separate but Equal*

Unlike American blacks or former French and British colonial subjects, Central Asian Muslims have never aspired to social integration with those who held power over them. The main factors working against the desirability of such integration have been not only the Muslim community (*umma*) spirit but also the relative social unattractiveness of the bulk of Russian settlers. The first point is quite clear; the second needs some clarification.

British or French settlers (except for the poorest among the *"petits français"* of Algeria) have always regarded themselves as socially superior to the native masses. Indeed, their way of life, their manners, style of dress, and recreational habits became symbols of "the good life" for the elite of the colonized groups as well. The Englishman set the life style in colonial India, and the American Southern gentleman was the symbol of life *"comme il faut"* in Virginia, even for blacks.

But this has not been the case with the Russians. While some upper-class Russians, especially the officers of the victorious Imperial Army, impressed the awed natives, the much more numerous lower-class Russian settlers failed to have such an impact on their Muslim neighbors. Thus theft and drunkenness, very rare in pre-Russian Turkestan, were imported into the area by the "little" settlers. While some native habits, like spitting tobacco, sitting on a rug, and eating with one's hands, seemed unsanitary to the Russians, lower-class Russian crudeness seemed equally "uncultured" to the natives. Finally, the economic gap between the living standards of Russian settlers and of the native Muslims (except for those on the lowest socioeconomic level) was much smaller than that prevailing in British or French colonies or in the American South between blacks and whites.

The narrowness of the economic and cultural gap also had its positive consequences. As soon as legal inequalities between the Russians and the Muslims were removed (roughly by the early 1920s), little discrimination remained in everyday life. Since then the natives have enjoyed equal opportunities in labor (specific key control positions excepted), housing, education, etc.[17] In addition, local "affirmative action" programs were in effect long before their controversial American counterparts came into existence. Thus Muslim job seekers and college applicants are favored within their own republics (but not outside).[18] This practice, well known to European settlers and resented by them, is obviously a result of a conscious political decision. Moscow is quite aware of the fact that individual Russian settlers may be discriminated against in the process, but considers it the necessary price to be paid for reducing Muslim opposition to the continued Russian presence.

Some Western scholars perceive the situation differently. Comparing Central Asia to developing Third World nations, Robert Lewis and his associates have argued that the Muslims do in fact suffer from "ethnic stratification." These scholars point to low levels of urbanization (from 14.6 to 31.0 percent of the Muslim groups) in Central Asia and the region's inferiority vis-à-vis European parts of the USSR in terms of per capita incomes, retail sales, services, health, culture and education, urban housing space, or numbers of specialists and technicians. In this apparent dominance of Muslims by Slavs, these scholars see the operation of a universal principle—namely, that "hierarchic ranking of nationalities along socioeconomic lines" results whenever a country (or area) includes more than one ethnic group.[19]

To be sure, we know that—on average—Europeans living in Central Asia enjoy higher salaries, more housing space, better access to higher education for their children, more skills, and better positions than the natives.[20] We also know that since Stalin's time, certain controlling positions within the local party and government (including security) apparatuses have been in the hands of Russians and other Europeans (see Chapter 9). But this involves a small number of jobs, while the segment of the job market where Muslims are given preference is numerically much larger.

Rasma Karklins's survey, recently conducted among Volga German immigrants from the Soviet Union (mostly from Kazakhstan, Central Asia, and the Baltic republics—in that order), provides more evidence supporting the theory of "affirmative action," as opposed to that of discrimination against the Muslims. She found that 67 percent of the German immigrants from Kazakhstan (a total of sixty-six persons was questioned) thought that Kazakhs are gaining in power within their own republic, as against only 2 percent who thought the contrary. For Central Asia proper the figures were 39 percent to 11 percent (for thirty-six respondents). Immigrants from the Baltic republics, on the contrary, perceived a growth of Russian power in that area. The contrasting views may be attributed not only to an objective perception of political reality but to the impact of the Central Asian demographic explosion on that perception.[21]

While Karklins's survey leaves the concept of "power" purposely vague, its results add to the arguments against Lewis's theories of social stratification in Soviet Central Asia along ethnic lines. Furthermore, the gap between the European settlers and the native Muslims in areas of health, education, skill levels, housing, living standards, and jobs has been narrowing. The Soviet authorities have clearly been working—and with considerable effect—to achieve economic equalization, not exploitation. The routine practice of making capital transfers to Central Asia and Kazakhstan and of returning the totality (rather than the standard one fourth) of proceeds from the turnover tax originated in those republics is symptomatic of such efforts.[22]

4. *Welfare Colonialism in Search of Allegiance*

Central Asian equality of socioeconomic opportunities is often cited by Moscow as the main proof that there is no colonialism in Soviet Central Asia. Indeed, on the surface the case seems rather unusual. Can one speak of colonialism without social exploitation of the colonized by the colonizer? Can one speak of colonialism when the colonizer reaps little or no economic benefit for himself? Such was not the case for Great Britain or France in their colonies. Charles de Gaulle, in his brilliant perception of the possible consequences of retaining Algeria as an integral part of France rather than an exploited possession, quickly extricated his country from this danger. But Moscow persists in maintaining its former colonial possessions not for the sake of economic gain or colonial exploitation but to preserve and expand Russia's geopolitical dominance of the northern tier of the Eurasian land mass. We are thus faced with the case of an imperialism that does not correspond to classical Marxist definitions, a political-military imperialism for which economic factors are secondary. Unlike classical colonial powers that sought political domination for the purpose of economic exploitation, Soviet Russia seeks political domination, even at the price of economic discomfort for its own citizens.

Thus while Russia as a country dominates Uzbekistan or

Lithuania, and those Uzbeks or Lithuanians who dare to oppose it wind up in Siberia, individual Russians (except for a few colonial apparatchiki) fail to benefit from this state of affairs. They do get a psychological boost from the chauvinistic sense of Russia's might, but this is about the sum total of their personal gain. The satisfaction derived from spreading communist dogma cannot be viewed as a factor; few Russians really believe in it any longer; those who do are more attracted by familiar code words than the waning significance of the credo itself.

With no national pride derived either from communist dogma or from the global might of the Russian Empire, Muslim allegiances are directed toward their own community. Alexandre Bennigsen attempts to classify these allegiances into three categories: (1) subnational, a feeling of belonging to a specific clan or tribe; (2) national, an allegiance to the Moscow-created Soviet national republics (Uzbekistan, Kazakhstan, etc.); and (3) supranational allegiance to the Islamic community of Central Asia as a whole.[23] According to Bennigsen, the first category persists, albeit as a survival of the past. The third is growing increasingly stronger. It is the second that is weak.

"National" allegiance was supposed to be personified in the ethnic union republics created after the national delimitations of 1924. The new republics, bearing no similarity to the historical state units of Turkestan—Kokand, Bukhara, and Khiva—were, according to Moscow, supposed to provide national homelands for the major Muslim nationalities of the area. From the Muslim point of view, they seemed rather an attempt to lessen Muslim supranational unity. The old state units, based on subnational factors, presented no such danger. But the new national entities, soon provided with all the external paraphernalia of statehood—from quasi-identical constitutions and alphabets (first Latin, then, conveniently, Cyrillic) to separate, closely Russian controlled "governments"—never managed to inspire a true sense of patriotism capable of competing with the supranational feeling of Turkestan Muslim (I am not speaking of Pan-Muslim or Pan-Turkic) unity.

What gave Moscow's initiative an unexpected turn was its own parallel policy of curtailing national-ethnic allegiances in favor of federal, all-Soviet loyalty. This led to an open clash between two Moscow-promoted policies, each one pulling in a contrary direction. The result was the weakening of both sets of Moscow-inspired allegiances. Moscow was faced with a curious dilemma in which the best way to combat the dangerous trend of supranational Islamic unity lay in upholding national patriotisms for individual Muslim republics that are in themselves dangerous to the unity of "the Soviet people—the new community of peoples." In the Baltic republics, the Ukraine, or in the Caucasus, in the absence of such a supranational dimension, local nationalists have only the "national" to oppose to the all-Union aspect of the "Soviet people, a new historical community of nations."

5. *Social Mobility in Ethnic Perspective*

The problem of cadres remains the most fertile ground for Muslim-Russian conflicts. The old ethnic division of labor preceded the October Revolution: Muslims always leaned toward agriculture and trade and shunned factory work; Russians concentrated on factories, railroads, and administration. After the Revolution Muslims entered the new regime, but the key positions remained in Russian hands, and Muslims were most often assigned to public-contact jobs in order to present an image of native self-government. An influx of Muslims into the factories did occur but was slower than desired, with Muslims still avoiding straight production-line jobs and selecting such sideline occupations as maintenance, storage, canteens, etc.[24]

At the professional and managerial levels, the sheer numbers (and percentages) of Muslim university and institute graduates grew from year to year, with Muslims competing especially in the tertiary sector (trade, services, etc.) and at all the levels of management. In addition, at least one of the Muslim groups, the Kazakhs, showed a better-than-average Muslim inclination toward engineering and began to compete in that field too.[25]

With the demographic explosion, growing numbers of native cadres started to fight for desirable jobs, often successfully dislodging the old settler's cadres. National-religious antagonisms increased the bitterness of the competition. But the Muslims appear to be winning the battle, and for several reasons:

a. Moscow, whose policy has consistently been based on the development of native cadres, cannot easily reverse it.

b. The shortage of manpower in Russia proper restricts the availability of new Russian cadres for export to Central Asia, and natives are absolutely unwilling to migrate to labor-hungry regions of Russia.

c. Many Russian and other European settlers, themselves either deported to Central Asia under Stalin or children of deportees, faced with growing Muslim competition and increased racial conflicts, are inclined to return to the European USSR (see Chapter 5).

d. Already entrenched Muslim cadres do their best to hire candidates not only from their own group but even from their own clan or tribe.[26] The Russians cannot reciprocate without provoking so much Muslim resistance as to endanger national-religious peace in the area. Simply speaking, the Russian manager is restricted by a kind of "affirmative action," while the native manager has no other restriction than approximate job qualifications; and such requirements can often be bent for the desired individual.

e. The specific positions which it is in Moscow's vital interest that Russians hold represent a very small percentage of the total "cadres."

f. Unlike Algeria, where during French rule Arabs preferred metropolitan Frenchmen to "*colons*," Muslims in Central Asia show preference for local Russians over newcomers, finding the former easier to deal with.

g. If unable to hire a qualified Muslim, native managers tend to favor other minorities over the Russians. It is one of the rare cases in the Soviet Union where even a Jew has a better chance of getting a job than a Russian (although a good part of his edge comes from the fact that he can also be more easily fired than the Russian).[27]

For Moscow the danger of the present situation lies in the steady erosion of Russian on-the-spot control. The presence of numerous Russian cadres at all levels of political, social, and economic life has been the mainstay of Russian policy in all the national republics. While the control levers remain untouched, the steady weakening of Russian presence at those levels presents a long-term danger to Russia's dominance.

6. *Conflicts*

Moscow's policy in Soviet Central Asia is based on a balance between all-Union (read: Russian) prerogative and local leeway. Thus Moscow would surely cut short any nationalist agitation questioning its rule; at the same time, it shows remarkable tolerance toward abuses of power by local native authorities against individual Russians.

Thus Moscow tries to play down individual incidents, closing an eye to their nationalist motivation. Even the famous Pakhtakor race riot in Tashkent (September 1969), which resulted in numerous arrests following assaults by Muslim crowds on Russian bystanders after a soccer game between the local "Pakhtakor" team and a guest team from Russia proper, would have been swept under the rug by both Uzbek and Russian local party leaders except for the outcry from frightened Russian settlers.[28] Similarly, on a much smaller scale, an ordinary traffic death involving a Muslim offender and a Russian victim led to an investigation in which Muslim officials unanimously defended and Russian ones unanimously accused the offender.[29]

Cases of corruption, so widespread in the area, often result in similar situations, with Muslims eagerly defending their own kind. In all such conflicts the Russians are at a disadvantage: they are restrained by Moscow's policy of letting the native get away with a variety of transgressions as a price for accepting (*nolens volens*) Russia's overlordship. But this "tolerance" tends to spread and is hard to contain. By now the Russians not only hear the classic "go home"——in this case "Kalinka go home to Samara"——but are sometimes even threatened by Muslim youth gangs.[30]

Added to the previously described "reverse discrimination" employment patterns, the status of those Russian settlers whose position is not high enough to insulate and protect them is deteriorating in comparison with Stalin's day. Unwilling to grant its Muslim dependencies genuine self-rule, Moscow cannot avoid enlarging the scope of its "tolerance" toward Muslim transgressions. While all forms of such tolerance are but a protective cloak for established Russian prerogatives that are of vital importance in assuring continued control of the area, it is only a matter of time before the quantitative changes taking place in Soviet Central Asia will force qualitative shifts in its relationship with Moscow.[31]

CHAPTER NINE

Government

1. *The Unequal Republics*

The Soviet Union is a federation of fifteen national "union republics." In addition, within the union republics there are twenty national "autonomous republics" and eight autonomous regions. Legally, all union republics have equal status. But geopolitical reality makes the Russian Republic superior to the others. The Russian Federative Socialist Republic is a federation of nations in itself, occupies the bulk of the Eurasian land mass of the USSR, and accounts for roughly half of the Soviet population. The five major non-Russian areas in the Soviet Union are all territorially connected to the RSFSR, but only in one case to each other.

The non-Russian areas are: (1) the Baltic region, with its three small republics of Estonia, Latvia, and Lithuania; (2) the Slavic lands of Belorussia and the Ukraine (the most populous of the non-Russian republics) and territorially adjacent but mostly non-Slavic Moldavia; (3) the Transcaucasian trio of Georgia, Armenia, and Azerbaidzhan, with the adjacent North Caucasian autonomous republics of the RSFSR; (4) the five central Asian republics; and finally (5) the five autonomous Volga republics of the RSFSR, an island within the latter's territory.

Each national union republic is supposed to enjoy the same rights and privileges as the others, the same degree of self-government, matched by the same degree of dependence on federal power. Only internal governance is supposed to show some minor variation based on national traditions and economic differences. But this has not been the case. Some republics clearly appear "more equal" than others, their party, government, and security apparatus being *de facto* freer from federal controls than their counterparts in other republics. This is particularly evident in the degree to which the cadres of the titular nationality of the republic are entrusted with key positions within their own republic and given access to important positions within the federal structure in Moscow.

Thus in the Muslim union republics (Central Asia proper, Kazakhstan, Azerbaidzhan), "parachuted" Russian cadres occupy a disproportionate share of key power positions (listed later on p. 125 ff.) and provide reliable "seconds" to assist (and supervise) local Muslim officials. To a lesser degree, the same pattern prevails in the three Baltic republics and in Moldavia. However, in the "fraternal" Slavic republics of the Ukraine and Belorussia, native communists are generally in charge of internal governance; and Russians in high positions do not appear to have been selected for the purpose of ensuring Russian control over specific domains, as is the case in non-Slavic republics, but as equal co-citizens of the same republic as their Ukrainian or Belorussian neighbors.

This variation in methods of control visibly divides the non-Russian union republics into three "reliable," two "doubtful," and nine "unreliable" units. The reliable republics are Slavic. The doubtful ones are the two Caucasian republics, whose incorporation into the old Russian Empire had been more or less voluntary (even as a "lesser evil choice"). Most of the inhabitants of the five more or less trustworthy republics profess the Orthodox faith, have strong cultural and historical ties with Russia, and were already relatively privileged (after the Russians themselves) during the times of the tsars.

The "unreliable" nationalities were conquered (or reconquered) rather recently, are of either Islamic or Scandinavian culture, mostly Muslim by religion (some Protestant and Catholic), and their incorporation into the Russian Empire was visibly contrary to the wishes of their people. Some were classified as *"peuples allogénes" (inorodtsy)* in tsarist times, a category combining nomads, primitive natives, and . . . Jews. The Moldavians are a special case, since their "republic" is an artificial concoction (like the old Karelo-Finnish Republic) created to justify the annexation of a chunk of Romanian territory.

Because the three Baltic nations are small, have been historically connected with Moscow, and, despite strong nationalist feelings there, present no visible threat to Russia's future, the most serious control problem is in the Muslim republics, with their large territories, rapidly growing populations, and rising nationalism fed by a dangerous combination of racial, national, and religious feelings. This is not to underestimate, of course, the upsurge of nationalism in the Ukraine or Georgia, whose ties with Russia, however unsatisfactory, still lack the colonial elements present in the Moscow-Central Asian relationship.

Whatever the variance in the position of each main nationality *within* its titular republic, its leaders certainly have little hope of acceding to the real seats of power in Moscow. There only fraternal Eastern Slavs (Ukrainians and Belorussians) are trusted enough to share power with great Russians. Nobody expects the representatives of non-Russian groups to compete for top positions within this leadership. Unlike the October Revolution and the 1920s, when many non-Russian leaders did emerge in Moscow, such a possibility is now widely discounted. Few non-Russians rise to high positions in unionwide organizations, especially within the Central Committee. Only two men (the Kazakh Kunaev and the very elderly Russified Latvian Stalinist Pelshe) "represent" the non-Slavs among the fourteen full members of the Politiburo, and no one does so on the ten-man Politburo Secretariat. The place for the non-Slavs is among the nonvoting alternates (three of eight alternates were non-Slavs in 1981). Nobody expects a Georgian, a Jew, or even a Ukrainian to inherit Brezhnev's chair. At the Moscow-USSR level it is the Soviet equivalent of an American WASP who has the best chance to reach the top of the career ladder; a non-Russian has hardly any hope outside his own constituent republic.

Finally, control by Russia exercised through almost purely Slavic-managed unionwide agencies and on the spot through specially selected Russian bureaucrats is the rule of the game. But this does not involve special privileges for individual Russians in non-Russian union republics nor any personal discrimination against local ethnic groups, except for security considerations. Russians are simply the dominant group, and their past, traditions, and institutions permeate the Soviet way of life. They occupy top unionwide positions and provide personnel for security-sensitive jobs within other union republics. But Russians also suffer from a degree of reverse discrimination in those union republics. Unlike the British and the French empires, the Soviet Russian system seems to have devised means of securing political domination without socioeconomic privileges for the dominant ethnic group. This might be one of the reasons for its continued survival, despite the growing resentment and unfulfilled expectations of its non-Russian components.

2. *The Colonial* Nomenklatura

The main method of control in the Muslim republics is the principle of staffing power positions (called *nomenklatura*), with Russians and other Slavs and "doubling" important Muslim functionaries with Slavic counterparts. This method survived both Stalin and Khrushchev and has remained the cornerstone of the Soviet control mechanism throughout the years of Brezhnev's leadership.

In accordance with this method, specific positions within the party apparatus, the governmental structure, the security and armed forces, and the key economic enterprises located in the Muslim republics are entrusted to European outsiders (see Table 22).

Let us look in more detail at these sensitive positions:

1. The key position of *party second secretary* (at both the republic and regional levels, and often even at district levels).

In 1979 all but two regional (*oblast'*) second party secretaries in Uzbekistan were Russians. The two exceptions were a Ukrainian second secretary in one region and a native second secretary under a Russian first secretary in another. Those district (*raion*) second party secretaries whose names I was able to trace were also Russians, a pattern confirmed by recent émigrés from the area.[1]

It is by now common knowledge that the second party secretary in Muslim areas plays a much larger role than does the analogous party functionary in Russia or the Ukraine. While the latter is a bona fide "second" to his boss, the second secretary in a Muslim area is entrusted with much greater powers. He not only assists his nominal boss but acts as a watchdog over the latter's willingness to respect Moscow's overlordship. Generally speaking, the Russian second secretary is supposed to steer the Muslim first secretary away from nationalist, religious, or simply local influences, but do so diplomatically. Furthermore, the more experienced and often better educated second secretary is supposed to assist the usually less qualified first secretary in managing his affairs. This was especially true in the old days, when qualified Muslim cadres were in very short supply. It is still the case when the first secretary has little on-the-job experience. On the other hand, a very influential native first secretary,

Table 22   **The Colonial Nomenklatura**
Uzbekistan and Georgia, 1980

Position	Name of position-holder, Russian[1] or *native*		
	Uzbekistan, 1946	Uzbekistan, 1980	Georgia, 1980
Second republic party secretary	Lomakin, N. A.	Grekov, L. I.	Kolbin, G. V.
Head, department of party organs	Kotov, T. G.	Okunskii, V. V.	*Khabashvili, Z. V.*
Head, department of administrative organs	—	Arkhangel'skii, G. V.	*Sadzhaia, V. R.*
Capital city second party secretary	Lukovani, M. G. [first secretary, Georgian]	Dudin, K. P.	*Gurgenidze, N. V.*
Regional second secretaries in Uzbekistan:			
Andizhan	Shubladze, K. K. [first secretary, Georgian]	Shendrik, L. P.	
Bukhara	*Mangutov*	Shriabin, Iu. S.	
Dzhizak	—[2]	Klemenov, E. A.	
Fergana	Bel'skii, B. I.[3]	Esin, V. P.	
Kara-Kalpak ASSR	Egorov, G. A.[3]	Kislov, V. V.	
Kashka-Darya	Iashin, G. I.[3]	Golobachev, I. I.	
Namangan	Gabrieliants, G. A. [Armenian]	Rudenko, A. G.	
Samarkand	Inzhelevskii, G.	Kuksenko, I. K. [Ukrainian]	
Surkhan Darya	Nikitin, S. A.	Mikhailov, V. K.	
Syr Darya	—[2]	Khaidurov, V. A. [first secretary]	
Tashkent	Zaiko, G. I.	Antonov, V. A.	
in Georgia:			
Abkhaz ASSR			*Alavidze, V. B.*
Adzhar ASSR			*Ungiadze, Iu. V.*
South Ossetian ASSR			*Odishvili, N.A.*[4]
First deputy prime minister	Glukhov, R. M.	Osetrov, T. N.	*Chitanava, R. M.*
Head, committee security	Baskakov, M. I.	Melkunov, L. N. [Armenian]	*Inauri, A. N.*

Source: Radio Liberty Research for 1980; for 1946, M. Rywkin, "The Soviet Nationalities Policy and the Communist Party Structure in Uzbekistan. A Study of the Methods of Soviet Russian Control, 1941-1946," Unpublished Ph.D. dissertation, Columbia University, 1960.

[1] In Uzbekistan, all the nonnatives are combined with the Russians, but their nationality is indicated in brackets.

[2] Not a separate region at that time.

[3] In 1944 or 1945. No data for 1946.

[4] A Georgian, not an Ossetian.

especially a Politburo member or alternate (Aliev in Azerbaidzhan, Rashidov in Uzbekistan, or Kunaev in Kazakhstan), is in a much stronger position vis-à-vis his Russian second.

At the same time, however, the Russian second secretary in a Muslim republic, region, or district increasingly identifies himself with his non-Russian colleagues and their local interests. Not only does their growing importance enhance his own, but Moscow would tend to fire a second secretary unable to establish good working relations with his peers.

It is worth noting that the method of dual leadership has a long tradition in Russia. Not only was it standard during the Civil War years, with the commander-commissar teams, but it existed in pre-Petrine Russia as well: then the system of two *voevodas* (governors), each watching the other, was widely used.[2]

2. The *head of the department of organizational party work (partiinykh organov)*. This department has a wide range of activity and is entrusted with checking compliance with party directives and selecting party cadres for lower party organs. An inner party department, hidden from the public eye but very much in view among the apparatchiki, this department has most often been headed by a Russian. It is significant that its officers are given the higher rank of "inspector" rather than "instructor," as is the case with lesser departments.

At the republic level, by early 1980 Russians headed the departments of organizational party work in most of the Central Asian republics, except for Turkmenistan, where the department was run by a man with a German-sounding name (possibly a Russian of remote German ancestry). In Kazakhstan a Kazakh was in charge. Outside of Central Asia, by comparison, Russians were in charge in Estonia, Latvia, and Moldavia; in all three Transcaucasian republics and in Lithuania, natives were entrusted with the job.

3. The *department of administrative organs*; a counterpart to organizational party work, but with more narrow functions, mostly limited to supervision of and appointments to the KGB, the militia (police), the justice apparatus, and possibly, the system of soviets. This department has often been in Russian hands (in early 1980 this was true of Uzbekistan, Kirghizia, Latvia, and Estonia while natives were in charge in the three Transcaucasian republics and in Lithuania, Tadzhikistan, and Turkmenistan).

4. Another control position is that of the *head of the special (security) section*, a connecting link to the state security ap-

paratus. All references to the section seem to have vanished from the press, but recent émigrés from the Soviet Union confirm its continued existence as a KGB liaison in charge of keeping protocols of party meetings at all levels. In Muslim areas the section is said to have always been in Russian hands.

Taken together, the positions of second secretary, heads of departments of organizational party work and of administrative organs, and heads of the special (or secret) section constitute a team capable of controlling the work of the Muslim majority within a given party committee, even if no other Russian department head is present, which is rarely the case.

5. The numerous economic departments of the republic central committees, each in charge of supervising corresponding branches of economic activity as well as the ministers responsible for them, present a mixed picture. They are divided into three groups: heavy industry and energy, light and consumer goods, and agriculture. Most of the heads of these departments have traditionally been Muslim. Nevertheless a Russian department head may be appointed if a particular line of economic activity in a given area is of outstanding importance to the all-Union economy or simply in need of closer attention at a given time, therefore warranting Russian guidance and supervision.

In Uzbekistan in 1979, out of eight economic departments in existence, Russians were in charge of three: trade and services (*bytovoe obsluzhivanie*), a field marked by corruption and nepotism and considered better managed when in Russian hands, and agriculture and irrigation, key economic fields in Uzbekistan, where Russian supervision over Uzbek ministers is felt highly desirable. By comparison, in Georgia all seven economic branch departments, except the combined department of transportation and communication, were in Georgian hands, a sign of confidence in the efficiency of the Georgian party apparatus in a republic considered more nationalistic and corruption-prone than Uzbekistan.

In addition, Muslim secretaries and department heads have usually been provided with Russian or other European assistants, so as not to leave any department without Russian watchdogs at decision-making levels. Again, a case can be made for their presence on the grounds of experience and expertise, but the practice has been too widespread and enduring not to look like a conscious effort to shadow native party functionaries with ethnically reliable personnel. The same method applies to governmental jobs as well, reinforcing the same impression.

According to a survey conducted by Grey Hodnett concerning the percentage of native occupancy of leading party positions by republics (1955—72), Central Asian republics rank lower than all others, except for Moldavia. Kazakhstan, with its large nonnative population, was worse off than its Muslim sister republics (a situation which seems to have changed later in the 1970s), while Azerbaidzhan occupies a position comparable to its Transcaucasian neighbors. In ministerial positions we find the same picture, except for Belorussia, which ranks lower than expected.[3]

3. *The Union Republic Ministries*

The Soviet Consitution distinguishes three kinds of ministries: (a) the all-Union ministries which function in Moscow and have no counterparts in Tashkent, Kiev, etc.; (b) the mixed union republic ministries, which exist both in Moscow and in the republic capitals; and (c) the republic ministries, which function exclusively in the union republics and not in Moscow and are, therefore, capable of exercising some degree of autonomy in the fields of their endeavor.

In accordance with the 1924 Constitution, agriculture, internal affairs, justice, education, health, and social security belonged to the republic group. The 1936 Constitution shifted justice, agriculture, and health into the mixed union republic category, leaving only education and social security in the, so to speak, exclusive hands of individual republics. In the early 1960s the union republics were granted more autonomy: internal affairs and seven economic ministries were shifted to the republic levels. In 1965 eight more ministries were classified as republican: public order (a new name for internal affairs), education, social security, and five economic units. Also, the freedom of action of state planning commissions of the union republics was enlarged. But simultaneously, seventeen new mixed ministries were created, raising their total to twenty-five, and eleven all-Union ministries were added, for a total of twenty-two.

These post-Khrushchev changes increased local autonomy in some fields while decreasing it in others. The constant shuffling of ministries from one category to another, the increasing and decreasing of the number of ministries, the renaming of old ones and the creation of new ones were rather confusing, but one can still distinguish some long-term trends. Thus the 1936

Table 23   **Exclusive Competence of Republic Ministries**

Field of competence	1924 Constitution	1936 Constitution	1965 Reforms	1977 Constitution
Agriculture	+	−	−	−
Internal affairs	+	−	+[2]	−
Justice	+	−	−[3]	−
Education	+	+	−	−
Health	+	−	−	−
Social security	+	+	+	+
Local economy (roads, auto transport, industry, services, housing)	(+)[1]	+	+	+

[1]Not specifically mentioned.
[2]Called "Public Order."
[3]Included in the early 1960s.

Constitution was an administrative setback for the union republics in comparison with the 1924 situation, while Khrushchev's era rectified, to some extent, the situation in favor of the union republics. Immediately post-Khrushchev changes appeared to move in the same direction. A number of public-relations-type concessions were made to appease native sensitivity. The renewal by the Supreme Soviet of the practice of publishing its acts in the languages of the union republics (abolished in 1960) could serve as an example of such a concession.[4] All these timid attempts at returning to "Leninist traditions," combined with generally unsettled ideas in the administrative field, as far as the union republics are concerned were characteristic of the administrative policies in that domain in the mid-1960s.

In the 1970s the pendulum swung back again. There was a growing tendency to increase the number of mixed ministries that function both in Moscow and at the union republic's level, while reducing the number of purely republic ministries that function without Moscow counterparts.[5] This has been partially compensated by a reduction in the number of all-Union ministries as well. But the administrative tendency toward centralization, so well known to Americans from the federal versus state power conflicts, is now taking place in the USSR. It obviously increases the importance of Moscow-based Russian bureaucrats at the expense of their mostly non-Russian republic homologues. Hélène Carrère d'Encausse has even suggested that the old method of controlling "unreliable" republics through keeping Russians in key control positions is giving way to control through centralized policy-making (i.e., "centralization" replaces "Russification").[6] It appears, however, that while governmental positions may be so affected, key party positions remain as firmly in Russian hands as they were under Stalin (see Table 23).

Within the government Russians are generally present in vice-ministerial positions, leaving the limelight to the natives. Still, some ministerial seats remain in Russian hands——more in the "unreliable" republics, fewer in the others. In Uzbekistan in 1979 Russians held the ministerial positions in auto transportation, services, communal economy, and industrial construction. They also headed state construction and state security. By contrast, in Georgia they were in charge only of services. Even the key state security position was entrusted to a Georgian, with only one of his aides being a Russian.

4. *The Centralized Judiciary*

In the judicial field the laws of the RSFSR often apply outside its borders, something unthinkable in the United States, where state laws never apply outside state borders. Until February 1957 the Criminal Code of the RSFSR covered not only Russia but Kazakhstan, Kirghizia, Latvia, Lithuania, and Estonia. Its Civil Code applied to the same union republics plus Turkmenistan and Tadzhikistan.[7]

Soviet journals specializing in public administration (such as *Soviet Government and Law [Sovetskoe gosudarstvo i pravo]*) tend to discuss unionwide and RSFSR laws interchangeably. Except for the lowest courts in non-Russian areas, the Russian language is also commonly used in Soviet court proceedings held outside the RSFSR. Local differences exist mostly in interpreting and applying the law. For instance, better opportunities exist for private legal or illegal economic initiative in Tbilisi (Georgian SSR) than in Tula or Riazan (RSFSR) because of regional differences in application and enforcement. Otherwise, the almost identical legal codes of individual national republics allow very limited variation in the uniform judicial system.

5. *Two Aborted Developments*

The short-lived Central Asian Bureau

The policy of economic decentralization inaugurated by Nikita Khrushchev and the resulting creation of regional economic units under local *sovnarkhozes* (councils of national economy) was applied in Central Asia as well. The result, in this particular instance, was the rebirth (by the end of 1962) of an institution that had ceased to exist in that area by the mid-1920s, namely, the Central Asian Bureau of the Central Committee of the CPSU. The bureau was given the task of political-economic coordinator of the four Central Asian republics, Kazakhstan excluded. Curiously enough, the Chimkent Region of Kazakhstan, formerly a part of the tsarist era Turkestan Krai, was also subordinated to the bureau.

Thus, for the first time in many years, the unity of Turkestan within its historical borders was unequivocally acknowledged. This had heretofore been considered politically undesirable, given the established policy of stressing the distinctive qualities of the Central Asian republics rather than their common historical, racial, religious, or linguistic backgrounds, a policy implemented in order to forestall all possible nationalistic phenomena of pan-Turkic or pan-Islamic nature. The Soviet military, however, did not find it necessary to engage in such subtleties and conveniently retained the old territorial boundaries of the Turkestan Military District, under Russian command, as usual.

The new Central Asian (one is tempted to say Pan-Turkestani) Bureau consisted of eleven members (a good number, traditionally used in Moscow's old Politburo), namely: a chairman and his deputy (both Russians); four first party secretaries of the four union republics; the Chimkent Obkom Party Secretary; the four Russian heads of specialized regional economic administrations, i.e., of the Council of National Economy (*Sovnarkhoz*), Construction Administration (*Gosstroi*), Directorate for Cotton Growing, and Directorate for Irrigation and Sovkhoz Construction.

Little was known about the extent of the bureau's powers and activities. However, one can presume that the very existence of such a suprarepublic agency restricted the power and the authority of the central committees of the union republics of Central Asia, if only by providing an intermediary power structure between Moscow and them. On the other hand, the existence of the bureau could not fail to underline the reality of traditional ties between the republics under its jurisdiction, regardless of the fact that native Muslim officials were in the minority in the bureau.

At any rate, the bureau did not outlive Khrushchev's fall. It apparently died without much notice, sometime between March and May 1965. Practically the only mention of this event was newspaper references to the transfer of V. G. Lomonosov, the former bureau first secretary, to the position of second secretary of the Central Committee of the Communist Party of Uzbekistan. Simultaneously, the former bureau's second secretary, S. M. Veselov, was recalled to Moscow and given a high party position there.[8] The reasons for the dissolution of the bureau are not too clear. Perhaps it was an attempt to eliminate an intermediary between Moscow and Tashkent or Dushanbe? Or a feeling in Moscow that the bureau's existence overemphasized the ties between the republics of Central Asia? Or an undoing of one more of Nikita Khrushchev's innovations? Curiously enough, a 1965 article in Tashkent's *Pravda Vostoka* commemorating the forty-fifth anniversary of the creation of the Turkestani Bureau did not even provide a clue as to the reasons for the dissolution of its heir.[9]

To downgrade the Kazakh Republic?

Another set of interesting developments connected with the so-called virgin lands program, also a pet idea of Nikita Khrushchev's economic and administrative reforms, was the creation of the Virgin Lands Territory as a specific administrative unit within the Kazakh SSR and changing the name of its capital from the Kazakh "Akmolinsk" to the Russian "Tselinograd." The territory included five regions,[10] contained almost one third of the population of Kazakhstan, and produced approximately two thirds of all the grain crops of the republic. It is heavily populated with Russians and other Slavs, and at one point rumors were circulated of the possible transfer of the area to the RSFSR.

Cold political reality, and not constitutional phraseology about the inviolability of the territory of the union republics, prevented this from happening. But the habitual pattern of having natives as first secretaries and Russians as second secretaries in the party setup was reversed there. In the Virgin Lands Territory Russians or Ukrainians were appointed first obkom secretaries, while Kazakhs were relegated to the position of second secretaries, a conspicuous sign of the disappearance of the usual ostentatiousness of native sovereignty. The same situation existed in the middle bureaucratic strata: a 1965 article describing a conference of agricultural managers from the territory failed to mention a single *Muslim* participant among the ten listed.[11] The *kraikom* secretary was himself a Russian, and in some oblasts of the territory, both party secretaries and the *oblispolkom* (regional executive committee) head were Russians (as in Tselinograd Region).

In October 1965 the Virgin Lands Territory was abolished, and its component regions returned to direct republic subordination, a shift to the pre-Khrushchev status.[12] However, even in the other regions of Kazakhstan outside the Virgin Lands Territory, Russian first secretaries were in power by 1965 in half of the regional party committees. As a result of this situation and contrary to the traditional practice maintained elsewhere in Central Asia, only one third of the regional party first secretaries in Kazakhstan were native Muslims.[13] Taking into account the meticulously bureaucratic manner of Soviet party and governmental administrative practices, one cannot doubt that Moscow at that time no longer considered Kazakhstan to be a "national" union republic in the full (however restricted) sense of the word.

Moscow's new leadership, however, clearly understood that given the present international situation, Kazakhstan cannot possibly be downgraded the way the Karelo-Finnish Republic was, even by continuous administrative semidetachment of a large chunk of its territory, as was the case during the existence of the Virgin Lands Territory. After all, one should remember that both the creation and the downgrading of the Karelo-Finnish SSR were due to foreign relations considerations, first the 1940 hope of absorbing all of Finland during the Soviet-Finnish War, and then the post-Stalin desire to show Helsinki that this is no longer a Soviet intention. Finally, the vigorous demographic recovery registered by the Kazakhs in the 1960s and 1970s removed all danger of "voluntary" downgrading of their republic. The ethnic imbalance among regional first party secretaries has been reduced. Thus by 1974 half of them were Muslims, instead of one third. Nevertheless Akmolinsk remains Tselinograd, as a reminder of that aborted attempt.

6. *The National Military*

The Soviet army's traditions are totally Russian, despite the growing proportion of non-Russian draftees from a population whose younger generations are becoming increasingly non-Russian. The military command, training, codes, and all other aspects of military life are drawn from Russian prerevolutionary tradition, with no allowance for the military past of other component ethnic groups of the USSR. (The decree of March 7, 1938, ended the "national units.") The language of command is Russian; military schools and academies operate in Russian. Ranks and uniforms are patterned after the old tsarist Russian army. This return to tsarist tradition was made during World War II, when most of the international "Soviet" characteristics of military life and behavior were dropped and replaced by pre-1917 Russian ones. Soviet elite regiments followed the same tradition: Guards, Cossacks, and even "national units," revived during World War II. But Lithuanian, Estonian, Georgian, Armenian, Azeri, and Kazakh formations, temporarily created in the image of the famous Latvian revolutionary sharpshooters, were again dissolved at the end of the war.[14]

The appearance of so-called "military commissars" of the Central Asian republics was a modest and partial fulfillment of a long-delayed postwar promise to create military forces for individual union republics (law of February 1944). This idea came to light during the creation of positions of "foreign ministers" of the union republics (done in the unfulfilled hope of getting all fifteen of them into the United Nations with voting rights). The exact duties of the so-called "foreign ministers" have never been too explicit, and those of the newly appointed "military commissars" have also not been clarified.

What jobs were they to do? Were there any troops under their command? What was their relationship (in the case of the Central Asian republics) with the Russian generals in command of their military district, one of whom was at the same time a member of the Central Committee of the Communist Party of Uzbekistan? All this was extremely unclear. We know only that the new "military commissars" of the union republics (not to be confused with the "people's commissars" of the past nor with the *Voen-koms* in charge of local draft boards) were natives like their comrades the "ministers of foreign affairs," that they attended some ceremonial gatherings, and that no specific military rank seems to have been attached to their function.[15]

By the 1980s the "military commissars" seem to have vanished,[16] while the high commands of the two military districts covering Central Asia and Kazakhstan appear as segregated as always. Thus, as of the beginning of 1980, the commander and all but one of the five deputies in the Central Asian Military District are Russians. Of thirty-two known staff members, only two are Muslims. In the Turkestan Military District the situation is even more extreme: no Muslims among the thirty-three staff members![17]

Muslims aside, among the higher army personnel non-Russians are generally not represented in proportion to their population. The figures of Jewish, Latvian, or Georgian revolutionary commanders and commissars such as Yona Yakir and Sergo Ordzhonikidze are memories of the past, as are those of Stalin and Leon Trotsky themselves.

7. *The Nature of Soviet Federalism*

The Soviet federal system was intended to be the first authentic *multinational* federal system. It is in fact unique because the American federal system is based on local, not ethnic criteria. The Swiss cantons did not emerge as national entities, since the four national-linguistic groups in the country are represented by five times as many cantons. In addition, the bulk of the population of the national groups inhabiting Switzerland live in neighboring countries outside the borders of the Swiss federation. Yugoslavia is not a full-fledged example because it is composed of "sister" nationalities: all but the Albanians are Southern Slavs.

Furthermore, the Soviet model displays other unique features:

a. the existence of a federation (RSFSR) within a federation (USSR);

b. nationalities organized in hierarchical territorial units depending on their numerical importance, preponderance in their native area, history, and economic cohesion (union republics, autonomous republics, autonomous regions, autonomous districts in descending order of importance).[18]

This system was supposed to solve nationality problems inherited from the Russian Empire, which to some extent it has done. Where it has failed, what has gone wrong has happened not because of, but *despite* the emergence of the federal system. For instance, the Civil War and subsequent reconstruction plus rapid industrialization have demanded a degree of centralized effort detrimental to the federal features of the system. But the most damaging factor has unquestionably been the principle of party centralized unity combined with party primacy over parallel governmental agencies. Thus supposedly autonomous governmental structures in the national republics were made subordinate to Moscow-ruled centralized party organs.

The Eighth Party Congress of December 1919 had ruled on this crucial issue: It was made clear that

> the Central Committees of the Ukrainian, Latvian, Lithuanian Communists . . . are completely subordinate to the Central Committee of the all-Russian Communist Party . . . [whose decisions] are unconditionally compulsory for all parts of the Party irrespective of their national composition.[19]

The creation of a "single centralized party with a single Central Committee" has probably been the most important move responsible for tarnishing the image of the Soviet federal system. With a genuine multinational federal system operating at one level and a centralized state system at a higher one, the latter kept enlarging its powers at the expense of the former. At first the power imbalance was to some extent compensated by the presence of a large number of non-Russians in the central party organs in Moscow (all-Union level). One must note, however, that Soviet Muslims were never too important at that level, unlike Georgians or Jews. But with time, and especially since World War II, the non-Slavic elements began to vanish. By now, except for some token representation, central party organs are firmly in Slavic hands, creating an even wider gap between the multinational federal system on record and the Russian centralized party apparatus that has the final word on major issues.

CHAPTER TEN

The Terminology
of Nationality Politics

1. The Traditional Triad:
Flourishing, Rapprochement, Fusion

Ideology has from the beginning been the cornerstone of Soviet life.[1] It has penetrated all domains, shaped all structures, guided all laws, touched everything down to the private lives of the most nonpolitical citizens. But at the same time, the ideological superstructure has begun to drift away from the reality of life (and vice versa), reaching a stage where the two no longer correspond. Simultaneously, the original ideological formulas have been evolving in their own way. Thus we see ideological signifiers disconnected not only from reality but also from the images they are still trying to convey.

Nationality affairs are strongly affected by this situation. Take, for example, the officially proclaimed right of the union republics to withdraw from the Union. This right, incorporated into the 1936 and 1977 Constitutions, is an ideological formula that does not correspond to reality, since any attempt to exercise (or to advocate the exercise of) such a right would automatically be considered treasonable and punished as such. Still, the paper right maintains its importance because its formulation conveys the notion of recognition of the republics' residual sovereignty. To deny the "right" would be to vitiate that sovereignty. Thus the terminology of nationality politics is important not for its reflection of reality, which is minimal, but for the messages it conveys, which in turn do affect reality, even if they are perceived as lies.

Since the time of Joseph Stalin, the terms used to label the three basic positions in Soviet nationality politics have been: *rastsvet* (flourishing), *sblizhenie* (rapprochement), and *sliianie* (fusion).

The term "flourishing" signifies autonomous development of each Soviet socialist nationality within the community of peoples of the USSR. It stresses national and cultural separateness without rejecting political-economic integration.

The second term, "rapprochement," is a movement away from the static stage of "flourishing" and toward eventual "higher" stages, variously defined as "fusion," "unity," "fusion in historical perspective," and so forth. Rapprochement is a transition, albeit one that might take generations. The manner and pace of the process are of primary importance. Slow rapproachment might last for the entire period of transition between socialism and communism, i.e., forever.

The utopian "fusion" is a stage of nationality development projected into equally utopian communism, eternally under construction. "Fusion" is theoretically supposed to take place around the Russian nation and its language. Its initial product, the new "Soviet people, a new community of nations," supposedly has already emerged from the continued "rapprochement" of its individual component nationalities, each meanwhile "flourishing" on its own under the conditions of "developed socialism."

The "flourishing—rapprochement—fusion" terminology applied to the USSR differs somewhat from the parallel triad applied to other socialist nations. Thus in the context of bloc politics, "flourishing" means separate development, "rapprochement" signifies integrated development, and "fusion" the ultimate merger of all socialist states (but not of peoples) after communism is reached. Within the USSR, as in the Soviet bloc, the inviolability of the Moscow-centered community of peoples is taken for granted, and each component is supposed to follow the road to communism under strict guidance from the pacesetting Russian *primus inter pares*.[2]

For the component nationalities of the USSR, rapprochement is supposed to lead to centralized unity[3] (i.e., to the ultimate disappearance of the federal structure and to the emergence of a socioeconomically and culturally uniform Soviet people). For the nations of the socialist bloc, led by the USSR, rapprochement allows for discrepancies in pace and manner of progress and is supposed to lead to a unity resembling the present-day flourishing of individual republics within the USSR. Finally, there is the heretic "own road" of national-communism, based on socioeconomic patterns similar to those prevailing in the USSR but excluding dependence on the latter. Followed by

China, Albania, Yugoslavia, to a lesser extent by Romania, and in a different way by Poland, this road excludes not only merger but even centralized unity of action with the USSR.

The non-Russian nationalities within the USSR are not in a position to aspire to either bloc or "own road" choices, and their best hope is simply the slowest possible movement from the relative comfort of flourishing along the thorny road of rapprochement. Thus every Soviet work on nationality problems that stresses the continuity of rapprochement at the expense of "unity" or "fusion" defends the national separateness of the component republics of the USSR.[4]

2. *Flourishing of Terminology*

The splitting of rapprochement

In his 1972 speech marking the fiftieth anniversary of the formation of the USSR, Leonid Brezhnev introduced new terms defining Soviet policy goals in the field of nationality affairs: *vsestoronnee sblizhenie* (all-around rapprochement) and *splochenie* (unity, cohesion). These new terms define the optimum stages of rapprochement on the road to *edinstvo* (unity).[5] His deliberate choice of high-level code words was an obvious reaction to the unsatisfactory pace of rapprochement between reluctant union republics on the one hand and Mother Russia on the other. Brezhnev's speech, coming *after* other leaders had already stated their views, showed the gap between his thinking and that of the union republic secretaries. Impatient with their reluctance, he warned against any kind of attempts to "slow down" (*sderzhivat'*) the process of rapprochement.

Brezhnev's speech had an immediate effect on the first party secretaries of the national republics, who came forward with a new set of modifiers for the elusive "rapprochement": *tesnoe* (close), *vse bolshee* (ever increasing); some new terms, including the complex pair *sblizhenie cherez rastsvet* (rapprochement through flourishing) and *rastsvet cherez sblizhenie* (flourishing through rapprochement); and the compromise formula of *rastsvet i sblizhenie* (flourishing *and* rapprochement).[6]

Additional adjectives were introduced in 1977—78 to define the elusive process of rapprochement, namely, *rastushchee* (growing), *neuklonnoe* (steadfast), *progressivnoe* (progressive) and *narastaiushchii protsess sblizhenia* (ever increasing process of rapprochement).

The unusual proliferation of rapprochement terminology was due to two factors: Brezhnev's desire to move the discussion away from the autonomy-oriented "flourishing" of the individual republics, and the reluctance of the leadership of these republics to abandon this theme for the dangerous-sounding "fusion." Thus "rapprochement" became the mutually acceptable compromise, a movement forward (to give Ceasar his due), but one so modified by different adjectives and so varied as to period and nature as to be interpretable to everyone's satisfaction.

"Full unity"

The next development was the appearance of the code word *polnoe edintsvo* (full unity), which takes Brezhnev's "unity" one step further. This seemingly illogical concept (unity is supposed to be indivisible by definition) was taken from Lenin's statement about federal union as a transitional stage toward full unity[7] by Professor Lepeshkin, who attempted to provide theoretical foundations for Brezhnev's views.[8] While the self-contradictory stage of "full unity" was adjuged unattainable in the foreseeable future, the author cautioned not only against "slowing down" (*sderzhivat'*) but also against "hurrying" (*toroplivost'*) the process of rapproachement leading toward unity.[9] He also defined its four basic premises: (1) economic unity; (2) intermigration of labor; (3) enlargement of both federal *and* republic powers; and finally (4) the process of rapprochement itself as carrier of its own momentum. Lepeshkin argued that both state and federal powers can simultaneously be enlarged, mainly by extending the system of mixed ministries, and he rejected the sensible arguments made by other Soviet scholars about the need for choices between self-excluding positions.[10]

On the positive side in the Brezhnev-Lepeshkin argument has been the replacement of the highest code word "fusion" by "unity" or Lenin's "full unity,"[11] terms much more preferable as far as non-Russian nationalities are concerned. In the first place, when he used the term "unity," Lenin meant a French-style centralized system of national government after the initial political necessity for a federal system disappears; he followed the traditional Marxist tenet that social justice would resolve ethnic issues, but he hardly thought of melting-pot fusion and never of assimilation or Russification. Second, in Russian the word *sliianie* (fusion) means the total blending of liquids that

141

lose their separate identities. Unity, on the other hand, is a static state of consolidation of separate solid entities (Soviet socialist nations) into one (Soviet people), but without mutual assimilation or Russification. The nonassimilative character of "unity" makes it preferable to melting-pot "fusion" and represents a major concession to the national sensitivities of non-Russian nationalities.[12]

Meanwhile, the already vanishing code-word "fusion" has been relegated to an even more distant future by adding the qualifier "in historical perspective," i.e., at the communist stage of historical development or never. Thus at the Twenty-fifth Party Congress (February-March 1976), nobody mentioned "fusion," a sure sign of its final demise. Brezhnev's key word was "unshakable unity." On that occasion Karen Demirchian, the leader of Armenia, outdid everyone in his subservience to Mother Russia by proclaiming (seriously or ironically): "May the sacred hour be blessed when the foot of a Russian stepped on Armenian soil."[13]

"Relative independence" and "limited sovereignty"

"Ideological" articles and speeches preceding and following the publication of the new all-Union constitution (1977) and the constitutions of the union republics (1978) brought forth a whole array of new expressions defining the basic process of nationality development.

The universally accepted stage of flourishing has been enriched by a significant neologism, "relative independence" (*otnositel'naia samostoiatel'nost'*), applied equally to all-Union and union republic statehood (*gosudarstvennost'*). The initiative came from Estonia,[14] but further discussion of this term has been rather disappointing; Moscow experts in the field of government and constitutional law have chosen to ignore it altogether.[15] The leading Soviet expert in the field, A. I. Lepeshkin, has argued against all conceptions of original "limited sovereignty," claiming that "limited state sovereignty results from voluntary transfer of some republic rights to the federal government."[16] Hence "relative independence," a concept based on "the organic interconnection of one objectively existing socioeconomic and political foundation"[17] (i.e., on present-day political reality, not on voluntary action by a union republic), seems equally distasteful to Lepeshkin.

In search of new definitions

A new code word *obschchnost'* (community, common character) appeared in several sources throughout 1978 and 1979;[18] in Trapeznikov's article it appeared twenty-five times, prevailing over every other nationality code word.

While "community" has not been Brezhnev's preferred choice, it could not have emerged without highest-level consent. It aims at establishing a transitional platform on the never ending road of rapprochement leading to the ever more remote "full unity" or clearly utopian "fusion."

Another innovation is the tendency to add an ending to the radical of "unity" (*edinstvo*), namely, *enie* (*edinenie* = unification),[19] thus forging a term signifying a higher level of the rapprochement process. Thus Sharaf Rashidov's 1978 *edinenie* and *splochenie*[20] are an obvious backtracking in comparison with Brezhnev's 1976 *nerushimoe edinstvo* (unshakable unity).[21] Although it has remained in the vocabulary of nationality politics, "unity" has been projected further into the future; at present only the process of *unification* is supposedly taking place. Quite a retreat in just a year or two!

3. The National Anthems
(in Plural)

The national anthems of the union republics (either published in new forms or approved in the new 1978 constitutions of union republics) are another excellent source for studying the code words of nationality affairs.

For the sake of comparison, I have analyzed the anthems of five Soviet republics (Armenia, Georgia, Belorussia, Uzbekistan, and Latvia), which are representative of various areas (the Caucasus, a "fraternal" Slavic republic, Muslim Central Asia, and the Baltic region).

Each text contains six four-line verses; all except the Georgian have a thrice-repeated refrain (four times for Latvia) accounting for three of the six verses. We are thus dealing with songs of identical length and form. Table 24 shows the frequency with which key terms in the anthems are repeated.

The Latvian anthem, while stressing partnership with Russia, puts its own identity first, tying its future to the "Soviet

Table 24	Content Analysis of National Anthems				
		Times mentions			
		own land or people		USSR or	Lenin
Republic	Russia or Russian	by name	by inference	Soviet people	or CPSU
Armenia	1	11	4	4	5
Georgia	0	1	15	0	5
Belorussia	1	3	9	7	7
Uzbekistan	1	4	10	7	7
Latvia	1	5	6	8	2

Source: Kommunist (Erevan), April 13, 1978, p. 1; *Zaria Vostoka* (Tbilisi), April 16, 1978; *Belaruskaia Savetskaia Entsyklapedyia*, vol. 3 (Minsk: Akademiia Nauk BSSR, 1971), p. 481; *Kommunist Uzbekistana*, 1978, no. 5, p. 76; *Dzimtenes Balss* 1978, no. 13, p. 1.

peoples" (in plural) rather than to the one Soviet people.

The Belorussian anthem underlines the common past and historical partnership with Russia. Its first line: "We Belorussians with brotherly Russia" sets the tone for what follows, claiming recognition for Russian (in the prerevolutionary sense of the word, encompassing Ukrainian and Belorussian) achievements.

The Georgian anthem is proud sounding; it refers to its own rich historical past and presents Georgians as active people. The Armenian song, while equally patriotic, does mention "the hand of friendship extended by Russia," an implicit reference to Russia's "big brother" role.

The Uzbek anthem is so colonial in its content that one finds it hard to believe that such a text could have been adopted in our time and age. It starts with the line "Salam Russian brother, great is your people." (Who has ever heard an anthem begin with praise for *another* nationality?) Verbs predicating Uzbekistan (or Uzbeks) are always in the passive voice. Uzbeks are the objects of attention from their trustees (Russia, Lenin, party), always at the receiving end and never active.

It is obvious that Georgian officials fought a battle for "their text" and won. They accepted all Soviet/communist signs and symbols, but no Russian ones. The Armenians did bow to Russia, but stubbornly stressed their own identity. The Belorussians did what was really expected from them: their anthem reflects their partnership with Russia and their limited national aspirations.

The case of the Uzbeks is characteristic of Central Asian

Muslim attitudes. They obviously did not care about "their" anthem, did not even bother to argue about the text. The anthem, as well as the other ideological paraphernalia of the Soviet state, is irrelevant to Uzbek reality.

Thus for the Central Asians, as for all the non-Russian nations of the USSR, the "national in form, socialist in content" formula has been reversed into a "socialist in form, national in content" reality. And the last element has become "national-religious" for the Muslims, to whom the "socialist" part of the formula (to use Alain Besancon's expression) is simply "surrealistic." Muslim national content is reflected in a non-European way of life, Islamic values, and national-religious traditions and aspirations. The Soviet governmental structure and the party are real in their physical presence, but Soviet-Russian ideology is to be recited (or sung, as in the anthem). "Bow to the conqueror and go your own way" has been the (traditional) way to survive in Bukhara or Samarkand since time immemorial.

Thus Uzbek lack of interest in their "own" anthem is not surprising. What *is* surprising is that Moscow selected such an ode, grossly concocted (to the point of sounding almost ironic), as the national anthem of their principal Muslim dependency.

4. *Terminology Redefined*

A decade ago, in relation to Russia, Soviet republics were sometimes classified in the West as "fraternal" (Ukraine and Belorussia), "friendly" (Christian Georgia and Armenia, who chose Russia as a "lesser evil" compared with Turkish domination), and those historically "unfriendly" because of their subjugation by tsarist Russia. Despite the upsurge of Ukrainian nationalism and of consequent purges, the category of fraternal Slavic republics remains; but the difference between the other two groupings has significantly narrowed. Not only have the nationalistic elements in formerly freer Georgia and Armenia been purged, but in contrast to the situation in the Ukraine, Moscow has appointed Russian and other Slavic functionaries to some key positions in both republics, a practice traditionally reserved, albeit on a larger scale, for Muslim and Baltic areas (see Chapter 9, "The Unequal Republics," pp. 122-25).

As we have already noted, the last two years have seen the appearance of several new formulas, code words, or catchwords characterizing national relations under the conditions of "de-

Table 25   Stages of Historical and National Development

Official stage of historical development	Corresponding terminology	Corresponding official stage of national development
Building socialism	*rastsvet* (flourishing)	autonomous development of separate nationalities within the USSR
Socialism	*sblizhenie* (rapprochement)	movement toward future integration
Developed socialism	*obshchnost'* (community, common character)	development of a common culture with national peculiarities
Transition from developed socialism to communism	*edinenie* (process leading toward unity)	movement from common culture with national peculiarities toward the creation of a "Soviet people, a new historical community of nations"
Further transition	*edinstvo* (unity)	"Soviet people, a new historical community of nations"
Communism	*sliianie* (fusion, in historical perspective)	"the community of nations" becomes one nation? (in historical perspective)

veloped socialism." But what is the practical relevance of all this terminological display? Here we have a very complex situation.

1. The terminology (i.e., the redefinitions of the "flourishing—rapprochement—unity/fusion"), while pervasive, has little in common with the reality of national relations in the Soviet Union. Barthes's "African grammar" deals with French colonialist vocabulary in Africa, but it is applicable to Soviet nationalities terminology as well:

> The official vocabulary . . . is purely axiomatic. In other words it has no communication, only intimidation value. It is a language that essentially functions as a code, the words having either no relation at all or inverse relation to their content.[22]

2. The above notwithstanding, the "myths" created in abstract ideological discussions do have a bearing on reality, influencing the attitudes of the opposing parties in national confrontations. For myths become slogans, slogans influence attitudes, and attitudes beget more myths, so that the terminology of na-

tionality politics is constantly redefined——it is both abstract and real in its dialectical opposition.

For example, the "flourishing" of an individual nationality within the USSR is not always a reality; but the myth of such flourishing, promoted for opposite reasons by Moscow and by the leadership of that nationality, becomes a slogan. To Moscow it is a slogan for the success of its nationality policy; to the nationality in question, a slogan in defense of its own cultural separateness. Moscow accepts the credit for real or imaginary "flourishing" but also perceives it as a slogan that runs against the "unity" it promotes, and this regardless of the mythic qualities of both "flourishing" and "unity."

The French historian Alain Besançon thinks that the non-Russian peoples of the USSR are governed by two powers, "compulsion and magic," and that the latter is essentially of a linguistic nature. It is the "magic" (or "myth") of the "friendship of peoples," argues Besançon, that spares Moscow the necessity of costly and dangerous direct Russian occupation by replacing it with "native self-occupation" carried out by non-Russian elites over their own people.[23]

Besançon's thesis sounds very attractive but is only partially correct. The warped and often inverted relationship between words and their content and the reality of Russian domination is undeniable. But the relationship between Russians and non-Russians is not a static affair covered by a semiotic fig leaf. It is a constantly changing balance between several elements: the Russian-dominated Moscow power structure; the "great" Russian people, themselves exploited in the process; and the principal non-Russian ethnic groups, with their own power elites. The non-Russians are not only well aware of the unreality of terminology used in Soviet nationality affairs but have learned to use it to their own advantage, sometimes quite successfully.

The present stage of Soviet socioeconomic development has been labeled "developed socialism in the USSR." Through rapprochement and further unification it has supposedly achieved the state of "community" for the component nationalities of the USSR. But nationalism is on the rise, while rapprochement remains questionable; its qualifying adjectives (Barthes's "adjectives of revigoration") are in need of constant renewal to overcome rapid "signs of wear."[24] Non-Russian leaders use the myth of flourishing to oppose Moscow's myth of unity and hope the rapprochement-unification process lasts forever. But if mythical unity (*edinstvo*) is not achieved in practice, then the ruling Russian people, with their failing birthrate and jingoistic tendencies that alienate their junior partners, will find themselves dangerously outnumbered and spiritually isolated within the confines of an increasingly antagonistic multinational community driven by centrifugal nationalistic forces.

Conclusion

Central Asia's growing geopolitical importance and recent demographic explosion are the primary reasons for the mounting attention it has attracted. Without these factors the area would scarcely be noticed in the West, as was the case only a decade ago. But geopolitical and demographic factors alone do not suffice to explain the emergence of Central Asia: the non-Russian identity and the doubtful allegiance of its Muslim population provide the indispensable ingredient that projects the entire area into the forefront of Moscow's internal preoccupations. If the Muslims of Soviet Central Asia shared a kind of all-Soviet identity with and allegiance to the Russians, the demographic and geopolitical developments in the area would turn purely to Moscow's advantage.

This is, however, not the case. Discussions of "differential demographic policies" and of "qualities" versus "quantities" of future Soviet generations, consistently conducted in the Soviet press,[1] show a growing Russian fear of a twentieth-century version of a "Mongol invasion." Incessant attempts to integrate the reluctant *Homo islamicus*——whether through practical measures (cooptation of Muslim elites, integration of labor forces, modernization of economies, educational equalization, promotion of bilingualism, etc.) or by ideological maneuvers (the terminology of integration: "Soviet people," "rapprochement," "unification," "fusion in historical perspective," "multinational literature," etc.)——have not produced the desired results. Continued Russian preoccupation with these issues is the best proof of their persistence. True, Soviet Muslims are not immune to those integration measures which are economically beneficial to them (and to a much lesser degree to the alien ideological paraphernalia accompanying these measures); but the end results, from

Moscow's point of view, have been far from satisfactory.

Here one must also mention the views of some young students of Central Asian affairs (Nancy Lubin, for example), who think that because the Muslims of Central Asia adhere to different sets of values, they have not attempted to climb the same economic ladder as the Russian settlers.[2] Content to leave industrial and technical labor to the latter, they concentrate on less bureaucratic and more money-making fields, such as agriculture (with its private plot advantages), trade, services, or cottage industries, with real competition between the two ethnic groups surfacing in administration and management. And even in these fields Moscow tends to satisfy native aspirations by keeping the Russians, whenever feasible, in positions subordinate to their often less qualified native superiors. If pursued to its logical conclusion, this policy should greatly reduce the danger of ethnic battles for job openings, at least until demographic pressures, educational progress, and economic shifts exhaust the demand for labor in the sectors Muslims favor. Still, the proponents of such views cannot deny the existence of growing racial antagonisms between the two nonintegrated (whether economically competing or not) communities, which brings us back to the basic problems of ethnic identity.

Not just the survival but the "flowering" of Muslim identity (with the word "Muslim" used here as an identification, not an affirmation of religious beliefs) is a fact of life, and its symbols are clearly visible: the national-religious symbiosis, the specific way of life, local ethnic solidarity, endogamy, etc. But scholarly attempts to classify Muslim allegiances and to construct a working system for their relationships have encountered serious difficulties.

Alexandre Bennigsen's three kinds of allegiance among the Soviet Muslims were discussed earlier in this study.[3] They are the subnational (or tribal), the national (directed toward their own national republics), and the supranational (in reality Pan-Islamic) variants. But a fourth allegiance, the federal one directed toward the Soviet Union as a whole, clashes with national allegiance. And the conflict between these two Moscow-promoted loyalties is as much at the crux of the identity problem as the national versus supranational contention.

While most Western scholars believe the feeling of Islamic unity is dominant, the Orientalist Michael Zand takes a totally opposite position. Zand sees the cultures (in plural) of the peoples of Soviet Central Asia as subtypes of the Russified Soviet subculture, the latter having emerged on the ruins of the Russian version of the Christian civilization destroyed by the October Revolution. This, according to Zand, has been achieved through the cooptatation of native elites who, by joining the communist "new class," have become as alienated from the rest of their ethnic milieu as the Russian apparatchiki are.[4] This view is shared by many Russian émigré intellectuals, who, regardless of ideological differences, see Soviet nationality problems as subordinate to the conflict that pits the party elite against either the entire people (Solzhenitsyn) or the still isolated but awakened intelligentsia (Zinoviev). In either case the Russian people emerge as the principal victim among the nations of the Soviet Union. Such views are structurally close to the official Soviet image of "the Soviet people, the new community of nations," in which the Russian nation bears the heaviest burden of all. Zand grants each Soviet Muslim cultural subtype its own *couleure locale* (Stalin's "national form") but perceives its content as being more akin to Moscow (Stalin's "socialist content"?) than to Teheran or Kabul, with allegiences obviously running the same way.

Among Western scholars, Gregory Massell aside, few share the view of successful cooptation of Muslim elites, with all the ensuring consequences.[5] Hélène Carrère d'Encausse, for her part, insists on the term *Homo islamicus* and sees this type as a non-integratable element in Soviet society thanks to its almost existential opposition to the ruling Russian (or Russified) *Homo sovieticus*.[6] Her *Homo islamicus* is closer to Teheran and Kabul than to Moscow or Kiev; but she does not attempt to follow Bennigsen's classification of Muslim allegiances, since it would only split the integrity of her *Homo islamicus*.

A basically different approach is taken by the Soviet ethnogeographer Lev Gumilev, who is not concerned with Central Asia in particular, but whose views are very pertinent to the whole discussion:

An ethnos is an energy field with a particular rhythm since another ethnos would be distinguished by another rhythm.[7]

According to Gumilev, one's "ethnic rhythm" is gradually acquired during the early stages of one's life. Until exhausted, this tradition (or habit) is capable of surviving under highly disadvantageous conditions, such as loss of native tongue, of culture, of rituals, and even of native land (as was the case with the Jews). The Muslims of Soviet Central Asia, who do not face such strong obstacles, are obviously not in danger of exhausting their "ethnic rhythm" within the foreseeable historical future. Therefore they seem unlikely to fall, Zand-style, into the common pit of Soviet subculture, nor need they choose between Bennigsen's competing allegiances. The simple inner feeling that "we are such and the others are different" (as Gumilev puts it)[8] is enough to maintain their identity. Gumilev sees short-term dangers to ethnic identity only in biological factors (numerical decline, intermarriage, etc.), which certainly do not threaten the Muslims of Soviet Central Asia at this time.

Despite the range of opinions, one element is universally accepted by all scholars: the existence of a simple feeling of opposition between "we" and "they," which is expressed in various forms by Bennigsen, Carrère d'Encausse, and Gumilev, and even, in his own way ("subtype of subculture"), by Zand. It is *the* essential element, however hard it is to define it more precisely, because as long as the Muslims of Soviet Central Asia clearly perceive themselves as *the opposite of* the Russians (even if not *in opposition to* them), the notion of a "Soviet people," promoted by Moscow as an acceptable identity-substitute for the USSR's non-Russian population, remains wishful thinking. This being the case, growing Muslim numbers, which represent an irreplaceable source of future Soviet manpower supply, at the same time endanger the traditional Russian-dominated Soviet power structure.

The Basmachi cavalry is not about to descend into the valleys and cities of Central Asia to challenge the Russians; but the growing weight of geopolitical circumstances, demographic reality, and Muslim ethnic "innate drives" will increasingly do so, in a less dramatic but no less dangerous way. In order to meet this challenge, Moscow has three possible options, none of which is very satisfactory:

1. To integrate the Muslims of Central Asia into the mainstream of Soviet life through increasing political, economic, and cultural concessions, gradually abandoning the present system of Russian presence in key power positions in the area and entrusting the natives with genuine self-government, with all the ensuing consequences. The risk of such a policy is undeniable: it may lead to separatism instead of integration. Or if the latter somehow takes place, to an unwarranted (from a Russian point of view) alteration in the traditional nature of the Soviet-Russian state.

2. To strengthen the Russian hold over the national republics, using as much repression as necessary while granting minimal concessions to the natives. Such a policy cannot be successfully conducted without a Stalin-style stick (*dubina*) and would undoubtedly lead to further alienation of the growing Muslim masses.

3. To maintain the present policies of keeping Russians in ultimate control, repressing "local nationalism," and fostering acculturation, while increasing (with obvious limits) concessions to the native elites, subsidies to local economies, and tolerance of local styles of life, profiteering included. All this as a price for preserving the foundations (but not the details) of Russian rule over the area. This post-Stalin policy has been, until now, relatively successful and has provided Moscow with its most expedient alternative. But it is operative only as long as Soviet Muslims remain numerically nonthreatening, economically dependent, and educationally under par, and their area remote from international centers of upheaval and tension. Some of those conditions are no longer valid or are in the process of being altered, thus endangering the continued success of Moscow's methods of handling its Central Asian dependencies.

A perpetually delayed refusal to alter existing policies under changing objective conditions will speed the process of alienation of local elites, promote ethnic tension, and create obstacles to a rational solution to economic problems, especially the labor resources imbalance between Russia and Central Asia. Finally, it may force Moscow to face the possibility of turning toward the first two alternatives, each unsatisfactory in its own right. Whatever Moscow's ultimate choice, Soviet Central Asia is bound to become its number one internal preoccupation by the last decade of our century.

Notes

Chapter 1: Tsarist Times

[1] V. I. Massalskii, "Turkestanskii krai," *Rossiia, polnoe geograficheskoe opisanie nashego otechestva* (St. Petersburg: A. F. Davrien, 1913), vol. 13, is the most complete general source for the period.

[2] N. A. Khalfin, *Rossiia i khanstva srednei Azii* (Moscow: Nauka 1974), pp. 49-50.

[3] Ibid., p. 18.

[4] M. K. Rozhkova, *Ekonomicheskie sviazi Rossii so Srednei Aziei 40—60-e gody XIX veka* (Moscow: Akademiia nauk SSSR, 1963), p. 139.

[5] While suppressing Kazakh revolts, Russian authorities in turn encouraged the Kazakhs to capture and enslave the Bashkirs, who had fled to the steppe after the suppression of the Batyrsha revolt in Bashkiria.

[6] Hélène Carrère d'Encausse, *Réforme et révolution chez les musulmans de l'Empire Russe* (Paris: Armand Colin, 1966), pp. 31 ff., 50.

[7] Khalfin, p. 278.

[8] F. F. Martens, *Rossiia i Angliia v Srednei Azii* (St. Petersburg, 1880), p. 22.

[9] L. P. Morris, "The Subjugation of the Turkomans," *Middle Eastern Studies* (London), vol. 15, no. 2 (May 1979), p. 199.

[10] Ibid., p. 203.

[11] The Samarkand-Tashkent-Andizhan section was built in 1895—99 and the Orenburg-Tashkent railroad in 1900—1905.

[12] N. V. Arkhipov, *Sredneaziatskie respubliki* (Moscow-Leningrad: Gosizdat, 1930), pp. 86-87.

[13] G. Safarov, *Kolonial'naia revoliutsiia (Opyt Turkestana)* (Moscow: Gosizdat, 1921), p. 42.

[14] E. B. Bekmakhanov, *Prisoedinenie Kazakhstana k Rossii* (Moscow: Akademiia nauk SSSR, Institut istorii, 1957), p. 168.

[15] Geoffrey Wheeler, *The Modern History of Soviet Central Asia* (New York: Praeger, 1964), p. 89.

[16] A. A. Kaufman, *K voprosu o russkoi kolonizatsii Turkestanskogo kraia* (St. Petersburg: MZ i G. I., 1903), pp. I-VII.

[17] Safarov, p. 42.

[18] S. D. Asfendiarov, *Natsional'no-osvoboditel'noe vosstanie 1916 g. v Kazakhstane* (Alma-Ata—Moscow: Kazakhskoe Kraevoe izd., 1936), p. 184.

[19] S. Brainin, *Amangeldy Imanov* (Alma-Alta-Moscow: Kazakhskoe Kraevoe izd., 1936), pp. 50 ff.

[20] Asfendiarov, pp. 77 ff., 101-5.

[21] Alexandre Bennigsen and Chantal Lemercier-Quelquejay, *Islam in the Soviet Union* (New York: Praeger, 1967), pp. 46-47.

[22] Quoted in G. P. Gooch, *History of Modern Europe 1878-1919* (New York: Holt, n.d.) p. 24.

Chapter 2: The Revolution

[1] Safarov, pp. 50 ff.

[2] The production of cotton had already fallen rapidly. See A. Aminov, *Problemy ekonomicheskoi istorii Srednei Azii i ee zarubezhnye kritiki* (Tashkent: Uzbekistan, 1972), p. 11.

[3] Safarov, p. 78. See also *Pobeda oktiabr'skoi revoliutsii v Uzbekistane. Sbornik dokumentov*, vol. 1 (Tashkent: Akademiia nauk UzSSR, 1963), p. 578.

[4] Safarov, pp. 82-84.

[5] S. B. Ginsburg, "Basmachestvo v Fergane," *Novyi Vostok*, 1925, no. 10-11, pp. 184-5.

[6] A. I. Ishanov, *Sozdanie Bukharskoi Narodnoi Sovetskoi Respubliki* (Tashkent: Akademiia nauk UzSSR, 1955), pp. 61 ff.

[7] K. Mukhammedberdyev, *Kommunisticheskaia partia v bor'be za pobedu narodnoi revoliutsii v Khorezme* (Ashkhabad: Turkmenskoe Gosizdat, 1959), pp. 66 ff.

[8] Safarov, pp. 86-87.

[9] Mukhammedberdyev, pp. 80, 90-92.

[10] Safarov, p. 100.

[11] Mukhammedberdyev, pp. 100-49.

[12] V. I. Lenin, *O Srednei Azii i Kazakhstane*, "Zamechaniia na proekte Turkestanskoi Komissii" (Tashkent: Gosizdat UzSSR, 1960).

[13] Alexandre A. Bennigsen and S. Enders Winbush, *Muslim National Communism in the Soviet Union. A Revolutionary Strategy for the Colonial World* (Chicago: University of Chicago Press, 1979), pp. 62-63. Sultan Galiev, a Tatar communist-nationalist who disputed Stalin's theories, was arrested in 1928 and kept in the Solovki concentration camp from 1929 to 1939. He disappeared in 1940.

[14] Alexandre Bennigsen and Chantal Quelquejay, *Les mouvements nationaux chez les Musulmans de Russie; Le Sultangaleyevisme au Tatarstan* (Paris-Hague: Mouton, 1960), p. 138.

[15] See Broido's speech in *Istoriia Khorezmskoi narodnoi sovetskoi respubliki (1920-1924 gg). Sbornik dokumentov* (Tashkent: FAN, 1976), pp. 34-35.

[16] V. I. Lenin, pp. 571-72.

[17] Mukhammedberdyev, pp. 154-66, 179.

[18] Ishanov, p. 59.

[19] Seymour Becker, *Russian Protectorates in Central Asia. Bukhara and Khiva, 1865-1924* (Cambridge, Mass.: Harvard University Press, 1968), pp. 292-93.

[20] Ishanov, pp. 71-85.

[21] Ibid., p. 142.

Chapter 3: The Basmachi Revolt

[1] Safarov, p. 91.

[2] Joseph Castagné, *Les Basmachis* (Paris: Ernest Leroux, 1925), pp. 12, 14.

[3] S. B. Ginsburg. "Basmachestvo v Fergane," *Novyi Vostok*, 1925, no. 10-11, pp. 187-91. Madamin-bek was caught during the summer of 1920 by the forces of Kur-Shirmat, turned over to another Basmachi chieftan, Khal-Hodja, and executed by the latter.

[4] Ibid., pp. 192-91.

[5] T. Kh. Keldiev, *Razgrom Kontrrevoliutsii v Ferganskoi i Samarkandskoi oblastiakh Turkestanskoi ASSR (1918-23)* (Tashkent: Gosizdat UzSSR, 1959).

[6] Akademiia nauk Uzbekskoi SSR, *Istoriia sovetskogo gosudarstva i prava Uzbekistana*, vol. 1, 1917-1924 (Tashkent, 1959), p. 55.

[7] T. Ryskulov, "Sovremennyi Kazakhstan," *Novyi Vostok*, 1926, no. 12, p. 112.

[8] Mukhammedberdyev, pp. 200-24 ff., 251-56.

[9] M. Irkaev, W. Nikolaev and Ia. Sharapov, *Ocherki istorii sovetskogo Tadzhikistana (1917-1957)* (Stalinabad: Tadzhik Gosizdat, 1957), pp. 77-79.

[10] Faizullah Khodzhaev, *Izbrannye trudy* (Tashkent: Akademiia nauk Uzbekskoi SSSR, vol. 1, 1970), p. 420 (letter to M. P. Tomskii, chairman of the Turkcommission).

[11] A. Briskin, *Strana Tadzhikov* (Moscow-Leningrad: Gosizdat, 1930), pp. 37-38.

[12] A. Kh. Babakhodzhaev, *Proval aggressivnoi politiki angliiskogo imperi-*

alizma v Srednei Azii 1917-1920 g. (Tashkent: izd. Akademii nauk UzSSR, 1955), p. 142.

[13] *Vtoroi Vseuzbekskii s″ezd sovetov . . . Stenograficheskii otchet* (Tashkent: TsIK Sovetov UzSSR, 1927), p. 131.

[14] A. Listovskii, *Boevye zapiski (iz dnevnika budenovtsa)* (Moscow: Ogiz Molodaia Gvardiia, 1934), p. 7.

[15] Vasilevskii, "Fazy basmacheskogo dvizheniia v Srednei Azii," *Novyi Vostok*, vol. 29, 1930, p. 134.

[16] Sh. Z. Urazaev, *Turkestanskaia ASSR i ee gosudarstvenno-pravovye osobennosti* (Tashkent: Gosizdat UzSSR, 1958), pp. 146-47.

[17] M. N., "Pod znakom islama," *Novyi Vostok*, 1923, no. 4, p. 93.

[18] D. Soloveichik, "Revoliutsionnaia Bukhara," *Novyi Vostok*, 1922, no. 2, p. 287.

[19] Ginsburg, pp. 195-98.

[20] *Istoriia sovetskogo gosudarstva i prava Uzbekistana*, pp. 74-80.

[21] Ginsburg, p. 199.

[22] Keldiev, p. 121.

[23] Ginsburg, p. 200.

[24] Anatolii Maier, ed., *Boevye epizody Basmachestva v Fergane i Khorezme* (Moscow-Tashkent: Gosizdat, 1934), pp. 65, 73.

[25] A. Briskin, pp. 44-46.

[26] *Pervyi Vseuzbekskii s″ezd sovetov . . . Stenograficheskii otchet* (Tashkent: TsIK UzSSR, February 1925), p. 27.

[27] *Vtoroi s″ezd*, pp. 21, 51, 53.

[28] *Pervyi s″ezd*, pp. 106-7.

[29] *Vtoroi s″ezd*, p. 86.

[30] Briskin, p. 60.

[31] Riszard Wraga, *Sowieckie republiki środkowo-azjatyckie* (Rome: Biblioteka Orla Białego), 1945, p. 92.

[32] T. R. Ryskulov, *Kirgizstan* (Moscow: Ogiz, Sotsegiz, 1935), p. 67.

[33] Iu. A. Poliakov and A. I. Chugunov, *Konets Basmachestva* (Moscow: Nauka, 1976), p. 166.

Chapter 4: The Economic Scene

[1] *Istoriia sovetskogo gosudarstva i prava Uzbekistana*, p. 23.

[2] S. Dimanshtein, "Desiat let natsional'noi politiki partii i sovvlasti," *Novyi Vostok*, 1927, no. 19, p. XVIII.

[3] John D. Littlepage, *In Search of Soviet Gold* (New York: Harcourt, Brace and Co., 1938). pp. 108-9.

[4] *Kazakhstan*, Introduction by Nurpeisov (Moscow: Sotsegiz, 1936), p. 150.

[5] Michael Rywkin, *Russia in Central Asia* (New York-London: Collier-Macmillan, 1963), pp. 64-65.

[6] T. R. Rakhimbaev, *Tadzhikistan* (Moscow: Sotsegiz, 1936), p. 50; Ryskulov, p. 89; M. Belocki, *Kirgizskaia Respublika* (Moscow: Sostegiz, 1936), p. 37.

[7] USSR People's Commissariat of Justice, *Anti-Soviet Bloc of Rightists and Trotskyites (Report of Court Proceedings)*, verbatim report (Moscow, 1938), pp. 223-24. See also Khodzhaev, vol. *3*, pp. 264-65.

[8] K. Bedrintsev, "Sotsial'no-ekonomicheskie problemy razvitiia proizvoditel'nykh sil Uzbekistana," *Kommunist Uzbekistana*, 1978, no. 12, p. 16.

[9] Nestor Korol, "The So-Called Virgin Lands of Kazakhstan," *Marquette University Slavic Institute Papers*, 1962, no. 14, pp. 10, 17.

[10] Bedrintsev, p. 13.

[11] According to *The Soviet Economy in Regional Perspectives*, edited by N. Bandera and Z. L. Melnyk (New York: Praeger, 1973), pp. 99 and 272 ff.

[12] S. N. Dosymbaev, "Uchastie soiuznoi respubliki v upravlenii promyshlennosti soiuznogo podchineniia," *Sovetskoe gosudarstvo i pravo*, 1971, no. 2, p. 64.

[13] S. M. Mirkhasimov, "Sotsial'no-kul'turnye izmeneniia i otrazhenie ikh v sovremennoi sem'e sel'skogo naseleniia Uzbekistana," *Sovetskaia etnografiia*, 1979, no. 1, pp. 7-8.

[14] E. Manevich, "Vosproizvodstvo naseleniia i ispol'zovanie trudovykh resursov," *Voprosy ekonomiki*, 1978, no. 8, p. 42: V. K. Kostakov and E. L. Manevich, *Regional'nye problemy naseleniia i trudovye resursy SSSR* (Moscow: Statistika, 1978), p. 98.

[15] *Narodnoe khoziaistvo Uzbekskoi SSR v 1978 g. Statisticheskii ezhegodnik* (Tashkent, Uzbekistan, 1979), p. 307.

[16] L. P. Kuprienko, *Vliianie urovnia zhizni na raspredelenie trudovykh resursov* (Moscow: Nauka, 1976), pp. 61, 97.

[17] K. Saidov, "Ekonomicheskaia rol' lichnogo podsobnogo khoziaistva v Uzbekistane na sovremennom etape," *Kommunist Uzbekistana*, 1979, no. 5, p. 28, and *Narodnoe khoziaistvo Uzbekskoi SSR, 1978 g.*, p. 78.

[18] U. Matruziev, "O razvitii kolkhoznogo proizvodstva v Uzbekistane na sovremennom etape," *Obshchestvennye nauki v Uzbekistane*, 1979, no. 2, p. 9; Saidov, p. 30.

[19] *Narodnoe khoziaistvo SSSR v 1978 g. Statisticheskii ezhegodnik* (Moscow: Statistika, 1979), p. 392, and Kuprienko, pp. 97, 61.

[20] *Narodnoe khoziaistvo Uzbekskoi SSR v 1974 g. Statisticheskii ezhegodnik* (Tashkent: Uzbekistan, 1975), p. 300. The 1978 annual (published in

1979) fails to provide this information by eliminating the corresponding table.

[21] L. P. Kuprienko, p. 90.

[22] For a more positive attitude toward private plots, see L. I. Brezhnev, speech at the October 1976 Plenum of the Central Committee of the CPSU. For Uzbekistan, see Sh. Rashidov's speech at the Tenth Plenum of the Central Committee of the Communist Party of Uzbekistan, July 1978. Also V. Voronin, "Lichnye podsobnye khoziaistva i torgovlia," *Voprosy ekonomiki*, 1980, no. 6.

[23] Radio Liberty dispatch of February 8, 1977, quoting *Ekonomicheskaia gazeta*, February 1977, p. 16.

[24] See K. Bedrintsev, p. 17, about the special importance of private plots in Uzbekistan.

[25] Martin C. Spechler, "Regional Development in the USSR, 1958-78," *Soviet Economy in a Time of Change. A Compendium of Papers Submitted to the Joint Economic Committee of the Congress of the United States*, vol. 1 (Washington D.C.: U.S. Government Printing Office, 1979), p. 145.

Chapter 5: Population and Manpower

[1] S. I. Bruk and V. M. Kabuzan, "Etnicheskii sostav naseleniia Rossii (1719—1917 gg.)," *Sovetskaia etnografiia*, 1980, no. 6, p. 26.

[2] S. S. Balzak, V. F. Vasiutin, and Ia. G. Feigin, *Ekonomicheskaia geografiia SSSR* (Moscow: Akademiia nauk SSSR, Institut ekonomiki, 1940), vol. 1, p. 152.

[3] A. Bennigsen, "The USSR and the Colonial Revolution," in *The Middle East in Transition. Studies in Contemporary History*, Walter Z. Laqueur, ed. (New York: Praeger, 1958), p. 410.

[4] Poles were arrested in the areas annexed by the USSR in 1939—40 and deported to Siberia as "socially dangerous elements." They were released after the German invasion of the USSR.

[5] *Samarkand. Kratkii spravochnik-putevoditel'*, compiled by I. I. Umniakov et al. (Tashkent: Gosizdat Uzbekskoi SSR, 1956), p. 66.

[6] S. I. Bruk, "Etnodemograficheskie protsessy v SSSR (po materialam perepisi 1970 goda)," *Sovetskaia etnografiia*, 1971, no. 4, p. 28.

[7] Ibid., pp. 14-15.

[8] Iu. V. Bromlei, ed., *Sovremennye etnicheskie protsessy v SSSR* (Moscow: Nauka, 1975), pp. 484-85; "Vsesoiuznaia perepis' naseleniia," *Vestnik statistiki*, 1980, no. 2, pp. 24-25; S. I. Bruk, "Etnodemograficheskie protsessy v SSSR po materialam poslevoennykh perepisei naseleniia," *Istoriia SSSR*, 1980, no. 5, pp. 42-43.

[9] Rein Taagepera, "National Differences Within Soviet Demographic Trends," *Soviet Studies* (Glasgow), 1969, no. 4, p. 486.

[10] Bruk, "Etnodemograficheskie protsessy v SSSR (po materialam perepisi 1970 goda)," p. 16.

[11] A. Kvasha and G. Kiseleva, "Tendenstii vosproizvodstva naseleniia SSSR," *Vozobnovlenie naseleniia nashei strany* (Moscow: Statistika, 1978), p. 7.

[12] Some Soviet authors predict a future decline in the Muslim birthrate. See, for example, D. Grazhdannikov, *Prognosticheskie modeli sotsial'no-demograficheskikh protsessov* (Novosibirsk: Nauka, 1974), pp. 100-101.

[13] "Vsesoiuznaia perepis'" (1980), pp. 24-25.

[14] V. I. Perevedentsev, "Sotsial'no-demograficheskaia situatsiia i vstuplenie molodezhi v trudovuiu zhizn'," *Rabochii klass i sovremennyi mir*, 1980, no. 3, pp. 85, 88-89.

[15] Murray Feshbach and Stephen Rapawy, "Soviet Population and Man-power Trends and Politics," in U.S. Congress, Joint Economic Committee, *Soviet Economy in a New Perspective* (Washington D.C.: U.S. Government Printing Office, 1976), p. 148.

[16] "Vsesoiuznaia perepis'" (1980), pp. 27 ff. For a discussion of the reluctance of Central Asians to migrate, see E. Chernova, "Zavtrashnii den' trudovykh resursov," *Sovetskaia Kirgiziia* (Frunze), June 29, 1977, and N. Khonaliev, "Migratsiia naseleniia," *Kommunist Tadzhikistana* (Dushanbe), March 17, 1977.

[17] John F. Besemeres, *Socialist Population Politics. The Politics of Demographic Trends in the USSR and Eastern Europe* (White Plains: M. E. Sharpe, 1980), p. 48, speaks of the so-called Leningrad-Kaluga experiment of strong-arm manpower control.

[18] Ibid., pp. 74-75.

[19] See V. Perevedentsev, "Migratsiia naseleniia i ispol'zovanie trudovykh resursov," *Voprosy ekonomiki*, 1970, no. 9. He had already discussed some of these themes in "Spor o perepisi," *Literaturnaia gazeta*, January 1, 1967. There is a list of three books and fourteen articles by Perevedentsev in V. I. Staroverov, *Sotsialisticheskie problemy derevni. Metodologiia, metodika, opyt analiza migratsii sel'skogo naseleniia* (Moscow: Nauka, 1975), pp. 263 ff.

[20] See R. A. Lewis, R. H. Rowland, and R. S. Clem, *Nationality and Population Change in Russia and the USSR: An Evaluation of Census Data, 1897-1970* (New York and London: Praeger, 1976), especially pp. 350-87.

[21] Between 1970 and 1975 the irrigated acreage in Soviet Central Asia and Kazakhstan increased by 12 percent, and between 1975 and 1978, by almost 9 percent, a much higher rate than in the 1960s. See *Narodnoe khoziaistvo SSSR v 1978 g.*, p. 240.

[22] Lewis, Rowland, and Clem, pp. 367-71.

[23] Ibid., p. 358.

[24] Ibid., p. 361.

[25] Murray Feshbach, "Prospects for Massive Outmigration from Central Asia During the Next Decade," paper for the U.S. Department of Commerce, Bureau of Economic Analysis, February 1977, p. 23.

[26] For confirmation of this finding in the case of Uzbekistan, see R. A. Ubaidullaeva, "Trudovye resursy v regional'noi ekonomike razvitogo sotsializma," *Obshchestvennye nauki v Uzbekistane* (Tashkent), 1978, no. 2, p. 8.

[27] Feshbach refers to V. G. Kostiakov, *Trudovye resursy piatiletki* (Moscow: Politizdat, 1976), p. 56, and *Planovoe khoziaistvo*, 1976, no. 11, pp. 19-22. At the same time, it should be noted that natural gas and cotton— Central Asia's most important resources—are still exported to the RSFSR in raw form for processing. See K. Bedrintsev, "Sotsial'no-ekonomicheskie problemy razvitiia proizvoditel'nykh sil Uzbekistana," *Kommunist Uzbekistana*, 1978, no. 12, p. 16, who estimates that Uzbekistan processes only 4 or 5 percent of the cotton it produces.

[28] This point is confirmed in the case of Uzbekistan by L. Sbytova, "Istochniki rabochei sily v sovremennykh usloviiakh," *Voprosy ekonomiki*, 1978, no. 6, pp. 36-37, 40.

[29] L. P. Kuprienko, *Vliianie urovnia zhizni na raspredelenie trudovykh resursov* (Moscow: Nauka, 1976), pp. 89-92.

[30] A. V. Topilin, *Territorial'noe pereraspredelenie trudovykh resursov v SSSR* (Moscow: Ekonomika, 1975), pp. 13 ff. and 122 ff. [Abridged English edition: "The Territorial Redistribution of Labor Resources in the USSR," *Problems of Economics* (White Plains: M. E. Sharpe), May 1980, vol. 23, no. 1.] Topilin contrasts present-day organized migration to that of the 1930s, when it accounted for 30-40 percent of the total. Organized migration includes *orgnabor* (organized recruitment, mostly of young singles with a profession) for jobs in not-too-distant areas; *pereselenie* (organized resettlement of entire families, mostly in agriculture); and *obshchestvennye prizivy* (public call-ups affecting technical graduates or demobilized draftees).

[31] According to Topilin, in the years 1959-70 approximately 113 persons entered Central Asia for every 100 who left. For the RSFSR as a whole, the imbalance was 124 to 100, and for Western Siberia, 159 to 100. Topilin, pp. 44-45, 56, 92.

[32] For example, he reports that the Central Asian republics of the USSR had the highest percentage of nonworking able-bodied people of working age: 16-20 percent, as against 7-10 percent for the RSFSR. Topilin, p. 45.

[33] Ibid., pp. 62-63.

[34] Ibid., pp, 120-29, 153.

[35] G. I. Litvinova, "Vozdeistvie gosudarstva i prava na demograficheskie protsessy," *Sovetskoe gosudarstvo i pravo*, 1978, no. 1, pp. 134-35.

[36] As reported by R. Galetskaia, "Demograficheskaia politika i ee napravleniia," *Voprosy ekonomiki*, 1975, no. 8, pp. 149-52.

[37] L. E. Darskii, "Sotsial'no-demograficheskie issledovaniia problem rozhdaemosti," *Sotsiologicheskie issledovaniia*, 1979, no. 3, pp. 12-13.

[38] E. Manevich, "Vosproizvodstvo naseleniia i ispol'zovanie trudovykh resursov," *Voprosy ekonomiki*, 1978, no. 8, p. 40; *Materialy XXVI s"ezda KPSS* (Moscow: Politizdat, 1981), pp. 54-55.

[39] See Juozas A. Kazlas, "Social Distance Among Ethnic Groups," in Edward Allworth, ed., *Nationality Group Survival in Multi-Ethnic States: Shifting Support Patterns in the Soviet Baltic Regions* (New York: Praeger, 1977), p. 246. A text of Mikoyan's interview was published in Emma Schwabenland Haynes, *The Restoration of the Volga German Republic*, Work Paper no. 11 of the American Historical Society of Germans from Russia (Lincoln, Neb.), April 1973, pp. 13 ff.

[40] See Iu. A. Bzhilianskii, *Problemy narodonaseleniia pri sotsializme, Politiko-ekonomicheskii analiz* (Moscow: Mysl', 1974), p. 177.

[41] Some Central Asian Germans are already moving either to West Germany or to ethnically more akin areas in the Soviet Baltic. See Sidney Heitman, "The Soviet Germans in the USSR Today," report prepared for the Office of External Research, U.S. Department of State, 1980, p. 86; Kazlas, p. 246.

[42] *Itogi vsesoiuznoi perepisi* (1970), vol. 4 (Moscow: Statistika, 1974), tables 11-14, 22-28. The figure for the Crimean Tatars is an estimate.

[43] Mobin Shorish, "Soviet Development Strategies in Central Asia," *Canadian Slavonic Papers*, 1975, no. 2-3, p. 410.

[44] James Critchlow, "Uzbeks and Russians," ibid., pp. 366-72.

[45] Based on *Itogi vsesoiuznoi perepisi* (1970), vols. 4 and 7.

[46] See V. V. Onikienko, *Kompleksnoe issledovanie migratsionnykh protsessov. Analiz migratsii naseleniia UkrSSR* (Moscow: Statistika, 1973), pp. 39, 152.

[47] L. L. Rybakovskii, *Regional'nyi analiz migratsii* (Moscow: Statistika, 1973), p. 61.

[48] Indications of "Uzbek" labor being used in the non-black-soil areas of European Russia are misleading. Most of the persons involved are Europeans residing in Uzbekistan (communication from Ann Sheehy, Radio Liberty, Munich). For a discussion of possible future Muslim *gastarbeiter*, see Jeremy Azrael, *Soviet Nationality Policies and Practices* (New York: Praeger, 1978), p. 371.

[49] The *tache d'huile* (oil slick) effect referred to by A. Bennigsen in a conversation with the author.

[50] This has been mentioned by two Soviet scholars. See B. S. Khorev and V. M. Moiseenko, *Sdvigi v razmeshchenii naseleniia SSSR* (Moscow: Statistika, 1976), pp. 82-83.

[51] This point is raised by Besemeres, *Socialist Population Politics*, pp. 47-48.

Chapter 6: The National-Religious Symbiosis

[1] Hans Kohn, *The Idea of Nationalism* (New York: Collier Books, 1969), p. 15.

[2] L. N. Gumilev, "O termine etnos," *Doklady geograficheskogo obshchestva SSSR*, issue 3 (Leningrad: Nauka, 1967), p. 4.

[3] See N. Ashinov, "Izmeneniia v kul'te. Evoliutsiia Islama v SSSR," *Nauka i religiia*, 1971, no. 9, p. 18, for the usage of "European" as opposite to Muslim; T. S. Saidbaev, *Islam i obshchestvo* (Moscow: Nauka, 1978), p. 196.

[4] Saidbaev, p. 194; Iu. V. Arutiunian and S. M. Mirkhasimov, "Etnosotsiologicheskoe issledovanie kul'tury i byta v Uzbekistane," *Obshchestvennye nauki v Uzbekistane*, 1979, no. 1, pp. 40-41; S. M. Mirkhasimov, "Sotsial'no-kul'turnye izmeneniia i otrazhenie ikh v sovremennoi sem'e sel'skogo naseleniia Uzbekistana," *Sovetskaia etnografiia*, 1979, no. 1, p. 14.

[5] Besemeres, pp. 81-82; see also Wesley Fisher, "Ethnic Consciousness and Intermarriage Correlates of Endogamy among Major Soviet Nationalities," *Soviet Studies*, July 1977, p. 398.

[6] N. Ashirov, *Musul'manskaia propoved'* (Moscow: Politizdat, 1978), p. 76.

[7] Alexandre Bennigsen and Chantal Lemercier-Quelquejay, *Islam in the Soviet Union* (New York: Praeger, 1967), p. 138.

[8] Maxime Rodinson, *Marxisme et le monde musulman* (Paris: Editions du Seuil, 1972), pp. 152-55.

[9] Israel Zangwill, *The Principle of Nationalities* (London: Watts, 1917), p. 39.

[10] Hans Braker, *Kommunismus und Weltreligionen Asiens*, I, 1, 2, *Religionsdiskussion und Islam in der Sovjetunion* (Tubingen: J. C. B. Mohr [Paul Siebeck], 1969), pp. 91 ff.

[11] Monteil, "Supplement à l'essai sur l'Islam en URSS," *Revue des Etudes Islamiques*, vol. XIII (Paris, 1953), p. 8, quoting *Mir Islama*, 1913, no. 9, pp. 269-71, and p. 46; Chantal Lemercier-Quelquejay, "Islam" (paper read at the Second World Congress for Soviet and East European Studies, Garmisch, October 3, 1980).

[12] Ashirov, p. 67.

[13] M. Dzhunusov, "Obshchestvo internatsionalistov—obshchestvo massovogo ateizma," *Nauka i religiia*, 1972, no. 9, p. 23.

[14] N. M. Baltina, "Sovetskii obraz zhizni i protsess preodoleniia perezhitkov musul'manskoi morali," *Voprosy nauchnogo ateizma*, issue 23 (Moscow, 1978), p. 114; Saidbaev, p. 221.

[15] *Dzhunusov*, p. 10.

[16] Alexandre Bennigsen, "Several Nations or One People," *Survey*, 1979, no. 108, p. 59; idem, "Soviet Muslims and the World of Islam," *Problems of Communism*, March-April 1980, p. 39; and Alexander Bennigsen and Chantal Lemercier-Quelquejay, "Muslim Religious Conservatism and Dis-

sent in the USSR," *Religion in Communist Lands*, 1978, no. 3, pp. 153-54.

[17] Gumilev, p. 16.

[18] *Saidbaev*, p. 180; Lemercier-Quelquejay.

[19] *Saidbaev*, p. 207.

[20] Michael Rywkin, "Central Asia and Soviet Manpower," *Problems of Communism*, January-February 1979, p. 13.

[21] Alexandre Bennigsen and Chantal Quelquejay, *Les mouvements nationaux chez les Musulmans de Russie; Le Sultangaleyevisme au Tatarstan* (Paris-Hague: Mouton, 1960), pp. 226 ff.

[22] Redzhep Karaev (interview), "Slovo zovushchee," *Nauka i religiia*, 1979, no. 4, p. 10.

[23] Rodinson, pp. 158-59 and 179.

Chapter 7: Culture

[1] Adoption of the Russian alphabet was considered but rejected at that time for fear of raising the question of attempted Russification.

[2] Serge A. Zenkovsky, *Pan Turkism and Islam in Russia* (Cambridge, Mass.: Harvard University Press, 1960), p. 2.

[3] For more detail, see Elisabeth E. Bacon, *Central Asians under Russian Rule. A Study in Culture Change* (Ithaca, N. Y.: Cornell University Press, 1966), ch. 7, pp. 189 ff.

[4] Leonard Barnes, *Soviet Light on the Colonies* (London: Penguin Books, 1944), pp. 213-15, and Hans Niedermeier, "Schriftreform und Nationalitaten in der UdSSR," *Osteuropa*, 1956, no. 6, p. 416.

[5] I. D. Desheriev, *Razvitie mladopismennykh narodov SSSR* (Moscow: Uchpedgiz, 1958), p. 218.

[6] A. Bennigsen, "Les limites de la déstalinization dans l'Islam soviétique," *L'Afrique et l'Asie*, 1957, no. 39, pp. 30-31, and E. Allworth, "The Soviet Russian Impact on Uzbek Literary Activity" (Ph.D. dissertation, Columbia University, 1959), p. 209.

[7] S. Wurm, *Turkic Peoples of the USSR: Their historical background, their language and the development of Soviet linguistic policy* (London: Central Asian Research Center in association with St. Anthony's College, Oxford, 1954), pp. 45-47.

[8] Desheriev, p. 224.

[9] Rakhmanqul Berdibaev in *Sotsialistik Qazaqstan*, as quoted by Soper, *Radio Liberty Report*, no. 20, Munich, August 1, 1979.

[10] H. Jämalkhanov's article in *Oqituvchilär gazetasi* of July 8, 1979, as quoted in *Radio Liberty Report*, July 20, 1979.

[11] Ann Sheehy, "National Languages and the New Constitutions of the Transcaucasian Republics," *Radio Liberty Research Bulletin*, no. 97-78, May 13, 1978.

[12] Ann Sheehy, "The Tashkent Conference and Its Draft Recommendations on the Teaching of Russian," *Radio Liberty Report*, no. 232/79, August 1, 1979; "After the Tashkent Conference: Additional Measures to Improve the Study of Russian in the National Republics," ibid., January 2, 1980 (Solchanyk). It should be noted that most of the 1979 recommendations had been suggested in 1975.

[13] "Vsesoiuznaia perepis' naseleniia," *Vestnik statistiki*, 1980, no. 2, p. 24.

[14] Hélène Carrère d'Encausse, *L'empire éclaté* (Paris: Flammarion, 1978), p. 192; Brian Silver, "Language Policy and Linguistic Russification of Soviet Nationalities," in Jeremy A. Azrael, ed., *Soviet Nationality Policies and Practices* (New York: Praeger, 1978), pp. 253, 301; Richard Pipes, "The Forces of Nationalism," *Problems of Communism*, January-February 1964, p. 6.

[15] For Uzbekistan, see *Narodnoe khoziaistvo Uzbekskoi SSR v 1978. Statisticheskii ezhegodnik* (Tashkent: Uzbekistan, 1979), p. 293.

[16] James Critchlow, "Signs of Emerging Nationalism in the Muslim Soviet Republics," *The Soviets in Asia, Proceedings of a symposium held at George Washington University, May 19-20, 1972* (Maryland: Cremona Foundation, 1972), pp. 21-22.

[17] Hans Kohn, *Pan-Slavism: Its History and Ideology* (South Bend: University of Notre Dame Press, 1953), p. 250.

[18] Rywkin, *Russia in Central Asia*, p. 94.

[19] Anna Procyk, "The Search for a Heritage and the Nationality Question in Central Asia," in Edward Allworth, ed., *The Nationality Question in Soviet Central Asia* (New York: Praeger, 1973), pp. 124-25.

[20] "Uzbek Writers Look to the Past for Inspiration," *Radio Liberty Report*, Munich, April 26, 1979, quoting Professor Ghulam Karimov on *Sharq yulduzi* of March 1979, pp. 206 ff.

[21] "Kazakhskii poet vystupaet protiv velikorusskogo shovinizma," *Nasha strana* (Tel-Aviv), August 28, 1978.

[22] Mobin Shorish, "Dissent of the Muslims: Soviet Central Asia in the 1980's," paper presented at the Twelfth National Convention of the American Association for the Advancement of Slavic Studies, Philadelphia, November 1980, p. 3.

[23] Robert J. Barett, "Convergence and the Nationality Literature of Central Asia," in *The Nationality Question in Soviet Central Asia*, p. 29; Chantal Lemercier-Quelquejay, "Soviet Muslims and the 'Islamic Resurgence,'" paper presented at the Carnegie Endowment for International Peace conference on "Soviet Muslims and their Political Destiny," New York, March 19-20, 1981.

[24] Aleksandr Iakovlev, "Protiv antiistorizma," *Literaturnaia gazeta*, November 15, 1972, pp. 4-5; Hedrick Smith, "Soviet Said to Punish Party

Aide for His Attacks on Nationalism," *New York Times*, May 7, 1973, p. 8.

[25] V. F. Samoilenko, *Druzhba narodov—istochnik mogushchestva sovetskikh vooruzhennykh sil* (Moscow: Voenizdat, 1972), p. 26.

[26] L. I. Brezhnev, *O piatidesiatiletii Soiuza sovetskikh sotsialisticheskikh respublik. Doklad. 21 dek. 1972 g.* (Moscow: Politizdat, 1972), p. 35.

[27] Rywkin, pp. 95 ff.

[28] Ibid.

[29] Iu. V. Bromlei, ed., *Sovremennye etnicheskie protsessy v SSSR* (Moscow: Nauka, 1975), p. 343.

[30] Rywkin, p. 97.

[31] Bromlei, p. 340.

[32] Iu. V. Arutiunian, "O nekotorykh tendentsiiakh kul'turnogo sblizheniia narodov SSSR na etape razvitogo sotsializma," *Istoriia SSSR*, 1978, no. 4, p. 103.

[33] Steven L. Burg, "Russians, Natives and Jews in the Soviet Scientific Elite. Cadres Competition in Central Asia," *Cahiers du Monde Russe et Soviétique*, 1979, no. 1, pp. 54-55, who presents the following data:

National Composition of Scientific and Technical
Cadres in the Uzbek Republic, 1960—75

	1960	1970	1975
Central Asians	4,510	13,744	17,749
	43.7%	54.4%	57.6%
Europeans	5,356	10,446	11,794
	51.9%	41.4%	38.2%

[34] Shorish, p. 3.

[35] Ibid.

[36] Carrère d'Encausse, pp. 255 ff.

[37] Following and adopting arguments developed by Gumilev, "O termine 'etnos,'" *Doklady geograficheskogo obshchestva SSSR* (Leningrad, 1967), issue 3, p. 4.

Chapter 8: The Sociopolitical Setting

[1] Joseph Stalin, *On the National Question* (London: Lawrence and Wishart, 1942), p. 29.

[2] T. H. Rigby, "Social Orientation and Distribution of Membership in the Communist Party of the Soviet Union," *The American Slavic and East European Review*, vol. 16 (October 1957), p. 275, presumes these principles to be the guiding force of the Communist Party.

[3] Vincent Monteuil, "Essai sur l'Islam en URSS," *Revue des Etudes Islamiques*, vol 12 (Paris, 1952), pp. 57-58.

[4] USSR People's Commissariat of Justice, *Anti-Soviet Bloc of Rightists and Trotskyistes (Report of Court Proceedings)*, verbatim report (Moscow, 1938), pp. 213, 239, 746.

[5] Roy A. Medvedev, *Let History Judge. The Origins and Consequences of Stalinism* (New York: Knopf, 1972), pp. 206-7, quoting *Ocherki po istorii kommunisticheskoi partii Kazakhstana* (Alma-Ata, 1967) and *Ocherki po istorii kommunisticheskoi partii Turkmenii* (Ashkhabad, 1965).

[6] Rigby, pp. 290 and 277.

[7] Caroe (Sir Olaf Kirkpatrick), *Soviet Empire. The Turks of Central Asia and Stalinism* (London: Macmillan, 1953), pp. 246-53. Jan Dubicki, *Elements of Disloyalty in Turkmenistan* [Russian text] (New York: Research Program on the USSR, 1954), pp. 44-47.

[8] Rywkin, *Russia in Central Asia*, p. 108.

[9] S. P. Trapeznikov, "Istoricheskaia rol' MTS v sozdanii i ukreplenii kolkhoznogo stroia," *Vosprosy istorii KPSS*, no. 2, 1958, p. 52. Under Khrushchev MTS machinery was sold to collective farms, and the MTS themselves were eliminated.

[10] Rywkin, p. 111.

[11] Joseph Stalin, *Marxism and the National Question. Selected Writings and Speeches* (New York: International Publishers, 1942), pp. 193-94.

[12] Ibid., p. 160.

[13] As quoted by C. Barghorn, *Soviet Russian Nationalism* (New York: Oxford University Press, 1956), p. 69.

[14] Rywkin, p. 114.

[15] A. Solzhenitsyn mentions this tendency in his *Arkhipelag GULag*, vol. 3 (Paris: YMCA Press, 1975), pp. 397-98.

[16] Eyewitness report.

[17] See Michael Rywkin, "Religion, Modern Nationalism and Political Power in Central Asia," *Canadian Slavonic Papers*, 1975, no. 2-3, p. 279.

[18] Eyewitness report.

[19] Robert A. Lewis, Richard H. Rowland, and Ralph S. Clem, "Modernization, Population Change, and Nationality in Soviet Central Asia and Kazakhstan," *Canadian Slavonic Papers*, 1975, no. 2-3, pp. 295-98.

[20] From discussions at the Conference on the Nationality Question in Soviet Central Asia, held at Columbia University's Program on Soviet Nationality Problems, New York, April 7-8, 1972.

[21] Rasma Karklins, "Nationality Power in Soviet Republics," Report to the National Council for Soviet and East European Research (1979), pp. 4, 10.

[22] Alec Nove and J. A. Newth, *The Soviet Middle East. A Model for Development* (London: Allen and Unwin, 1967), pp. 114, 120; Alexander Woroniak, "Regional Aspects of Soviet Planning and Industrial Organiza-

tion," in V. N. Bandera and Z. L. Melnyk, eds., *The Soviet Economy in Regional Perspective* (New York: Praeger, 1973), pp. 99 ff.; and Hans Jürgen Wagener," Rules of Location and the Concept of Nationality: the Case of the USSR," in ibid., p. 272.

[23] Alexandre Bennigsen, "Several Nations or One People," *Survey* (London), 1979, no. 108, pp. 51 ff.

[24] Eyewitness report.

[25] Eyewitness report.

[26] Alexandre Bennigsen, "Islam in the Soviet Union," paper presented at the Carnegie Endowment for International Peace conference on "Soviet Muslims and Their Political Destiny" (New York, March 19-20, 1981), mentions the dominant position of the Buguu clan in Kirghiz and of the Great Horde in Kazakh politics.

[27] Eyewitness report.

[28] B. Y. Kamenetskii, "The Pakhtakor Events," RFE-RL Soviet Area Audience and Opinion Research, October 26, 1979.

[29] A. Baran'ko, "Zigzag odnogo sledstviia," *Sovetskaia Kirgiziia*, December 27, 1979.

[30] Boris Kamenetskii, "Notes on Life in Uzbekistan," RFE-RL Soviet Area Audience and Opinion Research, background report no. 20-79, October 1979.

[31] Michael Rywkin, "Prospects for the Future and Implications for Western Policy," paper presented at the Carnegie Endowment for International Peace conference on "Soviet Muslims and Their Political Destiny" (New York, March 19-20, 1981).

Chapter 9: Government

[1] As compiled from *Pravda Vostoka*, January-June 1979.

[2] Michael Rywkin, "The Prikaz of the Kazan Court: First Russian Colonial Office," *Canadian Slavonic Papers* (1976), vol. 18, no. 3, p. 296.

[3] Grey Hodnett, *Leadership in the Soviet National Republics. A Quantitative Study of Recruitment Policy* (Ontario: Mosaic Press, 1978), pp. 101-3.

[4] Michael Rywkin, "Some Changes in the Administrative and Political Structure of Central Asia During and After Khrushchev," *International Review of History and Political Science* (Meerut, India), 1968, vol. 5, no. 3, pp. 42-43.

[5] Michael Rywkin, "The Russian-Wide Soviet Federated Socialist Republic (RSFSR): Privileged or Underprivileged," in Edward Allworth, ed., *Ethnic Russia in the USSR. The Dilemma of Dominance* (New York: Pergamon Press, 1980), p. 182.

[6] Hélène Carrère d'Encausse, "Nationality Issues on the Kremlin Agenda and Factors Likely to Affect Their Resolution," paper presented at the

Second World Congress of Soviet and East European Studies, Garmisch-Partenkirchen, September 30-October 5, 1980.

[7] Mark A. Shafir, *Kompetentsiia SSSR i soiuznoi respubliki* (Moscow: Nauka, 1968), pp. 99-100.

[8] Rywkin, "Some Changes," p. 38. The former second secretary of the Central Committee of the Communist Party of Uzbekistan, V. A. Karpov, made way for his more illustrious colleague. Veselov was made head of the Sector of Party and State Control of the Central Committee of the CPSU and USSR Council of Ministers.

[9] A. Azizkhanov, "Leninskaia zabota o Turkestane," *Pravda Vostoka*, July 20, 1965.

[10] Tselinograd, Kokchetav, Kustanai, Pavlodar, and North Kazakhstan.

[11] *Kazakhstanskaia Pravda*, June 22, 1965.

[12] Ibid., October 20, 1965.

[13] Rywkin, "Some Changes," p. 40.

[14] Theofil K. Kis, *Le féderalisme soviétique. Ses particularités typologiques* (Ottawa: University of Ottawa, 1973), p. 92; V. F. Samoilenko, *Druzhba narodov—istochnik mogushchestva sovetskikh vooruzhennyk sil* (Moscow: Voenizdat, 1972), p. 54.

[15] See, for example, the mention of S. Samsaliev as military commissar of the Kirghiz SSR in *Sovetskaia Kirgiziia*, February 23, 1965 (on Red Army Day).

[16] Carrère d'Encausse, "Nationality Issues."

[17] Radio Liberty Research data, 1980.

[18] Vernon Aspaturian, "Soviet Nationality Question in World Perspective," paper presented at the Twelfth National Convention of the American Association for the Advancement of Slavic Studies, Philadelphia, November 1980.

[19] John S. Reshetar, *A Concise History of the Communist Party of the Soviet Union* (New York: Praeger, 1960), p. 162. For a discussion of nationality issues at the Eighth Party Congress, see Frantishek Silnitsky, *Natsional'naia politika KPSS v period s 1917 po 1922 g.* (Munich: Suchasnist, 1978), ch. 6, pp. 235 ff.

Chapter 10: The Terminology of Nationality Politics

[1] Some of the material in this chapter was published as "Code Words and Catch Words of Brezhnev's Nationality Policy," *Survey* (London), 1979, no. 108.

[2] L. I. Brezhnev, "O piatidesiateletii Soiuza Sovetskikh Sotsialisticheskikh Respublik," *Kommunist*, 1972, no. 18, p. 13, defines the RSFSR as "first among equals" (*pervaia sredi ravnykh*) among union republics.

[3] For such articles, see I. P. Tsamerian, "Mezhdunarodnoe znachenie opyta KPSS," *Voprosy istorii KPSS*, 1970, no. 2; K. Hallik, "Rol' kul'-

turnykh sviazei v ukreplenii druzhby sovetskikh liudei," *Kommunist Estonii*, 1969, no. 9.

[4] P. Masherov (First Secretary of the Central Committee of the Communist Party of Belorussia), "O nekotorykh chertakh i osobennostiakh natsional'nykh otnoshenii v usloviiakh razvitogo sotsializma," *Kommunist*, 1972, no. 15, p. 19; A. Snechkus (First Secretary of the Central Committee of the Communist Party of Lithuania), "Velikaia sila sotsialisticheskogo internatsionalizma," ibid., 1972, no. 11.

[5] Brezhnev, p. 18.

[6] Sh. Rashidov, "Iazyk bratstva i druzhby narodov," *Kommunist*, 1973, no. 3, p. 21.

[7] V. I. Lenin, *Polnoe sobranie sochinenii*, vol. 41, pp. 164 and 438.

[8] A. I. Lepeshkin, "Sovetskii federalizm v period razvitogo sotsializma," *Sovetskoe gosudarstvo i pravo*, 1975, no. 8, p. 5.

[9] Ibid., p. 8.

[10] Ibid., pp. 10-11. For an opposite opinion, see I. M. Kislitsyn, in *Voprosy teorii i praktiki federal'nogo stroitel'stva Soiuza SSR* (1969), p. 134, as quoted by Lepeshkin.

[11] Lepeshkin, p. 4, arguing against P. G. Semenov's article in *Sovetskoe gosudarstvo i pravo*, 1961, no. 12, pp. 15 and 23 ff.

[12] Lepeshkin, p. 8; Brezhnev, p. 17, about "tolerance and delicate handling of national feelings."

[13] K. Demirchian (First Secretary of the Central Committee of the Communist Party of Armenia), speech at the Twenty-fifth Party Congress, *Pravda*, February 29, 1976, p. 5.

[14] "Nash bratskii soiuz," *Kommunist Estonii*, 1979, no. 3, pp. 2 ff.

[15] V. S. Shevtsov, "Nekotorye problemy teorii sovetskogo soiuznogo gosudarstva," *Sovetskoe gosudarstvo i pravo*, 1978, no. 4; and D. L. Zlatopol'skii, "Razvitie leninskikh idei o sovetskoi federatsii v novoi konstitutsii SSSR," ibid., 1979, no. 4.

[16] A. I. Lepeshkin, *Sovetskii federalizm (Teoriia i praktika)* (Moscow, 1977), pp. 277-78.

[17] *Kommunist Estonii*, 1979, no. 3, p. 4. Among the new expressions we find: monolithic brotherly friendship, mutual enrichment, full equality, brotherly cooperation, mutual assistance, ever increasing process of rapprochement, unwavering rapprochement, process of national consolidation, unshakable unity, and community (*obshchnost'*).

[18] K. Demirchian, "V sem'e narodov brat'ev," *Kommunist*, 1978, no. 16, pp. 25, 27; N. Tarasenko, "Sblizhenie natsii—zakonomernost' kommunisticheskogo stroitel'stva," ibid., 1978, no. 13, pp. 65 ff.; G. Trapeznikov, "Kul'tura novoi istoricheskoi obshchnosti liudei," *Kommunist Estonii*, 1979, no. 2, pp. 18 ff.

[19] See Tarasenko, p. 72 (all-around *edinenie* of nations and nationalities).

[20] S. Rashidov, in *Kommunist Uzbekistana*, May 5, 1978, pp. 72-73.

[21] Speech on the occasion of the sixtieth anniversary of the October Revolution.

[22] Roland Barthes, *Mythologies* (Paris: Editions du Seuil, 1970), p. 137.

[23] Alain Besançon, *Present soviétique et passé russe* (Paris: Le livre de poche, 1980), pp. 173-75.

[24] Barthes, p. 143.

Conclusion

[1] See Chapter 5, Notes 35-38, pp. 161-62.

[2] Nancy Lubin, "Assimilation and Retention of Ethnic Identity in Uzbekistan," paper delivered at the Twelfth Annual Convention of the American Association for the Advancement of Slavic Studies, Philadelphia, November 5-8, 1980.

[3] Alexandre Bennigsen, "Several Nations or One People? Ethnic Consciousness Among Soviet Central Asian Muslims," *Survey* (London), 1979, no. 108, p. 51.

[4] Michael Zand, "A Muslim Literature Sovietized. Tadzhik Literature during the First Three Decades of Soviet Rule," paper presented at the Symposium on the Soviet Union and the Muslim World, December 28-30, 1980, at the Centre for Russian and East European Studies, Tel Aviv University.

[5] Gregory Massell, "The Collective Identity of Soviet Central Asians. Patterns, Potentialities and Limits," ibid.

[6] Hélène Carrère d'Encausse, *L'Empire eclaté* (Paris: Editions du Seuil, 1979), pp. 255 ff.

[7] Lev Gumilev, "The Nature of Ethnic Wholeness" (Landscape and Ethnos, part XII), *Soviet Geography. Review of Translations*, September 1973, p. 472 (translated from *Vestnik Leningradskogo Universiteta*, 1971, no. 24, pp. 97-106).

[8] Lev Gumilev, "O termine etnos," *Doklady geograficheskogo obshchestva SSSR*, issue 3, Leningrad University, 1967, p. 5.

Selected
Bibliography

General

Allworth, Edward, ed. *The Nationality Question in Soviet Central Asia.*
New York: Praeger, 1973.
Azrael, Jeremy R., ed. *Soviet Nationality Policies and Practices.* New York:
Praeger, 1978.
Bennigsen, Alexandre, and Lemercier-Quelquejay, Chantal. *Islam in the
Soviet Union.* New York: Praeger, 1967.
Bromlei, Iu. V., ed. *Sovremennye etnicheskie protsessy v SSSR.* Moscow:
Nauka, 1975.
Carrère d'Encausse, Hélène. *L'Empire éclaté.* Paris: Flammarion, 1978
(published in English as *Decline of An Empire: The Soviet Socialist
Republics in Revolt.* New York: Newsweek Books, 1979).
McCagg, William O., Jr., and Silver, Brian D., eds. *Soviet Asian Ethnic
Frontiers.* New York: Pergamon, 1979.
Pipes, Richard. *The Formation of the Soviet Union. Communism and
Nationalism (1917-1923).* Cambridge, Mass.: Harvard University
Press, 1954.
Rodinson, Maxime. *Marxisme et monde musulman.* Paris: Editions du Seuil,
1972.
"Russian and Soviet Central Asia." A special issue of the *Canadian Slavon-
ic Papers* (Summer/Fall 1975).
Rywkin, Michael. *Russia in Central Asia.* New York-London: Collier-
Macmillan, 1963.
Wheeler, Geoffrey. *The Modern History of Soviet Central Asia.* New York:
Praeger, 1964.

Chapters 1 and 2

Becker, Seymour. *Russian Protectorates in Central Asia. Bukhara and
Khiva 1865-1924,* Cambridge, Mass.: Harvard University Press, 1968.
Bennigsen, Alexander A., and Wimbush, Enders S. *Muslim National Com-
munism in the Soviet Union. A Revolutionary Strategy for the
Colonial World.* Chicago: University of Chicago Press, 1979.

Carrère d'Encausse, Hélène. *Réforme et révolution chez les musulmans de l'Empire russe. Bukhara 1867-1924.* Paris: Armand Collin, 1966.

Khalfin, N. A. *Rossiia i khanstva Srednei Azii (pervaia polovina XIX veka.* Moscow: Nauka, 1974.

Massaiskii, V. I. *Rossiia, polnoe geograficheskoe opisanie nashego otechestva.* St. Petersburg: A. F. Darrien, 1913.

Safarov, G. *Kolonial'naia revoliutsiia (Opyt Turkestana).* Moscow: Gosizdat, 1921.

Chapter 3

Castagné, Joseph. *Les basmachis. Le mouvement national des indigènes d'Asie Centrale.* Paris: Leroux, 1925.

Poliakov, Iu. A., and Tchugunov, A. T. *Konets basmachestva.* Moscow: Nauka, 1974.

Chapter 4

Bandera, V. N., and Melnyk, Z. L., eds. *The Soviet Economy in Regional Perspective.* New York: Praeger, 1973.

Narodnoe khoziaistvo SSSR v 1979 g. Statisticheskii ezhegodnik. Moscow: Statistika, 1980.

Narodnoe khoziaistvo Uzbekskoi SSR v 1978 g. Statisticheskii sbornik. Tashkent: Uzbekistan, 1979.

Soviet Economy in a Time of Change. A Compendium of Papers Submitted to the Joint Economic Committee of the Congress of the United States, vol. 1. Washington D.C.: U.S. Government Printing Office, 1979.

Chapter 5

Besemeres, John F. *Socialist Population Politics. The Political Implications of Demographic Trends in the USSR and Eastern Europe.* White Plains: M. E. Sharpe, 1980.

Bondarskaia, G. A. *Rozhdaemost' v SSSR (etnodemograficheskii aspekt).* Moscow: Statistika, 1977.

Bruk, S. I. "Etnodemograficheskie protsessy v SSSR (po materialam poslevoennykh perepisei." *Istoriia SSSR,* 1980, no. 5.

Feshbach, Murray, "Prospects for Massive Outmigration from Central Asia During the Next Decade." Paper for the U.S. Department of Commerce, Bureau of Economic Analysis, February 1977.

Perevedentsev, V. I. "Sotsial'no-demograficheskaia situatsiia i vstuplenie molodezhi v trudovuiu zhizn'." *Rabochii klass i sovremennyi mir,* 1980, no. 3.

Rywkin, Michael. "Central Asia and Soviet Manpower." *Problems of Com-*

munism, January-February 1979.

Topilin, A. V. *The Territorial Redistribution of Labor Resources in the USSR.* Special issue of *Problems of Economics*, May 1980.

Chapter 6

Arutiunian, Iu. V., and Mirkhasimov, S. M. "Etnosotsiologicheskie issledovaniia kul'tury i byta v Uzbekistane." *Obshchestvennye nauki v Uzbekistane*, 1979, no. 1.

Bennigsen, Alexandre. "Soviet Muslims and the World of Islam." *Problems of Communism*, March-April 1980.

Saidbaev, T. S. *Islam i obshchestvo.* Moscow: Nauka, 1978.

Chapter 7

Arutiunian, Iu. V. "O nekotorykh tendentsiiakh kul'turnogo sblizheniia narodov SSSR na etape razvitogo sotsializma." *Istoriia SSSR*, 1978, no. 4.

Bacon, Elisabeth E. *Central Asians under Russian Rule. A Study in Cultural Change.* Ithaca, N.Y.: Cornell University Press, 1966.

Burg, Steven L. "Russians, Natives and Jews in the Soviet Scientific Elite. Cadres Competition in Central Asia." *Cahiers du Monde Russe et Soviétique*, June-August 1979.

Critchlow, James. "Signs of Emerging Nationalism in the Muslim Soviet Republics." In *The Soviets in Asia. Proceedings of a symposium held at George Washington University, March 19-30, 1972.* Maryland: Cremona Foundation, 1972.

Gumilev, L. N. "O termine etnos." *Doklady geograficheskogo obshchestva SSSR*, 1967, issue 3.

Chapter 8

Bennigsen, Alexandre. "Several Nations or One People." *Survey* (London), 1979, no. 108.

Rywkin, Michael. "Religion, Nationalism and Political Power in Central Asia." *Canadian Slavonic Papers*, 1975, no. 2-3.

Chapter 9

Hodnett, Grey. *Leadership in the Soviet National Republics. A Qualitative Study of Recruitment Policy.* Ontario: Moscaic Press, 1980.

Shafir, M. A. *Kompetentsiia SSSR i soiuznoi respubliki.* Moscow: Nauka, 1968.

Chapter 10

Besançon, Alain. *Present soviétique et passé russe*. Paris: Le Livre de Poche, 1980.

Lepeshkin, A. I. "Sovetskii federalizm v period razvitogo sotsializma." *Sovetskoe gosudarstvo i pravo*, 1978, no. 8.

Rywkin, Michael. "Code Words and Catch Words of Brezhnev's Nationality Policy." *Survey*, 1979, no. 108.

Index

Abdul-Kahar (mullah), 39-40
Absolute evil. *See* lesser evil
Acculturation. *See* Assimilation
Affirmative action, 53, 57, 74, 115-16, 120-21, 124
Afghanistan, 8, 9, 13, 14, 32, 36, 40, 43, 44, 102, 151
Africa, 44
Agriculture, 35, 46-48, 54, 56. *See also* Collectivization; Cotton; Irrigation; Land
Ak-Mechet (Aral'skoe), 9. *See also* Raim
Akmolinsk, 7, 8, 133-34
Alash Orda, 18, 22
Albania(ns), 136, 140
Algeria, 34, 72, 117, 120
Alexander I (tsar), 5
Aliev, G. A., 127
Alma Ata (Vernoe), 9
Alphabets: Arabic, 88, 93, 114; Cyrillic, 93-94; Latin, 93-94; shift from Arabic to Cyrillic, 93-95, 118
American Relief Administration, 36
America(ns). *See* United States
Andizhan, 13, 16
Anthems (of union republics), 143-45
Antinatalism. *See* Demography
Arifov, Abdulhamid, 39
Armenia(ns), 24, 25, 60, 85, 95, 122, 135, 140, 143, 144, 145
Army: Bukharan People's, 40;

discipline in, 34; First Uzbek Cavalry Brigade, 35-36; Fourth Red, 28-29; future recruits for, 69; military commisars of union republics in, 135-36; Muslims in, 36, 79, 110, 135-136; Volga Tatar Red Brigade, 35. *See also* Fergana Valley
Asia, 44, 102
Assimilation, 89, 98-99, 105-7, 151-53
Astrakhan Khanate, 3
Aulie-Ata, 11
Azerbaidzhan, 122, 123, 129
Azeri Turks, 18

Babakhan, Zinautdin ibn Ishan, 102, 135
Bagirov, M. D., 101
Balk, 3
Baltic republics, 60, 116, 119, 122, 123, 143, 145. *See also* Estonia, Latvia, Lithuania
Barthes, Roland, 146
Bashkirs, 18, 38, 95, 112
Basmachis, 26, 34-44, 108, 152
Baytursun, Akhmed, 18, 22
Bekovich-Cherkasskii, A., 4, 7, 9
Belorussia(ns), 60, 65, 85, 96, 122, 123, 124, 143, 144
Beneveni, Florio, 4
Bennigsen, Alexandre, 86, 98, 118, 150, 152
Beria, L. P., 101

Berlin, Congress of, 13
Besançon, Alain, 145, 147
Besemeres, John, 72
Birthrates. *See* Demography
Blacks, 115
Bokii, G. I., 28
Brezhnev, L. I., 76, 103, 124, 125, 140-43
Broido, G. I., 31
Bruk, Solomon, 66
Buddhism, 101
Bukeev Horde. *See* Kazakhs
Bukhara, 118, 145; attacked unsuc-successfully, 24; contacts with, 3, 8, 9, 10; defeated by tsarist troops, 12; education in, 104; Peoples Republic of, 32, 38-40; population and territory of, 10, 59; Russian protectorate of, 12; Soviet conquest of, 32. *See also* Basmachis, Communist Party of the Soviet Union; Jews
Bukharin, Nikolai, 109
Bukheikhanov, Ali Khan, 18, 22
Burns, A., 8
Butenev, K. F., 9
Byk, Iosif Moiseevich, 31

Cadres: Colonial *nomenklatura*, 125-29; coopting Muslim elite into, 111-15; in villages, 110-11; job competition in, 82, 116; jobs reserved for nonnatives in, 52-53, 125-26, *korenizatsiia* in, 79, 83; national rivalry in, 74, 119-20; native, 52, 57, 111-15, 125-29, Soviet *nomenklatura*, 110-11; party elite, 110; reliable-unreli-able, 113-15; *See also* Govern-ment
Catholics, 62, 123
Carrère d'Encausse, Hélène, 98, 106, 107, 131, 151, 152
Catherine the Great (empress), 5, 88
Caucasus (Caucasians), 24, 100, 119, 123, 140
Censuses. *See* Demography

Cheka, 28,
Cherniaev, M. G., 11
Chicherin, G. V., 38
Children. *See* Demography
Chimkent, 11, 132
China, 5, 18, 101, 140
Chinese Turkestan, 17
Chokay, Mustafa, 21-22
Cholpan, 100
Civil War, 127, 137
Collective farm market, 54-56
Collectivization, 44, 45-46. *See also* Land
Colonialism: attitudes of 24, 29; British, French, and Russian compared, 115, 120; welfare, 57
Colonization, 15-16, 29, 58-59, 64, 79, 100, 116, 120
Communist Party of the Soviet Union (CPSU): Bukharan CP sub-ordinated to, 38; Central Asian Bureau of, 49, 132-33; Central Committee (CC) of, 124; coop-ting party elite for, 111-15; cult of personality in, 108; depart-ments in, 102-3, 122-23, 127-28; formative years of, 108-11; *no-menklatura* in, 125-29; right op-position to, 109; secretaries of, 92, 125; Twenty-fifth Congress of, 142; Twenty-sixth Congress of, 76; workers in, 110. *See also* Cadres; Government; Purges; Tashkent; Turkestan; Uzbekistan
Constitution: of 1924, 129-30; of 1936, 129-30, 138; of 1977, 138; of 1978 (of union republics), 143
Cossacks, 5, 7, 8, 16, 23, 135
Cotton, 15, 20; and grain policies, 20, 47-48; directorate for grow-ing, 132
Crimean Tatars. *See* Tatars
Crimean War, 10
Culture, 93-107; *See also* Customs; Education; Islam; Language; Lit-erature

Customs, 74, 88, 90, 115. *See also* Islam

Daudov, Vasilii, 3
deGaulle, Charles, 117
Demirchian, Karen, 142
Demography, 58-83; antinatalism, 76; baby boom, 64-65; birth-rates, 64, 67, 72; censuses, 78; children, 66-67; differential policy for, 149; fertility, 65-66; future prospects for, 80-83; quantitative vs. qualitative factors, 149; urbanization, 116. *See also* Migration
Development. *See* Economy
Divorce, 66
Djany-bek, 36
Djulek, 11
Djunaid Khan, 25, 31, 37, 42-43
Draft. *See* Army
Dubicki, Jan, 104
Dulatov, Mirzakup, 22, 60
Dushanbe, 32, 101, 133
Dutov, A. I., 23

Economy, 45-57; enterprises of all-Union importance, 52-54; growth rates of, 49, 51; indicators, 50; industry in, 49; private, 54-57; turnover tax in, 51. *See also* Agriculture; *Gosplan*; *Gosstroi*; Labor
Education, 103-5; among Muslim women, 105; among natives, 104; conference on Russian language, 96; religious, 87, 104; universities: Alma Ata, 104; Samarkand, 101; Stalinabad, 101; University of Central Asia in Tashkent (SAGU), 104
Egypt, 47
Eliava, S. Z., 26, 28
Elite. *See* Cadres
England, 11, 13, 14, 31, 47, 58, 100, 117, 124
English language, 97

Enver Pasha, 38, 40, 42
Ermolov, A. P., 8
Estonia(ns), 97, 114, 122, 127, 131, 135, 142. *See also* Baltic republics
Ethnic allegiances, 37, 106, 118-19, 150
Ethnic groups, 67, 68, 77
Ethnic relations, 115-17, 150; *See also* Labor
Ethnic riots, 16, 22, 86, 121
Europe (Western), 64, 114

Federalism: autonomous republics and regions under, 122; nature of, 136-37; sovereignty, 138, 142; unequal republics under, 122-25
Fedotov, Ivan, 3
Fellagha, 34
Fergana Valley, 11, 14, 26, 34, 36, 40, 42; peasant army in, 35
Fertility. *See* Demography
Feshbach, Murray, 73, 74
Finland, war with, 134. *See also* Karelo-Finnish Republic
Fitrat, Abdurauf, 18, 100
Foreign Ministry (tsarist), 8, 12. *See also* Ministries; Turkestan
France, 100, 115, 117, 124, 146
Frolov, M. M., 26
Frunze, M. V., 28, 30, 31, 35, 43

Gaverdovskii, Lt., 8
Geok Tepe, 13, 14
Georgia(ns), 85, 95, 112, 122, 124, 126, 128, 135, 136, 143, 144, 145
Germans (Volga Germans), 85, 89, 96, 106, 116, 127, 131, 137
Germany, 79, 85, 100
Goloshchekin, F. I., 28
Gorchakov, A. M., 10
Gosplan, 75
Gosstroi, 132
Government, 122-37. *See also* Cadres; Communist Party of the

Soviet Union; Ministries
Greater Horde. *See* Kazakhs,
Gumilev, Lev, 85, 89, 151, 152

Herzfeld, 22
History reinterpreted, 99-103
Hodnett, Grey, 128
Housing, 54-55, 57

Ibragim-bek, 37, 40, 42-43
Ignatiev, N. P., 11
Ikramov, Akmal, 100
Imanov, Amangeldy, 17, 22
Incomes, 50
India, 8
Industry. *See* Economy
Inorodtsy, 18
Iran, 12, 100, 151
Irgash bey, 24
Irish, 85
Irjar, 12
Irrigation, 10, 72, 132. *See also*
    Agriculture; Land
Isatai, 7
Isfendiar (khan), 25
Ishimov, Kaip Gallia, 7
Islam, 84-92, 123; authorities in, 88;
    bida, 89; Dar-ul-Islam, 85; *hadj*,
    89; *homo islamicus*, 106; *kalym*,
    90; *khazi* courts, 42; Koran, 91;
    kufr, 89; Mir Arab medreseh, 88;
    modern, 84-85; *muhazzad*, 90;
    mullahs, 88; observance of, 84-
    85, 89-90; Ramadan, 89; *salad*,
    89; *Shariat*, 85; *sharaghad*, 90;
    shirq, 84; Soviet attitudes to-
    ward, 87; Soviet rituals in, 88-90;
    spirit of, 85; *umma*, 87; *zakat*,
    89. *See also* Tashkent
Ismaily, Mirzakalan, 101
Israil, 40
Italy, 85
Ittihad, 20
Ivan the Terrible (tsar), 3

Jadids, 18, 21, 37, 39
Japan, 18

Jenkinson, Anthony, 3
Jews, 60, 73, 80, 85, 89, 97, 120,
    123-24, 136, 137, 152; Bukh-
    aran, 10, 58, 60, 85
Judaism, 88
Judiciary, centralized, 131

Kabul. *See* Afghanistan
Kaganovich, L. M., 30
Kaledin, A. M., 23
Kalinin, Mikhail, 112
Kalmuks, 101
Kamenev, S. S., 38, 40, 42
Kandahar. *See* Afghanistan
Kapitonov, Ivan, 103
Kara-Kalpaks, 10, 97
Karelo-Finnish Republic, 123, 134
Karimov, Abdulla, 109
Karklins, Rasma, 116-17
Katta-Kurgan, 12
Kaufman, K. P., 12, 13
Kazakhs, 10, 17, 18, 22, 58, 104,
    119, 127; Bukeev Horde, 7; di-
    vided into provinces, 12; Greater
    Horde, 11; in the RSFSR, 71, 82;
    language, 97; law code of, 7;
    Lesser Horde, 5, 7; Middle
    Horde, 5, 7, 9; military forma-
    tions of, 135; revolts by, 7, 9,
    17, 22; Russian penetration
    of, 4
Kazakhstan, 36, 46, 48, 58-65, 78-
    83, 101, 109, 116-18, 123, 127,
    131, 132; attempts to down-
    grade, 133-34
Kazakov, A. A., 27
Kazembek, Muhammed, 27
Kenesary, Kasim, 7, 8, 9
KGB, 28, 127-28, 131
Khal Khodja, 35, 37
Khiva, 118; Bekovich-Cherkasskii
    expedition to, 4; khanate of, 3,
    10, 12; Khorezm, Peoples Re-
    public of, 31, 36; Perovskii ex-
    pedition to, 8-9; population and
    territory of, 10; recognition of,
    27; republic of, 37; Russian pro-

tectorate of, 13; Soviet conquest of, 37; tsarist education in, 104. *See also* Basmachis; Purges
Khodzhaev, Faizullah, 18, 37, 39, 40, 48, 92, 100, 109
Khokhlov, Ivan, 3
Khorezm. *See* Khiva
Khristoforov, A. N., 27
Khrushchev, N. S., 46, 48, 125, 129-30, 132, 133, 134
Khudoyar Khan, 12, 13
Kirghiz, 10, 17, 22, 39, 40, 42, 58, 95, 97, 100
Kirghiz Republic, 59, 79-83, 101, 104, 127, 131
Kiselev, A. S., 27
Kobozev, P. A., 25, 26, 27
Kokand, 118; khanate of, 7, 8, 10; Muslim government of, 22, 23, 34; population and territory of, 10; Russian conquest of, 11; Russian protectorate of, 13; Soviet conquest of, 23-24; Soviet in, 23
Kolchak, A. V., 28
Kolesov, F. I., 24, 25, 39
Kombedy, 28
Komsomol, 48
Koreans, 60
Korenizatsiia, 79, 83
Korovnichenko, P. A., 21
Koshmamed-khan, 31, 37
Krasnovodsk, 12
Kuibyshev, V. V., 28, 32, 37, 38
Kunaev, D. A., 124, 127
Kuram-bek, 43
Kuropatkin, A. N., 20
Kur-Shirmat, 35-36, 40, 42
Kzyl Arvat, 13, 14

Labor: cohorts in, 69; ethnic division of, 52-53, 78, 84, 119; manpower prospects for, 71, 82-83; migration of, 72-76; mobilized, 75, 82; supply, 68, 73. *See also* Economy; Ethnic Relations; Migration

Laiq, 102
Land: *amliak*, 10; collectivized, 44, 45-46; expropriated, 16-17; *miulk*, 10; ownership, 10, 45-46; private, 54; surplus, 14; *vakf*, 10, 42; virgin, 59-60. *See also* Irrigation; Virgin Lands
Language (language policies), 73, 75, 88, 91, 93, 94, 95-99, 101, 107; Tashkent conference on (1979), 72
Latvia(ns), 122, 127, 131, 135, 136, 137, 143. *See also* Baltic republics
Law: Kazakh code of, 7; *khazi* courts of, 42. *See also* Islam; Judiciary
Lenin, V. I., 28, 30, 33, 47, 102, 130, 141, 144
Lepeshkin, A. I., 141, 142
Lesser evil, theory of, 99-101, 145
Lesser Horde. *See* Kazakhs
Lewis, Robert, 72, 116-17
Lighthouse of the East, 102
Literacy, 93, 104, 112
Literature, 100-102
Lithuania(ns), 79, 118, 122, 127, 131, 135, 137. *See also* Baltic republics
Lokai Valley, 37
Lomonosov, V. G., 133
Lubin, Nancy, 150

Machiaveli, Niccolo, 97
Machine tractor stations (MTS), 111
Madamin-bek, 35
Malenkii, Semen, 4
Makambat, 7
Maksum, Faizullah, 40
Maksum, Nasrattulah, 43, 60
Manas, 100
Manpower. *See* Labor
Margelan, 13
Marriage, 66, 85, 86, 90
Marxism 100, 114, 141
Mary Oasis, 14
Massell, Gregory, 151

Mekhanizatory, 52
Mensheviks, 20, 21, 22
Metchi, 42
Middle Horde. *See* Kazakhs
Migration: active policy of, 75; balances, 78-83; Jewish, 73; mechanisms of, 75-78; prospects for, 69-74; rational/irrational, 75; to RSFSR, 80-82. *See also* Demography
Mikoyan, A. I., 78
Military. *See* Army
Ministries: all-Union, 137; of foreign affairs, 135; post-Khrushchev changes in, 129-30; republic, 129-31; union republic (mixed), 129-31. *See also* Foreign Ministry; Government; Turkestan
Mirmushin, 101
Mirzakulan, Izmaily, 101
Moldavian language. *See* Romania
Moldavia(ns), 91, 122
Mongols, 18
Monstrov, Konstantin, 35
Mosques, 87-88
Muetdin, 40, 42
Muftis, 102
Mullahs. *See* Islam
Muslim Committee of National Union, 39
Muslims, 68-69. *See also* particular group or Islam
Muslims of the Soviet East, 88
Muzzafar, Hanafi, 92

Namangan, 13
Napoleon I (emperor), 5
Narimanov, Nariman, 92
Nash sovremennik [Our contemporary], 102
Nasreddin (khan), 13
Nationalism, bourgeois, 46. *See also* Ethnic relations; Islam
Nauka i religiia [Science and religion], 88
Nechkina, M. V., 100

Negri, 8
New Economic Policy (NEP), 36, 42, 45
New York (city), 106
Niaz (shah of Khiva), 4
Nikiforov, 9
Nikon, 106
Nomenklatura. *See* Cadres
Novo-Aleksandrovsk, 7
Nurmat Ali, 37

Obruchev, N. N., 9
Old Believers, 103, 106
Ordzhonikidze, Sergo, 40, 136
Orenburg, 5, 7, 9, 11
Orlov, Vasilii, 5
Osipov, 26
Ospan, Kasym, 17

Palen, K. K., 16
Pan-Turkism, 118, 132
Party secretaries; *See* Communist Party of the Soviet Union
Paul I (tsar), 5
Pazukhin brothers, 3
Pelshe, A., 124
Peoples of the East, First Congress of, 30
Perevedentsev, V., 69, 72
Perfilev, E. L., 23
Perovskii, V. A., 8, 9
Peter the Great (tsar), 3, 4, 127
Peters, Ia., 30
Pipes, Richard, 98
Pishpek, 11
Poles (Poland), 60, 79, 85, 106, 140
Polo, Marco, 8
Pokrovskii, M. N., 100-101
Population. *See* Demography
Pravda Vostoka [Pravda of the East], 133
Private initiative, 54-57
Problemy nauchnogo ateizma [Problems of scientific atheism], 88

Protestants, 123
Purges, 108-9, 112; in Khiva, 37

Qairov, Pirumqul, 101
Quari, Munevver, 18, 100

Race relations. *See* Ethnic relations
Railroads, 13, 14
Raim (Aral'skoe), 9. *See also* Ak-Mechet
Rakhambaev, A., 30
Rakhman-Datkho, 37
Rakhmankul, 42
Rashidov, Sharaf, 127, 143
Reemigration, 76-80
Religion, 84-92. *See also* Islam and other religions
Republics or regions. *See* Federalism and individual republic names
Reverse discrimination. *See* Affirmative action
Revolution of 1905, 18; of 1917, 20-23; secured, 28-32; struggle for survival, 23-28
Rodinson, Maxime, 87
Romania(n), 96, 123
Romanov, Mikhail Fedorovich (tsar), 3
Rudzutak, Ia. E., 28, 42
Rumiantsev, 8
Russian chauvinism, 25-26, 29, 92, 102-3. *See also* Ethnic relations
Russian language. *See* Language
Russian settlers. *See* Colonization
Ryskulov, Turar, 27, 29, 100

Safarov, G., 20, 30, 92
Safonov, 37
Said Ali Khan, 32
Samarkand, 10, 14, 23, 42, 60, 101, 145; battle of, 12; early contacts with, 3
Sasvokasov, Smagul, 60
Segisbaev, Sultan, 109
Seid Abdulla, 31
Selim Pasha, 40, 42

Semireche, 16; settlers in, 22; Soviet regime in, 25, 26
Shamil, 100
Shorish, Mobin, 105-6
Siberia, 3, 8, 28, 82, 118
Silver, Brian, 98
Skalov, G. B., 31
Skobelev, M. D., 13, 14
Slavery, 7, 11
Slogans, 138-48
Social conflicts, 119
Social intercourse, 86
Socialism, developed, 145-46
Social mobility, 119-20
Social Revolutionaries (SRs), 20, 21, 27
Social status, 115
Sokolnikov, G., 30
Solomentsev, Iurii, 103
Solzhenitsyn, A. I., 103, 151
Southern Union of Cossacks, Mountain Caucasians, and Peoples of the Steppe, 23
Sovetskaia Rossiia [Soviet Russia], 102
Sovetskoe gosudarstvo i pravo [Soviet government and law], 131
Soviet bloc nations, 139-40
Sovnarkhoz, 132
Spechler, Martin, 57
Speranskii, M. M., 7
Stalin, I. V. (Stalinism), 33, 38, 60, 71, 96, 108, 111-13, 120, 124, 125, 131, 134, 136, 138, 151, 153
Stalinabad. *See* Dushanbe
Stoletov, N. G., 13
Stolypin, P. A., 17, 59
Sultanbekov, 60
Sultan Galiev, Mir Said, 29, 91, 92
Sultanmuradov, D., 31
Sweden, 4
Switzerland, 136

Tadzhikistan, 40, 42, 43, 78-83, 104, 127, 131

Tadzhik(s), 10, 58, 60, 95, 97, 102
Tanyshbaev, Makhmud, 22
Tarikats, 88
Tashkent, 5, 11, 102, 129; battle of, 12; conference on the role of Islam in (September 1980), 102; congresses of soviets in: Fifth, Sixth, Seventh, Eighth, 22-28; Council of Peoples Commissars in, 25; Muslim Congress in, 20; nationalist demonstrations in, 23; Pakhtakor race riots in, 121; railroad repair shops in, 21, 23, 36; Slavic population of, 59; Soviet of Workers and Peasants of, 20, 21; taken by tsarist Russia, 12
Tatars (Crimean Tatars), 18, 35, 38, 55, 60, 89, 96, 106, 112
Taxes, turnover, 51; from Kazakhs, 7
Tedjen Oasis, 13
Terminology. *See* Slogans
Textile industry, 14, 48
Third World, 116
Time of Troubles, 3
Tokmak, 11
Tomskii, M. P., 30
Topilin, A. V., 75
Transcaucasus, 80, 122, 127
Trapeznikov, G., 143
Trotsky, Leon, 136
Tselinograd. *See* Akmolinsk
Turcological Congress (Baku), 93
Turgai, 17
Turkestan, 106, 118, 132; Central Asian Military District of, 132, 136; conquest of, 11-13; Council of Peoples Commissars in, 25; Foreign Ministry of, 28; Fourth Party Congress in, 28; military district of, 136; population of 59; provinces of, 12, 14; Third Party Congress in, 27
Turkestan Commission, 16
Turkey, 4, 18, 38, 72, 100
Turkic Republic, 30
Turkmen, 10, 13, 24, 39, 58, 78-83, 95, 112, 127, 131

Turkmenistan, 59, 104, 109
Tursunkhodzhaev, Sagdulla, 27
Tursunzdad, Mirza, 102

Ukraine, Ukrainians, 58, 65, 80, 85, 119, 122, 123, 124, 125, 134, 137, 145
Ulema, 20
Umma. See Islam
Union of Toiling Muslims, 20
Universities. *See* Education
Ural River, 4
Ura Tiube, 12
Urbanization. *See* Demography
United Nations (UN), 135
United States, 64, 97, 115, 130, 136
Usman Khodja, 39
Uspenskii, K. Ia., 27
Uzbekistan, 43, 47, 54-57, 59, 78-83, 109, 117, 126, 127, 128, 131, 140; Central Committee of CPSU in, 128
Uzbeks, 10, 18, 24, 26, 39, 40, 42, 52, 60, 88, 91, 95, 104-7, 114, 118, 128, 144, 145

Validov, Zeki, 38
Veselov, S. M., 133
Victoria (queen), 13
Virgin Lands, 59-60; territory of, 133-34. *See also* Land
Volga Germans. *See* Germans

WASPs, 124
Welfare colonialism, 51, 57
Wheeler, G. E., 104
Witkewicz, Jan, 8
Women, 76; in education, 104-5; labor of, 74, 104
Workers. *See* Labor
World War I, 17
World War II, 44, 49, 60, 105, 110, 135, 137

Yakir, Yona, 136
Yany Kurgan, 11, 12

Yaqubov, Abil, 101
Yiddish, 96
Young Bukharans, 18, 32-33, 39
Young Khivans, 25, 26, 31-33, 37
Young Turks, 18, 38
Yugoslavia, 136, 140

Yusupov, Palvaniaz, 31

Zand, Michael, 150-51, 152
Zeravshan Valley, 10
Zinoviev, Alexandre, 151
Zinoviev, G. V., 36

About the Author

Michael Rywkin is Professor of Russian Area Studies at the City College of New York.

A World War II refugee in Samarkand, he attended the Uzbek State University for one year and lived in Central Asia for several years. Subsequently educated in France and the United States, he has published numerous articles on Soviet nationality problems in general and Central Asian affairs in particular. He has lectured extensively in the United States and abroad, and his previous book on Central Asia was published in a Turkish-language translation in 1975.